# *Your Home Business Can Make Dollars and Sense*

# Your Home Business Can Make Dollars and Sense

## Jo Frohbieter-Mueller

Chilton Book Company/Radnor, Pennsylvania

Copyright © 1990 by Jo Frohbieter-Mueller
All Rights Reserved
Published in Radnor, Pennsylvania 19089, by Chilton Book Company

No part of this book may be reproduced, transmitted, or stored
in any form or by any means, electronic or mechanical,
without prior written permission from the publisher

Designed by Arlene Putterman
Manufactured in the United States of America

Library of Congress Cataloging in Publication Data
Frohbieter-Mueller, Jo.
   Your home business can make dollars and sense / Jo Frohbieter
-Mueller.
       p.    cm.
   ISBN 0-8019-7995-1 (pbk.)
     1. New business enterprises—Handbooks, manuals, etc.   2. Home
-based businesses—Handbooks, manuals, etc.   I. Title.
HD62.5.F77     1990
658′.041—dc20                                            89-82095
                                                            CIP

1 2 3 4 5 6 7 8 9 0    9 8 7 6 5 4 3 2 1 0

*To my parents, Edwin and Sudie Frohbieter,*
*whose home business was to raise a brood of children*
*who cherish each other*

# Contents

## Part One / What Is Right for You?

# Foreword

The very fact that you are reading this book is indicative of major changes taking place in the American economy. Thirty years ago the idea of a home business was rare and certainly not the subject of a practical guide.

During the last half of the nineteenth century and the first half of the twentieth, the United States was basically a manufacturing economy. When you envisioned a "typical" business you thought of a factory that made something—cars, refrigerators, or other consumer goods. In order to produce more goods that could be sold at lower prices, companies turned to mechanization and standardization. Henry Ford conceived of the assembly line, which allowed Americans to buy the Model T Ford in any color as long as it was black. Larger and larger factories came into existence to house the increasingly complex machinery and operations. And Americans came to think of businesses as places you went to in order to work.

Of course, there were a substantial number of individual entrepreneurs. Many of these were shopkeepers and retailers. While they may have lived in quarters above or near the store, they didn't really have a home business as we think of it today since the shop was usually somewhat separate. In the period after the Second World War, this country saw the growth of retail chains and the resultant demise of the independent retailer. How many "Mom and Pop" grocery stores still exist in your neighborhood or community? How often have you noted that the shopping malls you visited in some distant city while on vacation have exactly the same stores as the ones in your home town?

In recent years, however, several new forces have been changing the nature of the American economy, and it is these forces that make the concept of home businesses practical and realistic today. First, our economy is more of a service-oriented economy as opposed to a manufacturing one. More and more people provide services to others, rather than making and selling physical goods. In general, services require much less equipment than manufacturing concerns and thus are much less *place*-bound.

Second, more of the economy is based on information and ideas than it was in the past. Computers and communications are the keys to this information economy. As an example, a legal researcher today can use a personal computer connected by phone lines to other computers to engage in legal studies which were previously possible only in a large law library. Everything, including texts of cases, indices, and word processing capabilities, is available on the computer. The home is just as appropriate a working environment as the office or law library.

Third, in the area of retailing there has been a tremendous growth in the fields of direct mail and telemarketing. Rather than going to the store, you can purchase a variety of items either by mail or over the phone. Again, this has reduced the importance of place in the conduct of business.

Fourth, there has been a resurgence of interest in high-quality, handcrafted items as opposed to mass-produced, machine-made ones. This is especially true in upscale markets for "luxury" items. People with moderate to high levels of disposable income are interested in buying handmade preserves, hand-knit sweaters, and so on. Many of these items are produced by people working at home.

Finally, a growing number of companies are discovering the advantages of letting their people set up offices at home, an arrangement which saves a company office space and related expenses and makes for happier employees. With computers on each end, an employee can tie into the company via modem and come into the office only when meetings are required. This is another indication of the lessening in importance of place in the conduct of business. Also, some companies are reducing their staffs, relying on freelancers instead; in so doing, the companies save on benefits and office space, and pay for only the services performed. As a home worker, you may be the freelancer hired by another company or the proprietor of a home business that hires freelancers.

Clearly, the climate today is as favorable for working at home as it has ever been. Perhaps it is right for you. No one claims that it will be easy. As with any business endeavor, a good and realistic plan, sound financing, and a liberal dose of hard work are required. You will find in this book much to assist you, including thoughts and ideas to motivate and inspire your efforts as well as proven methods for getting a business up and running.

*Dr. Dale Jon Hockstra*
*Dean, School of Business*
*University of Evansville*

# Acknowledgments

I wish to express my indebtedness to those who helped and encouraged me throughout this endeavor, especially my husband, Wayne, for his dedication and hard work on my behalf. I am also grateful to the many home business owners who shared their experiences with me, and for the patience of my family and friends, who found I had little time to spend with them.

# Introduction

If you want to start a business at home, or if you want your home business to be more productive, this book is for you. It offers advice on how to start, develop, and stay in a business. It takes you through a step-by-step list of what you must do to get a home business up and running and explains in detail how to go about making each step work for you. It also explains how to make your business grow once it has been started.

This book is written for anyone who is looking to the future with a special purpose, knowing he or she has something to offer and anxious to hang out a shingle. It is written for those of you who are thinking about offering a service—whether it is repairing automobiles, writing newsletters, or selling by mail—as well as those considering making and selling handcrafted or machine-made products. It is also written for artists and writers who know their creative juices flow best when they are working in their own home zone.

A home enterprise is not a get-rich-quick scheme, but it *is* a good way to live and work. Your home business will give you a chance to do the kind of work you enjoy, on your terms. Working at a home business means working for yourself and enjoying the benefits of your labor. A home business means flexible hours in a setting where you can flex your creative and independent spirit. Of course, as you might expect, it takes discipline, dedication, and a "can do" attitude.

There are many business people who are just barely surviving because they don't know how to make their businesses "take hold." Surviving is one thing; flourishing is quite another. This book will provide you with the guidelines you need to start a business and make it flourish. It will show you how to succeed where others have failed.

The entrepreneurial spirit is alive and well in America, with the number of small businesses increasing at an amazing rate. A phenomenal 99 percent of all American business firms are small, according to the Small Business Administration (which defines a small business as one with fewer than 500 employees), and many of these small businesses are operated out of homes. The Bureau of Labor Statistics estimates that approximately 14 million taxpaying businesses are home businesses, which is over 50 percent more than just a decade ago. Moreover, it has been predicted that the number of people working at home will nearly double by the turn of the century. In 1986, the advertising firm of D'Arcy Masius Bento and Bowles made a survey and asked the question, "If you could have your dream job, what would it be?" The choice of most men was to own and manage a business (followed by being a professional athlete), and the favorite among women was also to own and manage a business. People want to own a business because, as David Birch, an MIT research director of entrepreneurship says, "It means you are controlling your own destiny." Since starting a business at home is safer, easier, and has a greater chance of succeeding (see Chapter 1) than those in commercial space, it is not surprising that many people are seeking their dream jobs at home.

Small businesses are the backbone of our free-enterprise system. They employ 50 percent of the private work force and are responsible for 38 percent of the gross national product. Their health is a reflection of the health of our economy, and this is one reason our federal and state governments actively work to preserve and help small business development. The Department of Commerce and the Small Business Administration are charged with aiding small businesses, and their support ranges from management and financial assistance to help in securing government contracts.

Big corporations also recognize the importance of small businesses. Many small firms, some operating out of garages and basements, supply parts and materials to large manufacturers, and large businesses also depend on small ones to distribute and service their output. Studies show that small business workers have a higher rate of innovation than do workers in large corporations. Small business has been responsible for more than half of the new products and service innovations developed since World War II, including fiber optic examination equipment, artificial heart valves, aerosal spray cans, double-knit fabrics, the heart pacemaker, the personal computer, and soft contact lenses.

According to a study by AT&T, over 40 percent of home businesses have an income of $30,000 or more per year. Thus, home businesses are no longer considered a way to earn a little "pin money" but have become an integral part of the American economy and a way to "get ahead." Some families use their home business as their primary source of income, while others work at home to supplement Social Security or investment income, or to supplement their earnings from another job. The number of part-time entrepreneurs has increased five-fold in recent years, and most of these entrepreneurs work from home businesses. Obviously, the economic impact of American home businesses is significant.

Different segments of our population are coming home to work. People living in the heart of large cities, as well as those in remote rural areas, work from their homes and apartments to earn a living. Some home businesses are started by people who are driven by a dream, while others are started by those disenchanted with away-from-home work. Some people who start home businesses are anxious to start a second or post-retirement career, while others are still trying to develop a first career. Minorities, including blacks, Hispanics, and Asians, are creating their own opportunities by opening home businesses, and retirees, homemakers, hobbyists, disabled people, and those interested in a second income are finding there's no place like home to hang out a shingle and bring in the bread.

Although some families operate small manufacturing businesses from a garage or basement, the largest number of home businesses offer a service. Some of these are based on brain, others on brawn. There is a growing industry linked to the high-technology market. Computers have become both "user-friendly" and affordable in recent years, and people are developing the available computer technology into home-based work. Computers and word processors are being used to publish newsletters, write books, and compose articles for newspapers and magazines. Many home workers are exploiting the advances in tele-communication technology and becoming *telecommuters*, defined by *Business Week* as those who work at home but "commute" to a central office via computer. The enormous progress made with computers, communications equipment, and facsimile (fax) transmitters has made it possible for people at home to perform jobs that were formerly performed only in traditional work places. This rapid advance in technology has spurred a dramatic surge in the number of U.S. companies employing telecommuters to do such tasks as process purchase orders, handle accounting, prepare tax returns, and control inventory—all for an employer who is rarely seen in person.

Child care has become a huge cottage industry as mothers returning to work seek care for their children. The continuing movement of women into the work force is one of the most significant trends in the American economy. With more than 50 percent of mothers with infant children working outside their homes, we can expect child care to remain a strong field for home businesses. But there is a change occurring in this industry. Until recently, many homeworkers who provided child care did not report their earnings to the Internal Revenue Service (IRS). Now, however, parents get a tax break if they report the money spent on child care, which means the care providers must also report *their* earnings. Many of the care providers are grumbling about this governmental intrusion because it may reduce their earnings, but in all probability this change in policy will result in a more professional approach to the business of child care. It will force those who provide child care out of the closet, where too many have been hiding from the IRS, and put them in the mainstream of the business world. Parents will feel more secure in placing their children with someone who must conform to certain expectations and regulations.

It takes a lot of effort to make a business successful. As you consider embarking on your own business adventure you must recognize up front just how much hard work, time, and dedication goes into making a home business successful. Too many people think that if they work part-time or in their spare time they will make $40,000 a year. It doesn't happen that way. If you intend to earn a living working at home, you will need to work at it every day, all day. Of course, some of you may not intend to earn your total income from your home business and will only operate on a part-time basis, and that works fine, too.

The words in this book come from years of experience. I have worked at home for over 25 years and am well acquainted with the advantages and disadvantages of home work. For 10 years I conducted cancer research in my basement laboratory, working with mice and protozoans. Mine was the only laboratory of this sort in the country. Household appliances were lined up with centrifuges and other research equipment, and it was a regular routine to throw in the wash while centrifuging cells or injecting animals. My children played in the area but never crossed a line painted on the floor, beyond which hazards lurked for the unsuspecting. My work was supported by grants from scientific organizations, and I published scores of articles in scholarly journals. This led to a love affair with the printed word. More recently I have published hundreds of articles, and this is my fifth book. Also, I have had experience operating a manufacturing business. Several years ago, my husband, my daughter, and I developed a manufacturing business in our home that grew beyond our wildest dreams. Within two years we had hired 54 sales representatives to sell goods produced by other home workers to whom we subcontracted the production of our inventory. We recently sold this business as a fully operational company in order to make time and space for other ventures, including consulting, writing, and teaching others how to make a run for the gold.

You can't do it alone. You need help, and this book can provide that help. It will lead you to the free assistance, information, and resources that are available. It will give you tips on how to succeed and warn you of pitfalls to avoid. It will help you to determine whether you are socially, mentally, and economically equipped to operate a home business and show you ways to protect your time while maintaining a semblance of normalcy around the household. It will encourage and urge you on.

It's not enough to *start* a business. The real test of success is seeing that business alive and thriving in one, five, or ten years down the road. This book will teach you how to start and *sustain* a home business, and how to make it grow as you grow. If you already have a business under way, this book can give you tips on how to increase your efficiency and profit.

Resources are presented at the appropriate places throughout the book rather than being grouped together at the end of it. As you study each chapter, try to relate the subjects and ideas to your own home and convert the suggestions to your own use. Then plan your attack and get to work.

# Part One

## *What Is Right for You?*

# 1    Are You Programmed for Success?

The rewards and recognition that come from owning and successfully operating a business have inspired many people to venture into business ownership. All proprietors seek the reward of good profits. Some individuals are rewarded by the satisfying nature of their work and by being their own boss. Another type of individual may seek status in the community by being a successful entrepreneur. These are all good reasons for going into business, but why start a business at home? Why not open an office on Main Street or a shop in a commercial zone? You need to recognize your own reasons for wanting to work at home, because there is strength in understanding motives. Are you aware that working at home may have some disadvantages? And that it takes a lot of energy to make a business succeed? Are you prepared to evaluate your strengths and weaknesses and realistically consider your chances of success? This chapter will discuss the advantages and disadvantages of home work and the personal traits needed to be a successful entrepreneur.

## The Advantages of a Home Business

There are many reasons why millions of Americans have chosen to live and work in the same place, and these reasons reflect different backgrounds, goals, abilities, limitations, and responsibilities.

One important advantage is that home is a refuge. People feel safer starting a business at home, away from public scrutiny, where they have the time to search repeatedly for the approach that brings success. This is especially true of women who have been away from the business world for many years and aren't sure how to launch a business. While working at home they can gain the expertise, experience, and confidence needed to compete in the modern marketplace.

Some people are motivated to work at home because they seek the freedom to do the kind of work they enjoy. They are dissatisfied with their present jobs and feel their skills and talents are being wasted. Being in this type of job trap can be very frustrating. People working at home can do the things they do best without a boss watching every move.

Responsibilities can be met by working at home. There is the impression that women are much more involved in home businesses than are men, but 51 percent of those currently earning money at home are men; thus, this is not a women's issue. However, women, especially mothers, are exploiting the home-based work environment as they strive to mold a career and fulfill the traditional roles of wife and mother. Women are starting small home businesses at three times the rate men are as home businesses become known as a logical and workable way to resolve the conflict caused by the need to meet family obligations and earn money.

Some women who start home businesses have never been a part of the business community. Instead, they have remained at home raising their children and maintaining a household. Starting an enterprise at home allows them to enter the business world without giving up the independence they have grown to enjoy. Other women return home to work because they want to regain control of their lives. They have grown weary of the 9 to 5 crowd, the early morning rush hour, and juggling schedules and kids. They've discovered they have more control over their lives when they work at home. It gives them the flexibility to eat lunch with their children or take in a school event without jeopardizing their jobs.

Most people work at home to both earn and save money. Money motivates most of us, and a home business has good earning potential. Some people actually feel that earning money is of minor importance—that it's a by-product of their business, something that happens as a result of doing what they want to do. Even if money is not your motivating force at the outset, it will probably become increasingly important as your business develops because most businesses must make money to survive and grow.

A home business is a great way to save money. The biggest savings is in the use of home space for business operations, and that savings gives the home business a winning edge. Surveys by the Small Business Administration indicate that home businesses have a better chance to succeed than those located in commercial space. An individual planning a business can be intimidated by the rate of small business failure. According to Dun and Bradstreet's Business Failure Record, an awesome 82 percent of small businesses fail within 10 years (in other words less than 20 percent survive for a decade!). But the chance of success is greater at home, due partly to the economic advantages of rent-free business space. Overhead can overwhelm a small venture, but it is significantly reduced in the home-based business. In fact, a home business actually reduces your taxes because you can deduct the cost of maintaining space used for business in your home as a business expense.

Another advantage of a home business is that the home worker can save time—a lot of time. How much time do you spend going to and from work each week, month, or year? If your work is 30 minutes from home, travel consumes 60 minutes each day, which is 300 minutes each week and 15,600 minutes each year. This equals 6.5 forty-hour weeks! Commuting to work also costs money because an automobile must be kept in good repair and full of gas. A family of home workers can usually get along with fewer personal-use vehicles.

Some people work at home because they want to strengthen family ties. They look forward to developing a family business with all members contributing to its success. Children who participate in this type of venture learn first hand what it takes to make a living, how our free-enterprise system works, the meaning of supply and demand, and a host of other valuable lessons. Children who grow up with a business will have a decided advantage in the business world when they are grown and on their own.

Creative people are attracted to home businesses because they need long periods of solitude and a serenity that cannot be found in the marketplace. They thrive at home, where they can become immersed in the pursuit of their art and where the pressures of business matters are less daunting.

Many disabled people have discovered that a home business enables them to enter the business world and to lead economically productive lives. Too often the physically impaired have difficulty finding employment, but a home business can be adapted to their special needs, allowing them to participate in the business community.

And finally, retired people are finding that their productive years can be extended by starting a home business. The most popular age for retiring and taking Social Security income is 62. At this age some people are tired of working, while others feel they have a lot to offer and want to remain in the work force. The people in the latter group believe in work as a way of life and are uneasy at the thought of spending their days in idleness. These unretired retirees have a good chance to succeed because they have a lifetime of experiences and know-how to contribute to a business.

## The Disadvantages of Working at Home

Some of the advantages people seek when they start home businesses can become disadvantages. Flexible hours—and the freedom to follow your own schedule—is one of the pleasures of working at home, but if you aren't careful, this freedom can lead to poor work habits with frequent interruptions and breaks, resulting in an insufficient amount of work being accomplished. On the other hand, some home workers become workaholics and never know when to stop. To combat either extreme it might be necessary to set work hours and make a resolution to keep them. Developing a habit of beginning and quitting work on time is a worthwhile goal.

However, although you won't want to work nonstop, the truth is that it takes a lot of hard work to make a business succeed, and you should realize that you may have to put in many extra hours so your business doesn't founder. But it has been said that "Nothing is really work unless you would rather be doing something else"—and if you'd rather be doing something else, don't start a home business.

It gets lonely working at home. If you are working in a smoke-filled office, surrounded by workmates who talk too much and a boss who demands too much, you are probably longing for the solitude of home. It may surprise you to learn that among the first things home workers miss is their fellow workers and the professional and intellectual stimulation of a busy office. Even if your kids are playing within hearing range, you will feel isolated if you do not find peers with whom to interact.

Also, at home you must do all the work yourself. Home business people miss having an office support system—someone to handle photocopying, correspondence, collating of materials, answering the telephone, and often, most of all, someone to bounce ideas off of.

When business is booming, you will be so busy that you won't have time to notice the absence of workmates; however, when business is slow, isolation can lead to depression, and it's very easy to get into the habit of taking long naps, eating throughout the day, or engaging in a host of other unconstructive activities. Some people who find themselves alone don't bother to maintain their personal appearance and they may lose some of their social skills, but there are ways to fight isolation and bad habits, as you will learn in Chapter 22.

A home business is not the right type of work for someone who must have immediate and regular paychecks. That regular paycheck that you have grown accustomed to may not be so regular when you work at home. You must understand that when you first start a business there will be little, if any, profit for awhile. If you cannot support yourself and your family during the start-up phase, maybe a home business is not the right move for you, at least until you have saved enough to get through this almost inescapable lean period. Even after the business is up and running, bills and helpers get paid first, and if there is anything left over, then you get paid. Of course, the goal is to bring in enough business to more than cover expenses and to make a profit that can jingle in your pockets.

Another disadvantage of home work is the loss of benefits. If you have worked outside of your home, you may take for granted the many benefits your employer has subsidized. It is necessary to pay for these benefits yourself when you work at home, unless your spouse works "out there," in which case you can usually be included in your spouse's benefit package.

These are the main disadvantages to working at home. After weighing the pros and cons of a home business, many people feel the advantages outweigh the disadvantages, and that is why so many are turning homeward to make a living.

## Assessing Your Characteristics and Chances for Success

It's a big step to go from the security of somebody else's business to the relative insecurity of your own, and it's worth pondering what lies ahead. Do you have the personal qualities needed to turn your plans into a reality? Many studies have been made in search of a list of personal traits that an individual should have in order to succeed in self-employment, and while there is no definitive list, most successful business owners seem to possess a few traits in common. These traits include initiative, energy, optimism, stubbornness, a willingness to take risks, an ability to organize, an agreeable personality, technical competence, administrative and communications abilities, good judgment, restraint, leadership qualities, patience, and preownership experience. Do you recognize yourself?

A characteristic not listed above, but one that is perhaps the most important for success in a home business, is *a willingness to work hard.* Being your own boss means that you do not punch a time clock and work from 9 to 5, but that you must do what is necessary to be successful—which could well mean long hours and preserverance, at least during the formative years of your business. If you like to work and find satisfaction in a job well done, you are a natural for a home business. Many people prefer to watch television or pursue a hobby instead of working. These people should stay away from starting a business unless the business is based on a hobby. (And even then they must realize that a hobby will seem like work after spending every day with it.)

Your background could play a part in your future success. Studies have shown that a family business background is the single most important factor in predicting success. Being raised in a family of entrepreneurs orients you toward achievement. If you have this experience in your background, take advantage of it; if you don't maybe you will give rise to new line of entrepreneurs.

How do you feel about money? Generally, successful entrepreneurs view money as a measure of accomplishment. Do you keep your personal finances in order? Have you always had a head for financial matters, perhaps starting very young earning money babysitting or delivering papers? What did you do with the money you earned as a child? Did you immediately spend it, squirrel it away in a piggybank, or deposit it in a bank account where it earned interest? Do you have a little nest egg or retirement income you can live on as your business gets underway? Some people who want to start a business are surprised to learn they cannot borrow the total amount they need to get started. You are expected to have at least half the money needed to start a business before approaching a lending institution for the remainder.

What kind of a student were you? Interestingly, exceptional students rarely grow up to operate their own businesses. In fact, it's the poorer students or the ones who gave their teachers "fits" who are more inclined to venture out on their own. They bucked the system in school and are willing to swim against the tide as they start and operate a business.

Even though you think you have the background and characteristics needed to operate a business, I urge you to answer the following questions as a means of evaluating your personal traits. Spend a few moments thinking about the questions and try to answer them as objectively as possible, because in some ways your success depends on an accurate assessment of your qualifications.

1. Do you like being the boss?
2. Do you like to make decisions?
3. Do you like to work alone?
4. Do you think you have good ideas?
5. Have you saved a little money?
6. Do you learn from mistakes?
7. Do you learn from others?
8. Do you like to try new adventures?
9. Can you usually determine what needs to be done?
10. Are you organized?
11. Do you have a special skill or trade?
12. Did your parents own a business?

The more of these questions you can answer yes to, the better your chances of succeeding with a home business. These are the characteristics needed to make a business work, and if you can honestly say, "Yes, that describes me," then you are programmed for success. On the other hand, if you answered "no" to many of them, you may not be cut out for a home business, and it might be wise to reconsider the type of work you are planning. Actually, very few people fit completely into one group or the other, and you probably possess a mix of the characteristics. The test is of value because knowledge is strength, and knowing your weaknesses will enable you to apply your energies to compensate for your deficiencies.

## Building a Business Plan

Before you delve any deeper into this book, it is a good idea to pause and look at the "big picture." The overall focus of this book is to guide you as you build a detailed and informed business plan that will help translate your dream of a home business into a reality. When you start a trip you are more likely to get to your destination if you refer to a map to plan your route. Your business plan will be the map that guides you as you get your business adventure under way, and it will make the trip somewhat easier and more direct.

A business plan is needed for several reasons. In the first place, it will help you visualize your business before it actually gets off the ground and will allow you to get a better idea of its overall operation. In addition, a business plan is required when you seek financial help from bankers or other investors because they want to make sure the business idea has been well researched and well thought out. Most importantly, by gathering the information required to create a business plan, you will learn if the business you have in mind has a reasonable chance of succeeding. If you discover that the potential for profit does not exist, then you can look for a better opportunity without risking your savings and energy on an ill-fated project.

The steps involved in developing a business idea into a concrete business plan, which will be explained in detail as you go through the chapters of this book, are as follows:

*Step 1:* Define your business mission and your business goals. Just what is it that you hope to accomplish?

*Step 2:* Select the kind of business you want to start, taking into consideration your background, the location of your home, and other factors.

*Step 3:* Determine how much profit you want from your business. Be realistic.

*Step 4:* Determine if there is an adequate market for your business. Can you generate enough sales to yield the projected profit?

*Step 5:* Check zoning codes and legal issues that may affect your business. If necessary, apply for a special-use permit and/or a business permit.

*Step 6:* Decide how to organize your business (sole proprietorship, corporation, etc.).

*Step 7:* Determine whether your house or apartment is large enough to accommodate living quarters and the business you are considering.

*Step 8:* List the assets required to operate your business, and assign a dollar value to each. Determine how much money you will need to meet all the start-up expenses, including your living expenses during the start-up phase.

*Step 9:* Identify funding sources for your business.

*Step 10:* Name your business, register the name, and get stationery printed.

*Step 11:* Design an adequate accounting and bookkeeping system.

*Step 12:* Locate and price supplies and equipment required to get the business started.

*Step 13:* Decide if you will need additional personnel to help get your business under way.

*Step 14:* Design a pricing structure and a promotional program.

*Step 15:* Investigate how and where you will sell the products or services you intend to offer.

*Step 16:* Consider the terms of sale you will offer. Would selling on credit be a good idea for your business?

*Step 17:* Evaluate the risks involved with the business you are considering and decide which kinds of measures you need to take to cope with the risks.

Fill in the steps of your plan as you read this book and do the research suggested (as it applies to your business). The business plan that evolves from these steps in the end should be a highly detailed statement as to why the business is being formed, what personal and monetary goals it can realistically achieve, and where and how it will operate.

After using the information in this book to complete your plan, study it with an open mind. If the plan looks good, then put it into action; however, if the numbers are sobering and the project lacks promise, then you should probably reconsider your options and look for a different type of business.

# 2     Selecting the Right Business

What's the best home business for you? The desire to do a specific kind of work attracts some people to a home business, while others haven't the slightest notion of the kind of business they might start and may only know they either want or need to work at home.

Selecting the right business takes introspection and honesty. You need to find an occupation that will fit into your life and home, taking into account your personal goals and the special circumstances of your life and household.

## *Identifying Goals*

The kind of business you select to develop will depend upon your goals. The only way you can know when you have arrived at your destination is to know where you are going; the only way you can know if you have accomplished your goals is to know what they are. Your business goals should be an integral part of your life goals. Think about where your life is now and where you want it to go. Your business will be the vehicle that will enable you to realize some of your life goals. Ask yourself a few questions in order to define your goals. The answers to these questions will give you a standard against which you can measure success or progress, and they will give you direction and purpose, and energize your efforts. Following are the types of questions you might ask yourself as you identify life and business goals:

- What kind of a life do I want?
- What do I want to do each day? What kind of work? How much?
- What do I want to be doing in two, five, or ten years?
- What skills and what level of competence do I seek to obtain?
- What role will other people play in my life, including family, friends,

business associates, customers, and general members of the community?
- What do I want people to think of me?
- How much money do I need in order to do what I want to do?

With your goals in mind, you can plan a business that will help you accomplish them.

Money is the first goal of a business objective, and it is essential for accomplishing life goals. How much money do you expect to earn—not just gross revenues, but gross profits? Of course, there is no way, at this stage, that you can predict what you will earn, but you can determine how much you *want* to earn. With that figure in mind, you can evaluate the possible businesses you might start and decide which of them has the greatest chance to fulfill the financial goals necessary to accomplish your life goals. A business is worth pursuing only if it can fulfill your financial goals.

## Factors Affecting Your Choice of a Business

If there is a single word that should guide you as you select a business, it's *background*. Plan to build on your background, using your skills, experiences, hobbies, interests, and contacts. Take inventory and examine in detail all you have ever done, from part-time summer jobs to professional full-time positions and everything in between. Each experience contributes to what you are today and has its own level of skill that can be called upon in your home business. Assessing your background will be discussed later in this chapter.

The type of business you undertake will certainly be influenced by the type of space available. Some businesses require very little space, while others demand a large amount and a special kind of space. The typical office requires little more than room for a desk and chair; a typewriter, computer, or word processor; a facsimile machine; a photocopier; supplies; and filing cabinets. Thus, an office could fit nicely into even a small apartment.

Other kinds of businesses require a large area where noisy and dirty equipment can be used. This is particularly true of some types of manufacturing. Not only is space needed for the manufacturing process, but also for the storage of raw materials and finished products. Besides that, a packing and shipping area is necessary, as well as an office for planning business strategy, doing bookkeeping, handling accounts, and organizing sales promotion.

Some businesses require an outside entrance with parking space for clients. Toilet facilities must be provided if clients visit your home or if employees work on the premises, and the work area should be arranged so that clients and employees remain out of the family living quarters and your home remains secure. Zoning approval may be necessary if employees or clients frequent your home.

The wide variety of service businesses can require a wide range of space needs. Many require only an office where phone calls can be received and records kept, since the service is actually performed at the client's home or business. Other service businesses demand more space because the service is performed on the home business premises. For example, an auto mechanic would need garage and parking space, but a roofer would need only a phone to receive client calls and a truck to carry supplies to the job site. As you can see, the amount and kind of space you have available to convert to business use must be taken into account as you consider what type of business to pursue.

Evaluate your financial situation. The amount of money you have to invest will certainly influence the kind of business you start. Also consider your courage, your personality traits, and your other responsibilities as you ponder the various businesses you might undertake. You should certainly select a business you will enjoy, one that will allow you to do the things you like to do while making a profit. And it is important to "go where the money is," that is, to select a business that has profit-making potential.

Home businesses fall into several main categories, including service, manufacturing, and creative work. Some home workers purchase a franchise or a distributorship, and others operate mail-order businesses. Another option is to be hired by a business that allows its employees to work at home. A discussion of each of these options follows.

## The Service Industry Is Coming Home

The majority of home businesses offer some type of service, and this category includes many diverse occupations. Some occupations require a minimum of space because the service is performed elsewhere—usually at the customer's home or business (wallpapering, interior design, heating/air conditioning maintenance)—but others require more space because the service is performed at the home office or shop (dentistry, literary agency, auto repair, accounting). Many service businesses can be started with little money, but some require a significant investment in equipment. Service businesses are usually people-oriented, and a key ingredient to their success is the rapport the seller establishes with the buyer. If you are considering a service business you should enjoy working with and for people.

The following factors should be considered as you think about a service you might offer:

• Your job skills and experience
• Your hobbies and special interests
• The location of your home
• The equipment and tools you own
• Your education and special training
• Your aggressiveness
• Your empathy for and willingness to help others

## DESIGNING A SERVICE BUSINESS AROUND JOB SKILLS AND EXPERIENCE

The skills you developed while working for an employer can be the foundation for your own business. In fact, some people take a job just to learn a skill that can be converted into a home business. Maybe you already have a marketable skill that you acquired on the job, but if not, consider taking a training job before starting your own business. You will not only learn a skill, but you will also be able to save the money needed to get your business under way.

To help you recall your skills, make a list of every job you have done and make another list of the duties performed and skills learned for each job. The easiest way to make sure you don't miss important experiences is to list the jobs you have performed in chronological order, starting with the most recent and working back to your earlier years. Don't forget to include volunteer jobs. The list (or part of the list) might look something like this:

Sept. 1987 to present: Secretary for legal assistant
    Did typing
    Used IBM computer
    Did research, using computer searches with modem
    Organized information
    Handled legal documents
    Made appointments, kept schedule for boss
    Met with clients to gather information
    Became acquainted with many people in the legal profession
Summer 1987: Printing company employee
    Learned printing procedures
    Ran copy machine; learned maintenance of copier
    Learned to make layouts
    Dealt with customers, taking orders and complaints
    Learned billing procedures

After making a list of the jobs you have had and the skills acquired, study the list and think about how the skills can be expanded to provide the basis for a home business. While thinking about your background, keep in mind contacts that can be called upon as you start your new venture.

Many of the women reading this book may have been working at home as mothers and housewives. If you are in this group you may feel that you haven't developed skills that can be used in a business, but that certainly isn't the case. If you have kept a home intact and have raised or are raising a family, you undoubtedly have many marketable skills, which may include cooking, delivering, baking, cleaning, performing child care, decorating, organizing, and sewing, to mention only a few. Such skills can be put to use to start a child care center, a catering operation, a decorating or consulting business, and so on. If you need to acquire more skills, they are as close as the nearest community college, technical school, or library; don't hesitate to go after them.

## BUILDING YOUR BUSINESS AROUND A HOBBY

Many happy people have converted a favorite hobby or special interest into a business. If you elect to do this, you probably already have the necessary equipment and skills, and it's "just" a matter of expanding what you have been doing for fun into a profit-making venture. Hobbies that might be converted to a business include photography, finding junk/selling antiques, writing, making crafts, and many of the other things we wait for the weekends to do.

## WHERE YOU LIVE CAN HELP TO DETERMINE WHAT YOU CHOOSE TO DO

Where do you live? What is going on in your neighborhood? Do you live in the country, or near a school, factory, stadium, or shopping center? Who passes your house? What do these people need? If you look closely, you may discover that a business is just waiting to happen right in your yard or kitchen, because of where your house is located.

A room or two in a home near a highway or business district could be converted into a bed and breakfast (B and B). After decades of staying in nondescript motel rooms, people are rediscovering the charm of B and Bs (which used to be called "tourist homes"). B and Bs are especially appealing to business people who are frequently on the road, because they offer a touch of home atmosphere and personal attention. Some B and B operators find that certain business people become regular customers with whom they develop friendships. Besides being a good spot for a B and B, a location near a highway might be a good place to offer emergency engine repair or tire changing.

If you live near an auditorium or stadium you might consider renting parking space on your side lot, or selling snacks, cushions, or whatever seems to be needed by passing fans. Even youngsters can make a few dollars by transporting spectator's drink coolers several blocks in little red wagons. Preparing light lunches might fill the bill for someone who lives near a factory or office building where lunch facilities are inadequate. Or, if you live on a road that leads to a popular fishing hole, what about selling bait and supplies?

People who live away from the city on a little acreage can use the land to make money in ways other than farming, although farming remains the largest cottage industry. A lake could be stocked and opened for fishing, and extra space in the barn could be used to stable horses. Once a few horses are stabled, there are other possibilities for making money, such as grooming and exercising; or you might keep horses and sell riding time. Someone who lives on a farm could also choose to operate a guest ranch or to offer hay rides.

## PUTTING YOUR EQUIPMENT TO WORK

You probably own tools and equipment that can be used to start a business. For example:

Ladders: do painting; clean windows and gutters
Snowplow: clear walks and drives
Van: deliver people or things
Boat: be a fishing guide; do lake maintenance
Truck: pick up, deliver, and move things
Sewing machine: be a seamstress, do alterations
Camera: take passport photos; photograph weddings and gatherings
Chain saw: clear woodland and cut firewood
Lawn mower: do domestic and commercial lawn care
Typewriter: do secretarial work; prepare résumés
Computer: keep records, write books and articles; write computer programs; desktop publishing; newsletters
Equipped kitchen: cater or have other food-based business
Air compressor: clean furniture and equipment: spray paint
Garden tractor: turn soil for gardeners; grow crops and sell to grocery stores or from a roadside stand
Musical instruments: teach and/or perform
Hand tools: do repair work and home maintenance
Video camera: film new homes for sale, reunions, holiday gatherings

## BUILDING A BUSINESS ON KNOWLEDGE

Don't give away information you can sell. You might be surprised to discover that you can convert information and knowledge into a commodity with a price tag. If you run a successful business, other people will pay to find out how you got started. If you can decorate fancy cakes, people might want to know where you get supplies and how you use decorating tools. If you grow a magnificent garden, people might pay to learn your secrets. If you catch fish, where you catch them and what lures or bait you use might be of interest to others who fish.

As a successful author, I am regularly accosted at parties and social gatherings by unpublished writers who need advice. These people are anxious to learn how to get their work published, and some even slip a sheet of paper in my hand expecting a quick review of a poem or query letter. I have become very adroit at not giving on-the-spot advice; instead I offer assistance through my home literary service, and I have learned that people are willing and anxious to buy information. Yes, you can cash in on the knowledge you have worked to acquire.

## USING YOUR SMILE AND STYLE TO BUILD A SALES BUSINESS

Selling is truly *big* business, with approximately 2 million retail stores in operation in the United States. In addition, sales are made door-to-door and through the mail. A home-based business can be built around selling. You might consider operating your own marketing business by functioning as a sales representative or by selling products directly from your home or studio. Or you could distribute goods through parties, such as those given to demonstrate Mary Kay cosmetics or Tupperware. Another option is to open a resale shop in your garage.

There is much to learn about the business of selling. Where do you acquire merchandise? How does a sales representative function? What commission can you expect? The field of selling is too involved to explain in a few pages, but many excellent books on the subject can be found in your local library. If you have any interest in the business of selling, take a look at the inspiring book *Selling Power of a Woman*, by Dottie Walters, now in its 13th edition and available from Royal Publishing, Inc., P.O. Box 1120, Glendale, CA 91740 ($14.95). You will probably conclude, "Well, heck, I can do that!" Also, send for the following free pamphlets: *Pyramid Schemes: Not What They Seem; Customers Mean Business—Tips for Direct Marketers;* and *Promises—Check 'Em Out!* (all available from Direct Selling Education Foundation, 1776 K St. NW, Suite 600, Washington, DC 20006).

### HELP YOURSELF BY HELPING OTHERS

The personal service industry is booming because people need help. This is a growth industry for several reasons. In the first place, more people are working now than ever before in the history of our country, and there is more expendable income. As a result, many people are willing to pay others to perform everyday tasks they previously did for themselves. Secondly, people seem to be busier than ever before, and many of them either aren't willing or don't have time to do the chores that must be done to run a household. Another factor contributing to the burgeoning service industry is the movement of women out of the home and into the work force. This movement has redefined the division of labor in our society. While these women are struggling to climb the corporate ladder, they are leaving behind homes that need to be cleaned, children that need to be cared for, and families that need to be fed. Home-service businesses are quickly filling the gap created by these working women.

Glenn Partin and Richard Rogers, two corporate dropouts in Winter Park, Florida, are taking advantage of this service opportunity. In 1988 they founded a company called At Your Service, through which they perform a wide variety of tasks, from returning videotapes or driving people to the airport to fixing a light switch or buying groceries. A phone call will bring them to the rescue of their clients. They have removed a live lizard from an oven, delivered a 59-cent package of hot dog buns to a picnic (and charged $20 for the service), and taken care of many other curious jobs that their clients either can't or won't perform but will willingly pay to have done.

## The Business of Manufacturing

Manufacturing often requires a substantial outlay of funds to purchase machinery and raw materials, but the kinds of manufacturing undertaken by most home businesses are accomplished with only a modest investment in tools, using instead a manufacturing process that is labor-intensive. A manufacturer's customers may be wholesalers, retailers, industries, the general public, governmental agencies, or foreign markets.

There are several things to consider as you evaluate products to manufacture. How labor-intensive is the manufacturing procedure? Will hired help be needed to make the product? How much equipment will be required, and how expensive is it? Who will buy the products you produce? Is a strong market established or does a market need to be created? Can the products be developed, made, and marketed at a profit? While considering the various products you might manufacture, take into account where you will be working and how it will affect the household. Will the work be noisy and dirty, or relatively quiet and clean? Will it be located in a basement or garage or in a spare bedroom? Before deciding on a manufacturing business, be sure to study the free booklet *Business Plan for Small Manufacturers*, which is available from the Small Business Administration, P.O. Box 30, Denver, CO 80201.

There are several places to look for product ideas. Government-owned patents are available to the public on a nonexclusive, royalty-free basis. Many of these are for products that require a large initial tooling-up process, but it could be worth the initial large cost if the product offers the prospect of long-term profits. Information on government-owned patents may be obtained from the U.S. Patent Office, Department of Commerce, Washington, DC 20231.

There is a continuous supply of private patents available for licensing or sale, and they are listed as they become available in *The Official Gazette* of the U.S. Patent Office. For information or for copies of the *Gazette*, write to the Superintendent of Documents, Government Printing Office, Washington, DC 20402. Ideas can also be found at inventors' shows that are usually sponsored by the chambers of commerce in large metropolitan areas. To learn when and where such events take place, write to the Office of Inventions and Innovations, National Bureau of Standards, Washington, DC 20234, or call your local chamber of commerce about dates for the next show. New products sometimes have a difficult time trying to find their place in the market because people are reluctant to buy innovative or unfamiliar products. For that reason, it may be wise to consider manufacturing a variation of a product that is already established in the marketplace.

Producing components to be used in a product manufactured by other companies is another option for the small manufacturer. Many large companies subcontract small companies to make specific parts for the products the large companies manufacture. If the large company is reliable and well established, this is perhaps the safest route available to the small manufacturer. However, the smaller company will grow only at the rate the large company does unless the small company uses the association as a base and expands into different areas as resources become available. If you are interested in working as a manufacturing subcontractor, contact manufacturing businesses in your area to learn what components and in what quantities they are interested in purchasing.

Manufacturing also includes making handcrafted products, and these are commonly produced at home. Handcrafted items fall into several categories. Original compositions take longer to produce and can be quite expensive. This type of crafting will be discussed along with other creative work later in this chapter. Other handcrafted products are made by home workers who use designs they have found in design books or magazines, although some craftspeople work from patterns of their own design. These kinds of items are usually very trendy. One year you will find hundreds of craftspeople sewing together curious-looking rabbits, and the next year these same people will be making miniature Christmas-tree ladders or ducks wearing scarves. A couple in Stevensville, Michigan, makes potholders, keeping the basic potholder pattern from year to year but changing the design sewn on the front as the popularity of one type of figure wanes and another takes its place. Over the years they have used owls, sheep, loons, ducks, and alligators. By adapting to new trends, their product stays in demand.

Some handcrafted items are mass-produced on an assembly line in a factory-type setting, but more often than not they are produced by home workers who are subcontracted to do piecework (meaning the individual is paid a fixed fee for each item produced). Many home business manufacturers use this type of help. For legal purposes, these workers are considered subcontractors, not actual employees. Using this type of help, a home business can increase the size and volume of its business without adding production space and without paying benefits or doing the paperwork required for in-house employees. The piecework workers (or subcontractors) are responsible for reporting and paying taxes on their earnings. The number of people tucked in garages, sewing rooms, basement workrooms, and behind dining room tables doing this kind of work staggers the mind and is much greater than most of us realize. This kind of manufacturing can result in the output of a large number of products. Consequently, multiple outlets are needed to sell the goods, and the products are usually sold through catalogs or retail shops with sales representatives making the contacts. (See Chapter 17 for a discussion of sales representatives.)

## Creative People Thrive at Home

Creative careers especially suited to a home business include writing, arts and crafts, and research and development.

### WRITING

Freelance writing takes many forms. Large businesses, local governments, schools, and churches use freelancers to put together special projects, brochures, newsletters, promotional material, etc. These same groups also use editing services for in-house written material.

The number of written words published in this country is awesome, and many stories, books, and articles are crafted by writers sitting at home in front of word processors or typewriters. Generally, a writer can make more money writing nonfiction books on subjects that fill a need—especially how-to books, such as this one. Books provide an ongoing income with royalties paid every year for as long as the book continues to sell, while magazine articles are paid for only once, although they can be resold after a little rewriting. Some writers make a living doing newsletters, newspaper columns (poor paying), and instruction and organizational manuals for businesses and civic groups. Some authors not only write the material, but in the case of newsletters may also print and distribute it. Some home entrepreneurs write and print greeting cards, while others write and publish small books, usually on specialty topics aimed at a specific audience or age group.

Writing is a tough business. The competition is stiff and it takes more than good compositions to get published and to earn money on a regular basis. A writer needs to produce a lot of material in order to make writing a full-time, profit-making undertaking, because a sale now and then won't provide a steady income. Good marketing procedures are essential to surviving in this business. If you are planning a writing career, you must learn how to use marketing tools and how to sell your work. The *Writer's Market* and other writer's guides can help you find outlets for your work, and you might find it useful to join a writer's guild to learn how others succeed in this business. (See "Marketing Written Work" in Chapter 17.)

## ORIGINAL ART

Making original art and crafted objects has been a traditional home business, partly because original work requires such an extraordinary commitment of time and energy that it becomes economically infeasible in most commercial settings. Another reason this type of work is done at home is because creative people need private time in order for the "creative juices" to flow.

Artists who make a living from their work have discovered that there are many not-so-obvious routes to pursue. There is a market for functional art, including original furniture, pottery, weavings, worked leather, and needlework. Freelance commercial artwork is another outlet. Businesses need artwork for such things as advertising copy, brochures, book covers, and logos. Public art is another outlet for the artist who has the capacity to fabricate monumental works.

Business-wise artists orchestrate their careers to create [  ] for their work. I have observed members of the art circle in [  ] munity as they have plied their trade. The best artists don't n........., earn the most money, perhaps because they are better at art than at business. The most economically successful artists are the ones who have pieces hanging in outlets all over town, including the airport terminal, restaurants, medical facilities, hotels, dinner clubs, concert halls, libraries, and even on rented panels in large shopping malls. They sell their work because a lot of people see it. Also, since they make more sales, they can let a piece go for less than the artist who rarely sells anything.

Some artists have discovered the economic advantage of having limited prints made of their work. Although the initial cost for prints is substantial, the profit potential encourages artists to use this method of selling because it can provide numerous sales from a single painting. Selling prints is particularly effective if the subject of the original painting is of special interest to a large number of people. A southern Indiana artist, Evelyn Steinkuhl, is riding the wave of nostalgia that is currently in vogue by painting subjects that evoke fond memories, such as prominent public structures, churches, and old buildings that have been razed or are nearing their final days. She then has limited edition prints made of her paintings and presents them to a faithful clientele, whose members buy her work as they strive to put together a collection of "the old city." Smart!

There are several ways to sell art. An artist who lives and works near a tourist area can open a studio/showroom at home and tend shop while working. Seeing the artist at work is often the catalyst that brings a sale. But few artists are located in a tourist area. A co-op of several artists can operate a gallery, or an agent can place items in galleries or other appropriate areas for viewing and sale. Still, with all these options, most artists sell their own work at art shows and fairs. (See "Marketing Strategies," Chapter 17.)

## INVENTIONS AND RESEARCH AND DEVELOPMENT

A business can be built around the development of original ideas. This field requires a keen awareness of the latest technologies upon which new developments can be built. You might design new products or improve old ones. Many successful young companies are based on technological advances, one of the most famous being Apple Computer. This company, and many others, started in a garage, where inventors with the right components created a formula for success.

There are different ways to earn money through inventions. New inventions and variations of old ones are sought by industry, private manufacturers, governmental agencies, and research institutes. Inventions can be sold outright; they can be produced and sold by another company, with the inventor receiving royalties for each item sold; or the inventor can produce and sell the invention.

Ideas have to be managed well in order to bring financial success. You should be aware that to turn an invention into a profit-making venture requires some business know-how. Engineers and inventors are usually more interested in their ideas than in the profit the ideas might generate, and for that reason investors tend to shy away from engineers and inventors as business operators. If you plan to build a business on a new idea or product, be sure to learn the necessary business skills or gather around you people who can bring your business plan to fruition.

## Consider a Franchise

The International Franchise Association (IFA) defines *franchising* as "a continuing relationship in which the franchisor provides a licensed privilege to do business, plus assistance in organizing, training, merchandising, and management in return for a consideration from the franchise." Some franchises can operate from a home as well as from a storefront. The ones that are especially adaptable to a home business are those that deliver a service, such as Servicemaster or Superlawns, Inc.

According to statistics compiled by the Bureau of Industrial Economics, franchised businesses accounted for $640 billion in sales in 1988, and retail franchising makes up slightly more than a third of the total U.S. retail sales. Franchise sales are growing at a phenomenal rate. In 1988, there were 91 percent more franchise sales than in 1980. The following terminology is used in franchise arrangements:

*Franchise:* Authorization granted to a distributor or dealer
*Franchisor:* The owner of a product, procedure, or service who sells a license to others to market the product, procedure, or service
*Franchisee:* The person who buys the license to become an affiliated dealer

Examples of well-known franchises are McDonalds, Better Homes Realty, Kwik-Kopy, Budget Rent-A-Car, and Servicemaster Industries. A Classified Directory of Members of IFA can be obtained free from the International Franchise Association, 1025 Connecticut Ave. NW, Washington, DC 20036. Also, *Franchise Opportunities* lists nearly 1,000 franchises with descriptions and other valuable information. The publication is available from Sterling Publishing Co., Inc., 2 Park Ave., New York, NY 10016, for $9.95.

## WHAT DOES A FRANCHISE OFFER?

A franchise offers an idea—somebody else's idea that you can use as the foundation for your own business. It is a form of licensing and a way to get into business even if you are inexperienced and lacking adequate capital. The owner (franchisor) of a method, service, or product agrees to have the method, service, or product distributed through affiliated dealers (franchisees). A franchisee (who may be you) pays for the privilege of being an affiliated dealer and is sometimes given exclusive access to a geographical area. The franchisor maintains control over the marketing methods as well as the brand name that identifies the product, method, or service. This type of operation frequently resembles a large chain-store operation with trademarks, uniforms, equipment, and standardized products or services and procedures, as outlined in a franchise agreement. The franchisor may provide some or all of the following:

Location analysis and counsel
Store development aid, including lease negotiation
Store design and equipment purchasing
Initial employee and management training
Continuing management counseling
Advertising and merchandising counsel and assistance
Standardized operating procedures
Centralized purchasing with consequent savings
Financial assistance in the establishment of the business

Franchising is considered to be a convenient and economic way to get into business with a minimum of risk while using a proven product or service and proven marketing methods. However, in order to maintain uniformity between the franchises, much of the methodology of operating the business is a part of the franchise agreement, and, as a result, the owner of a franchised business may sometimes feel that he or she is not the boss, but only the errand runner for the home office. There are advantages to this. By maintaining strict quality control, the individual franchisee can share in the goodwill built up by all of the other outlets that bear the same name.

## HOW RISKY IS A FRANCHISE?

Magazines and newspapers are filled with advertisements promising instant success with a franchise even to those who have no experience in the field. But, *let the buyer beware.* The Better Business Bureau, a nonprofit organization supported by dues from members in the business community which functions as a watchdog for businesses engaged in unethical or deceptive practices, preaches, "Before you invest—*investigate!*" That is sound advice. If you are considering investing in a franchise, you should know the risks. Some franchises carry a greater risk than others. Some are offered by companies with a track record of successful operations, but there are also high-risk franchises offered by new companies. The truth is, the economic landscape is littered with the wreckage of small businesses that have been ruined by franchisors who do not offer a viable product, method, or service and others who are dishonest and anxious to make a fast buck from unsuspecting clients. Hence, you should be very wary when considering a franchise.

If you buy a franchise, you should understand that in this type of venture you must rely on both the business skills of the franchisor and also on you own business aptitude and experiences. For that reason, you should evaluate your own potential for success, as well as that of the franchise you are considering. Compare several franchises that offer the same type of business. The handbooks mentioned above briefly describe hundreds of franchises. Read them to get a general idea of what might interest you, and then continue your investigation by writing to several of the companies for their disclosure statement or prospectus. Examine earnings claims carefully and ask for written substantiation. Of course, many factors contribute to the profit an individual franchisee makes, and you should realize that you may not earn as much as some of the other franchisees—or you may earn more.

Before you decide on a particular franchise you should assemble and evaluate the following information:

1. A thorough description of the franchisor and its affiliates, including a description of the franchisor's business experience.
2. The names and addresses of other franchisees; write to them to learn how they feel about the franchisor.
3. Records of lawsuits or bankruptcies in which the franchisor and its officers have been involved.
4. A detailed list of all initial payments and fees required to obtain the franchise.
5. A description of the continuing payments required after the franchise opens.
6. Restrictions on the quality of goods and services used in the franchise and from whom they may be purchased. Are you required to purchase from the franchisor or its affiliates?
7. A description of services available from the franchisor and the costs of these services.
8. A description of territorial protection granted to the franchisee and your legal recourse if the territory is "invaded."

9. Conditions under which the franchise may be repurchased or refused renewal by the franchisor, transferred to a third party by the franchisee, or terminated or modified by either party.
10. The financial statements of the franchisor.
11. Training offered by the franchisor. Carefully scrutinize this for depth and content.
12. The number of franchisees terminated during the past year or two and the reasons for their termination.

After you have learned all you can about the franchises that interest you, see a lawyer. Buying a franchise is a big step and one that should be taken with a lawyer holding your hand. The cost of legal advice will be relatively small compared to the total initial investment for a franchise. Also, the cost of this advice at the outset will certainly be less than the cost of later legal representation to solve problems that could have been avoided at the outset.

## Mail Order: A Business in Your Mailbox (and Spare Room)

Mail-order sales represent about 12 percent of all consumer purchases, which means that over 1 billion dollars worth of products and services are purchased each week by mail. Many of these sales are made by people working at home. A mail-order business does not require a storefront or an office in the business district. Such a business can fit nicely into a home where there is a room to store goods and process orders and an office to plot strategy and keep records.

Some people conjure up visions of huge profits when they think of mail-order businesses. Maybe you've heard some of the mail-order success stories that have made the news—and there are many. Some of these successes did indeed get started on a dining room table and go on to make a fortune. However, you should also know that not everybody who ventures into this business succeeds at making money. Mail-order profits can vary greatly, depending on the personal skills, aggressiveness, ability, imagination, business judgment, capital resources, and determination of the proprietor. It is a way of doing business that has been profitable for many people, and it might be right for you.

How do you get started? What can you sell? How do you advertise? Who is your market? How much money is needed to get under way? These are some of the questions that need to be answered as you consider this type of business. The following few paragraphs touch upon these questions, but for a thorough examination of the mail-order business, refer to the resource books listed at the end of this discussion.

## DIFFERENT METHODS OF SELLING THROUGH THE MAIL

There are several different approaches to the mail-order trade. Some mail-order companies sell a specialty product line, while others print catalogs listing a whole array of items. The most common products sold through catalogs are women's clothing and gifts, but many mail-order companies appeal to buyers with specialized interests and sell very defined lines, such as car parts or gardening tools. Some companies advertise in newspapers and magazines, while others send brochures and catalogs directly to potential customers.

Home businesses can get involved with mail order in several ways. Some businesses function as distributors by purchasing merchandise from manufacturers or importers and selling it to customers who order by mail or phone. Others use mail-order techniques to sell their own home-manufactured products, and some home manufacturers sell their goods to mail-order businesses who in turn sell the items to consumers. The latter method is a good way to get products distributed, but sometimes the small manufacturer must sell at below wholesale prices in order to entice catalog companies to carry their products.

Services are also sold by mail. You've probably seen the advertisements in several men's magazines that offer locksmithing or small engine repair lessons through the mail. These ads assure graduates of their programs that they will be able to start a business with their newly acquired skills. The ads usually claim that graduates earn large incomes, and often include testimonials from pleased past participants. These advertisements lead the reader to believe that the classes originate in some "institute" where people wear lab coats and work with fancy equipment, but many of the "schools" are housed in small home offices and are operated by people whose only uniform is maybe a jogging suit or an apron. I once knew a university engineering professor who offered a metal-plating class by mail. This old gent taught metallurgy classes by day but spent his evenings grading papers from his mail-order students and writing more lessons.

## EFFECTIVE ADVERTISING AND REPEAT BUSINESS LEAD TO PROFIT

The success of a mail-order business depends on the effectiveness of its advertising campaign. The advertising media normally used are newspapers and magazines, wherein classified or display ads are placed. Many mail-order companies rely solely on classified advertising, while others use classified ads to determine the best copy appeal and then use this information to develop display ads and printed matter. Other mail-order companies don't use advertisements in publications, but instead purchase mailing lists directed to specific markets and send brochures or catalogs directly to these potential customers.

The most profitable mail-order businesses are those with customers who buy over and over again. Customers will reorder from a company that offers good prices, good service, and *products that are consumables*. For example, companies that sell foods, vitamins, cosmetics, and proprietary drugs can expect repeat business because these items are consumed and need to be repurchased periodically. If customers are satisfied with the products and service they receive with their first order, there is a high probability they will order more goods if they continue to receive mailings from the company.

If the mail-order business appeals to you, then study the market and try to find a product or service you might offer. Answer advertisements, particularly those for goods or services similar to those you are interested in selling, and study the catalogs, sales letters, brochures, and other literature you receive in an effort to learn what allows these companies to survive in a competitive market. For more information see

*Mail Order Moonlighting*, by Cecil C. Hoge. 1976. Order from Ten Speed Press, Box 7123, Berkeley, CA 94707. Paperback, $7.95. This is a classic that can serve as a guide for beginning mail-order entrepreneurs.

*How To Start and Operate a Mail-Order Business*, by Julian Simon. McGraw-Hill, 1221 Avenue of the Americas, New York, NY 10020. Hardcover, $24.95. This book offers basic techniques and sound advice for starting a mail-order business. It lists hundreds of products that sell well through the mail and explains how to go about selling them.

**TABLE PAD MANUFACTURERS: SINGLE-PRODUCT, SINGLE-ORDER MAIL-ORDER SURVIVORS**

Table pad manufacturers do practically all of their business by mail. Many of the companies selling table pads are home businesses that place small display advertisements in national magazines. The pads are usually priced between $50 and $125 (even though the advertisement might claim they cost only $29.95). Most customers can use only a single pad, so this type of business is built on the one-time customer. These companies survive without repeat business because there is a large profit margin on their product, and that margin provides the money to reinvest in more advertising. This type of operation is an exception to the rule of thumb that most profitable mail-order businesses are based on repeat business and are rarely profitable with a single product such as a table pad.

*Memo to Mailers,* a free newsletter from the U.S. Postal Service. Request a copy on business letterhead from Memo to Mailers, P.O. Box 1, Linwood, NJ 08221.

Also, the National Mail Order Association compiles reports of value to mail-order entrepreneurs. Membership includes subscriptions to two newsletters. For a free brochure write to National Mail Order Association, 5818 Venice Boulevard, Los Angeles, CA 90019.

## Working at Home for Someone Else

Another approach to home work is to be employed by a business that allows you to work in your own home. This is appealing to the person who wants to work at home but doesn't want the responsibility of owning and operating a business. Many mothers of preschool and school-age children are favoring this type of employment.

The advantages of working for another business rather than running your own include security in the form of a regular paycheck while working in your own home. Also, your personal savings won't be committed to the business, and there is less likelihood of your evenings and weekends being interrupted with work. The disadvantages are that (1) you are an employee of somebody else and probably can't do the work that most appeals to you, (2) there isn't much opportunity to accumulate wealth, (3) there is less recognition and prestige, and (4) you don't have the exhilarating challenge of making your own business succeed.

There are several reasons businesses have begun hiring home workers. An increasing number of small to medium-sized companies

---

**REPEAT SALES PLUS LIMITED ADVERTISING EXPENSE EQUALS MAIL-ORDER SUCCESS**

Home-Sew is a mail-order company that was built through customer loyalty, repeat sales, and good mailing lists. It is a small business that operates out of Bethlehem, Pennsylvania, and sells a wide array of sewing supplies—things that are consumed and need to be replaced. Home-Sew advertises very little, but it is known for low prices, reliable quality, and fast service. Enclosed with each order is a small catalog that contains an order form. On the bottom of the order form is space to write in the name and address of someone who might enjoy receiving the catalog. This is a cost-effective way to expand the mailing list, because most people who sew know others who would be interested in learning of a good source of inexpensive supplies. Thus, this company thrives through repeat sales and a well-targeted, customer-supplied mailing list.

**Home-Sew**

**BETHLEHEM, PA 18018**
(Please Print or Write Plainly)

**ORDERS SHIPPED SAME DAY AS RECEIVED**

DATE _____

NAME _____

DELIVERY
ADDRESS _____ APT. NO. _____
Please give full address so that Parcel Post or UPS can deliver to your home

CITY _____ STATE _____

ZIP CODE _____

| Item No. | Size | Color | Name of Item | How Many | Price Each | Total |
|---|---|---|---|---|---|---|
| | | | | | | |
| | | | | | | |
| | | | | | | |
| | | | | | | |
| | | | | | | |
| | | | | | | |
| | | | | | | |
| | | | | | | |
| | | | | | | |
| | | | | | | |
| | | | | | | |
| | | | | | | |

**SC5 — Sample Club**    If you are not a member, and wish current trimming samples, add 50¢ ➤

**FREE:** $1.00 in merchandise for each $15.00 of your order.
HOME-SEW choice or yours. _____

| | |
|---|---|
| **Total For Merchandise** ( Minimum Order $5 ) | |
| **Pa. Tax** | |
| **Add Postage and Handling** *POSTAGE FREE* on orders over $30. | **.95** |
| **Amount Enclosed** | |

FOR ITEMS DELIVERED TO PA. ADD 6% TAX. (Omit items that are used in making wearing apparel) ➤

**REQUEST EXTRA CATALOGS TO GIVE YOUR FRIENDS, OR WE WILL MAIL THEM FOR YOU.**

Please mail a free catalog to my friend (please print):

Name _____

Address _____

City _____

State _____ Zip _____

*Order form from Home-Sew. This form is enclosed with each order, encouraging the customer to provide both a new order and names for the company's mailing list.*

operate through a network of home-based workers with very few in-house employees because this arrangement allows them to expand without the cost of adding office or production space. Urban traffic is another reason people are permitted to work at home. In 1989, Los Angeles started allowing some city employees to work at home in an effort to reduce community traffic and office expenses. Information-based companies also hire workers who can work at home just as well as in an office complex. Some newspaper journalists rarely see their editors because they work at home and telecommute their stories to the editor's desk. And, it's a common practice for sales representatives to work from home and communicate with the home office through the telephone and through computer linkups.

One of the most compelling reasons for allowing workers to work at home is the resulting reduction in employee turnover. More and more companies are finding it difficult to hire and retain skilled employees, and for that reason are promoting programs that will reduce turnover by accommodating workers who, for one reason or another, cannot or do not wish to meet the traditional work schedule. These programs include flexible work hours and the opportunity to do some or all work at home. For example, IBM Corporation allows flexible work hours and the opportunity to work at home, and General Electric uses home workers as consultants. Both companies report that these programs result in greater worker loyalty and higher productivity.

I am acquainted with an engineer named Greta who has worked at General Electric (GE) for several years. She had planned to stop working for a brief time for the birth of each child and then hire a sitter and return to work. Greta had not anticipated the joy of motherhood, and she soon discovered she did not want to leave her infants and return to work. However she has not had to choose between her career and motherhood, because GE has hired her to work at home as a consultant. Both she and GE are pleased with the arrangement; she is happy because she can continue to work while raising her children, and GE is happy because the company is spared the expense of finding and training another engineer. And, while there is no commitment on either party's part, GE probably expects that Greta will return to the office when her child-rearing days are over.

If you like your current job but want to work at home, discuss this possibility with your boss. It might be wise to start by working part-time at home until you convince your employer that you are just as effective at home as you are in the office. Also, don't be reluctant to discuss the employment details of the arrangement *before* you start working at home because conditions taken for granted when you work on the business premises may not be the same when you work at home. Before you turn in your time card, pay schedules and work benefits should be clearly defined, along with the number of hours you will work. You need to know if you can move back to the office and if you will continue to be promoted even though you aren't working in the office. Also, whose equipment and office supplies will you use, and who will be responsible for maintenance? What are and are not reimbursable expenses? Who pays for the telephone, photocopying, faxing, and out-of-pocket expenses? Must you work precise hours? Clearly, there are a lot of issues to consider. Still interested? See *The Work-At-Home Sourcebook: How to Find "At Home" Work That's Right For You*, 1987–88 edition, by Lynie Arden (Live Oak Publishers, 6003 N. 51st St., Boulder, CO 80301).

## A Look Ahead

Part 2 of this book lists and describes many specific occupations that can be the basis of a home business. At this point, if you do not have one or two ideas about what you want to pursue, you should study the list and select an occupation that seems appropriate for you and your circumstances. (Even if you do have a fairly solid business idea, you may find the list interesting as it may suggest some occupations that hadn't occurred to you as you made your initial choice.)

The remaining chapters in the book (contained in Parts 3 through 7) deal with how to set up and run a business. It would be to your advantage to have a business in mind, at least tentatively, before you read beyond Part 2; that way, as you read, you can relate the information and tips provided in the remaining chapters to your particular idea to help flesh out your business plans.

# Part Two

# *Suggestions for Home Businesses*

# 3 A List of Suitable Occupations for Home Businesses

This section lists over 200 occupations that can be operated from a home. There are two lists. The first list provides service occupations organized by category to help you place them in the service industry. Most of the occupations from the first list are included in the second list, which is organized alphabetically. These lists are by no means complete, but they should help you become aware of the diversity of job opportunities that exist for home businesses. All of these businesses can be based in the home, but some require the work to be done elsewhere (such as wallpapering), while others can be accomplished at home (such as accounting). In the alphabetical list, a few comments are presented about some of the occupations, and library resource materials are listed for others. Many need no explanation.

## Category List

### COMMERCIAL AND RESIDENTIAL BUILDING SERVICES

Air conditioner installation/maintenance

Carpenter

Chimney sweep

Electrician

Furnace maintenance

Floor, carpet, and drape cleaning

Interior decorator

Lawn care and landscaping

Painting, exterior and interior

Pest control

Plant and garden maintenance

Plumber

Refuse removal

Security

Snow removal

Swimming pool maintenance

Television maintenance and repair

Upholsterer

Wallpapering

Window washing

## BUSINESS SERVICES

Accounting
Appraiser
Advertising
Attorney
Auctioneer
Bookbinding
Bookkeeping
Commercial photography
Computer consultant
Computer repair
Computer trainer
Copywriting
Credit and collection
Data Processing
Duplicating
Employment agency
Graphic design and illustrations
Income tax preparation
Information detective
Investment counseling
Messenger service
Office and shop equipment repair
Postal and delivery service
Printer, and quick printer
Public relations agent
Sales representative
Secretarial services
Signs, design and fabrication
Telephone answering
Telemarketer
Wholesaling and retailing

## REPAIR AND COMMUNITY SERVICES

Alarm systems
Appliance repair
Automobile detailing
Automobile repair
Baking, specialty items and wedding cakes
Bed and breakfast
Dating service
Day care for children, the infirm, or the aged
Garden rototilling
Hauling
Insurance agent
Machine and equipment repair
Newspaper delivery
Photographer
Piano tuning
Real estate agent
Relocation consultant
Shoe repair
Travel agent
Videographer
Water conditioning

## EDUCATIONAL SERVICES

Acting school
Aerobics/exercise instruction
Craft instruction
Language instruction, spoken and signing
Literary agent
Martial arts school
Modeling school
Musical instruction
Newsletter
Pollster
Remedial learning assistance
Researcher
Tutor
Writer
Vehicle driving school
Yoga instruction

## ENTERTAINMENT SERVICES

Balloon decorator
Catering parties and picnics
Dance studio
Entertainer

Event promoter
Hayrides and sleigh rides
Party planner
Talent agent

## HEALTH SERVICES

Companion for shut-ins
Convalescent home
Convalescent therapy
Dentist
Dietician
Meals for shut-ins

Nursing
Physician
Psychological testing and coun-
    seling
Wheelchair, hospital bed, etc.
    rental

## PERSONAL SERVICES

Babysitting
Butler
Chauffeur
Closet organizer
Cook
Dating service
Elder care, daily telephone checks
Elder care, catered meals
Family financial advisor
Hair stylist
Home cleaning

House sitting
Image consultant
Income tax preparation
Laundry and ironing
Manicurist
Masseur
Seamstress
Shopping service
Skin-care consultant
Telephone wake-up
Video editing

## PET SERVICES

Dog walking
Pet boarding
Pet grooming

Pet sitting
Pet training
Veterinarian

## TRANSPORTATION SERVICES

Car, truck, trailer rental
Chartered aircraft
Chartered bus or van
Limousine
Parking lot

Personal shopping for aged
School bus
Taxi
Transporting children
Transporting disabled

### TOOL RENTAL SERVICE

Agricultural equipment
Air compressor, generators
Backhoe
Chain saw

Construction equipment
Sewer cleaner
Sump pump
Tools, hand

### SPORT SERVICES

Billiard room operator
Boat rental
Camp and recreational vehicle
  (RV) grounds operator
Fishing guide

Sport equipment rental
Sports training school
Tennis and racquetball courts op-
  erator

## Alphabetical List

*Accountant:* An accountant can work at home just as effectively as in a downtown office. Many home office accountants do work for other home businesses, but some serve businesses in commercial zones. See the booklet *Establishing an Accounting Practice;* $3.00 from Bank of America, Dept. 341, P.O. Box 3401, San Francisco, CA 94137.

*Acting School Director:* A family room or finished basement can serve as a stage for teaching young people acting skills; a troupe of actors could prepare shows for parents and friends.

*Advertising:* Handling promotion and advertising for other businesses can be easily accomplished at home.

*Advising:* If you have expertise in some area, you can use that knowledge to build a business advising others. Advice services might range from helping high school students locate the best college scholarships and overseeing applications to helping hunters track game and fishermen locate the best streams in which to cast their lures.

*Aerobics/Exercise Instructor:* Get paid for flexing and stretching and moving to the music with a group of exercise addicts. Lease a public recreation center or a church activities room, and either work as an independent instructor or buy a franchise, such as Jazzercise. See *Dance Exercise Today,* 2437 Morena Blvd., 2nd Floor, San Diego, CA 92110, (619) 275-2450. Also ask about the Aerobic and Fitness Association of America at the same address.

*Agricultural Equipment Rental:* If you own tractors, plows, and other pieces of farm equipment, you might consider renting them to others. You might also hire out to do plowing or other agricultural work. If you have a rototiller you can prepare garden soil for a fee.

*Air Conditioner Maintenance:* Many home businesses combine this work with furnace maintenance in order to extend employment throughout the year. See *Furnace Maintenance* for reference.

*Alarm Systems:* These systems are used for medical emergencies as well as for crime detection and prevention. Both uses are growing in popularity. To learn about this business contact the National Burglar and Fire Alarm Association, 1120 19th St. NW, Suite LL20, Washington, DC 20036, (202) 296-9595. Also see *Security Distributing and Marketing Magazine*, 1350 E. Touhy Ave., Des Plaines, IL 60018, (312) 635-8800.

*Alterations:* Taking a nip here and a tuck there, replacing zippers, and altering all type of wearing apparel is a needed service that can produce a profit. You can do this independently or by commission in conjunction with a clothing store or dry cleaning establishment that offers alteration service.

*Antique Dealer:* A truck or hatchback to carry the pieces and a knowledge of antiques will help start this business. See *Buying and Selling Antiques*, by Don Cline and Sara Pitzer, 1986, Storey Publishing, Pownal, VT 05261.

*Appliance Repair:* This can include repairing items such as toasters, vacuum cleaners, television sets, sewing machines, heaters, lamps, refrigerators, and microwaves. A business could specialize in repairing a single type of appliance or a wide range, depending on the abilities of the proprietor.

*Appraiser:* Serving as an appraiser of residential and commercial property for banks and realtors is a viable home business. For further information contact the American Institute of Real Estate Appraisers, 430 N. Michigan Ave., Chicago, IL 60611, (312) 329-8559.

*Art, Commercial:* Freelance artists produce a wide variety of materials for a broad spectrum of commercial publications. See *Artist's Market*, in bookstores. Also see the catalog in the next listing.

*Art Gallery:* See free catalog from Dynamic Graphics, Inc., 6000 North Forest Park Drive, Peoria, IL 61656.

*Auctioneer:* Some auctioneers work out of their own warehouse-type facility with clients bringing the items to be sold, but others hold the auction on the client's premises. In the latter case the auctioneer needs virtually no space, and the only equipment required is a vehicle to travel to auctions and a portable amplifier. Also, a helper is needed to function as record keeper and cashier.

*Automobile Dealer, New or Old:* Buying, repairing, and reselling automobiles, especially vintage automobiles, has proven to be a good home business for auto mechanics.

*Automobile Detailing:* According to the Automotive Vehicle Manufacturers Association, people are keeping their cars an average of 7.5 years, up from 5.5 years in 1970, and they are taking care of them better. The International Carwash Association estimated carwash revenues at $8 billion in 1986. You can either open an independent car care center or buy a franchise, such as Tidy Car that operates out of Florida. For more information, contact the International Carwash Association, 1 Imperial Place, 1 E. 22nd St., Suite 400, Lombard, IL 60148, (312) 495-0100.

*Automobile Mechanic:* See *Find a Career In Auto Mechanics*, by C. William Harrison; Putnam, New York, NY.

*Automobile, Truck, or Trailer Rental:* This business could be started with a single vehicle or a fleet of them. Be sure to check with your insurance agent before venturing into this business.

*Babysitting:* See *Child Care.*

*Baking:* Baking specialty items for weddings and parties or for restaurants can be developed into a home business. See *Cooking for Profit—The Business of Food Preparation* (trade magazine), P.O. Box 267, Fond du Lac, WI 54935.

*Balloon Decorator:* Balloon decorating provides a living for thousands of entrepreneurs. These entrepreneurs usually start selling balloon bouquets, delivered along with a singing birthday wish. Now fancy parties have fancy balloon decorations, from columns to arches. See *Balloons Today*, P.O. Box 43472, Jacksonville, FL 32201, (904) 388-9060.

*Barber:* Just as beauticians develop a neighborhood clientele, so can barbers. This home business takes little space and would fit nicely into a side porch.

*Beauty Salon:* See *Start and Run a Profitable Beauty Salon: A Complete Step-by-Step Business Plan*, by Paul Pogue; paperback, $14.95 from TAB Books, Blue Ridge Summit, PA 17214.

*Bed and Breakfast:* See *Start Your Own Bed and Breakfast Business*, by Beverly Mathews; 1985, paperback, $5.95 from Pocket Books, 1230 Avenue of the Americas, New York, NY 10020.

*Beekeeping and Honey Sales:* See *Beekeeping—An Illustrated Handbook*, by Diane G. Stelley; paperback, $12.95 from TAB Books, Blue Ridge Summit, PA 17214.

*Bicycle Repair:* The increased number of bicyclists has produced a need for more repair shops.

*Bill Collecting:* Many small businesses hire freelance bill collectors to recover past-due accounts. To attract clients, list such a business under the heading "Collection Agency" in the Yellow Pages.

*Boat Rental:* A lot of city folk without a boat would like to spend a day or weekend fishing, and this service would meet their needs. Boats could be kept on the water and rented by the hour or day, or they could be stored elsewhere and the renters could take them to the water.

*Bookbinding:* See *Simplified Bookbinding*, by Henry Gross; 1976, Scribner, New York, NY.

*Bookkeeping:* Keeping books for several small businesses can be a very profitable home business. This can be combined with other secretarial services to make it even more appealing to customers.

*Book Producer:* Some bestsellers are produced by people working at home. A book producer takes a manuscript and converts it into a bound book, which is then marketed and distributed by a publisher or distributor. For more information contact the American Book Producers Association, Fourth Floor, 319 E. 52nd St., New York, NY 10022, (212) 982-8934.

*Camp and RV Grounds Proprietor:* A little ground near a well-traveled road is needed for this service. It is helpful to have your facility listed in campground guidebooks and directories. Consult guidebooks to learn who publishes them and to find out how to be included.

*Camping Equipment Rental.*

*Canned Specialties:* There is a big demand for "Granny's" jellies, pickled goodies, and the like. They can be sold from your home, or you can develop a larger market by selling through retail shops and delicatessens. Pricing is the key to making a profit, but a little jar of something special can bring a goodly sum.

*Carpentry:* See *Opportunities in Carpentry Careers*, by Roger Sheldon; 1987, VGM Career Horizons, Lincolnwood, IL.

*Carpeting, Floors, and Drapes—Cleaning and Installing:* Installing and cleaning floor coverings and drapes has become a popular home business. See *The Contract Cleaner Companion*, a free brochure from the American Institute of Maintenance, 1120 East Chevy Drive, P.O. Box 2068, Glendale, CA 91209. Also ask for other related publications.

*Catering Weddings, Parties, and Picnics:* See *Cater From Your Kitchen*, by Margorie P. Blanchard; 1981, Bobbs-Merrill, 866 Third Ave., New York, NY 10022. Also see *Professional Course in Bartending for Home Study*; paperback, $9.95 from Harvard Common Press, 535 Albany Street, Boston, MA 02118. Also see *Catering Today Magazine*, P.O. Box 222, Santa Claus, IN 47579, (812) 937-4464. For more information contact the National Institute for Off-Premise Catering, 1341 N. Sedgwick, Chicago, IL 60610, (800) OFF-PREM.

*Charter Aircraft or Bus.*

*Chauffeur.*

*Child Care:* You can work at this business full-time or part-time, and care for a single child or a group of children.

*Chimney Sweep:* See *Chimneys and Stove Cleaning*, Garden Way Publishing, Charlotte, VT 05445.

*Chiropractor:* This requires special, extensive education and licensing. See *Opportunities in Chiropractic Health*, by R. C. Shafer; 1987, VGM Career Horizons, Lincolnwood, IL.

*Closet Organizer:* According to *Entrepreneur* magazine, there are approximately 344 million closets in American homes. Most of these could probably use some organizing—and yes, people are paying for this service.

*Commercial Photography:* A listing in the telephone directory will bring jobs from other businesses in need of this service, which can range from taking employee portrait photographs to documenting new construction or a new product.

*Commercials—Radio and Television:* While national commercials are produced in fancy studios in metropolitan areas, writing and producing commercials for local television and radio is a service that can be easily done in a home studio.

*Companion for Shut-ins.*

*Computer-Oriented Occupations:* These occupations might include writing programs, processing data, keeping books, and writing with the word processor. Many books are available that explore this broad field.

*Computer Consultant:* If you have accumulated a base of knowledge about computers, you can sell your expertise. Most firms need computers (if they don't already have them) but haven't any notion which system best serves their needs. Maybe you can guide them and help them get into operation. For more information contact the Independent Computer Consultants Association, 443 N. New Ballas, P.O. Box 27412, St. Louis, MO 63141, (314) 997-4633. Also see *Consultants News*, Templeton Rd., Fitzwilliam, NH 03447, (603) 585-2200.

*Computer Repair:* Corporations are reconsidering the expensive maintenance contracts with computer manufacturers and are looking for less expensive ways to maintain their computers. If you have the skill to repair computers, you're in business! See *Computer/Electronic Service News*, Box 428, Peterborough, NH 03458, (603) 924-9457.

*Computer Trainer:* Computer trainers teach everything from basic word processing to difficult maneuvers around data bases to beginning computer users. See *Data Training*, 38 Chauncy Street, Boston, MA 02111, (617) 542-0146.

*Concrete Work.*

*Construction.*

*Consultant:* See *Consulting: The Complete Guide to a Profitable Career*, by Robert E. Kelly; 1981, Scribner, 866 Third Ave., New York, NY 10022. Also see *Advice—A High Profit Business*, by Herman Holtz; 1986, Wiley, New York, NY 10158.

*Convalescent Home:* Operating a convalescent home requires meeting many governmental regulations, but once these regulations have been satisfied the government and insurance programs pay for the care of many elderly and convalescing patients, and this practically ensures that this home business will make a profit.

*Convalescent or Physical Therapy:* This occupation takes special education and licensing.

*Cook:* See *Freelance Foodcrafting: How to Become Profitably Self-Employed in Your Own Creative Cooking Business*, by Janet Shown; 1983, paperback, $10.95 from Live Oak Publishers, 6003 N. 51st St., Boulder, CO 80301.

*Copy Writing:* Writing advertising copy can be combined with other writing activities to provide an ongoing business.

*Cosmetology:* Caring for skin and selling skin care products is sometimes done through organizations such as Mary Kay Cosmetics and Avon. While this means working for another company, much of the work can be done at home and on a flexible schedule.

*Counseling:* This type of business can range from marriage counseling to teaching proper dress and wearing apparel. Some types of counseling require more training and/or licensing than others.

*Crafts—Making, Selling, and Instructing:* See *Career Opportunities in Crafts*, by Elyse Sommer; 1977, paperback, $6.95 from Crown Publishers. Also see *How to Start Your Own Craft Business*, by Herb Genfan and Lyn Taetzsch; 1974, Watson-Guptill Publications, New York. Also see *Craft Supply Directory*, P.O. Box 420, Englishtown, NJ 07726 ($40), and *Gifts and Decorative Accessories Directory*, available in many libraries and bookstores. Many other books are available on this subject.

*Dance Instruction and Studio:* Ballet, ballroom, tap, and other dancing can be taught in classes or individually. Students of ballet and tap will be more inclined to excel and to continue their study if they can show their skill in recitals. Organized dances for students of ballroom dancing will encourage them to bring friends who might become students. A room can be rented at a community facility and a disk jockey hired for this kind of event.

*Data Processing and Other Computer-Based Occupations:* See *Make-Money-With-Your-Computer-Package*, which is free from the Association of Electronic Cottages, 677 Canyon Crest Drive, Sierra Madre, CA 91024. Many other publications on this topic are available in bookstores and libraries.

*Dating Service:* The matchmaker is still needed today.

*Day-Care Center Operator:* It may take remodeling to meet licensing regulations, but a home can easily accommodate a day-care center. Keep in mind that it makes more business sense to care for several children, rather than for a single child. A well-run center will quickly develop a waiting list of parents seeking trustworthy care for their children. Day care can also include care for the aged and infirm. For information contact the Day Care Council of America, 5730 Market Street, Oakland, CA 94608. Also see *Family Day Care: How to*

*Provide It in Your Own Home*, by Betsy Squibb; paperback, $10.45 from Harvard Common Press, 535 Albany Street, Boston, MA 02118.

*Debt Counseling Services:* Use your financial expertise to help clients bring income and expenditures into balance.

*Delivery Service:* Many small businesses hire an independent delivery service rather than using in-house employees.

*Desktop Publishing:* This is just one of the many writing careers a person with writing skills might pursue at home. Market-research firm Dataquest forecasts that the sales of desktop publishing equipment, which were only $2.5 million in 1985, will hit $5 *billion* in 1990! Find a niche and fill it, whether it's keeping people informed about the latest medical developments or the best videotapes being released. See *Publish, PC World,* and *MacWorld,* all published by PCW Communications Inc., 501 Second St., Suite 600, San Francisco, CA 94107, (415) 546-7722.

*Dietician:* See *Opportunities In Nutrition Careers*, by Carol C. Caldwell; 1986; VGM Career Horizons, Lincolnwood, IL.

*Dress Design and Custom Sewing:* Clothing for special events, special clothing for people confined to wheelchairs, and clothing in unusual sizes all require custom sewing.

*Driving Instructor:* Teaching adults who never learned to drive or teenagers anxious to get on wheels will require extra insurance protection.

*Dry Cleaning, Laundry, and Ironing:* This service is increasingly in demand as more people work outside the home and have less time to do work for themselves. Pickup and delivery will increase the value of this service.

*Duplicating:* This service is needed by many businesses, and the initial cost of going into business is the cost of a copy machine. Pickup and delivery of copied material would make this an attractive service.

*Editing:* If you are skilled in the craft of writing and are a careful reader, you can function as an editor or copy editor. Contact publishers and writers who are in need of editorial assistance by advertising your services and by soliciting work from companies listed in *Writer's Market* (available in bookstores and libraries).

*Elderly Care:* See *Manual for the Homemaker/Home Health Aide*, by Elizabeth Willborn; 1988, Lippincott, Philadelphia, PA.

*Electrical Equipment Repair.*

*Electrician:* See *Exploring Careers as An Electrician*, by Marilyn Jones; 1987, Rosen Publishing, New York, NY.

*Employment Agency and Service:* Matching people with jobs is a service people are willing to pay for and one that fits nicely into a home office.

*Entertainer:* If you like to perform and have special skills or talents there are numerous opportunities to use them. Consider the need for singing, playing a musical instrument, dancing, playing a clown for parties, performing as a magician, and many other types of entertaining.

*Event Promoter:* Each town needs several promoters to book traveling shows and local events. This takes a lot of nerve, a few good contacts, and hard bargaining to get the best deals. Make sure the promotions are based on a percent of income.

*Excavating:* This could include horizontal or vertical boring, trenching, or backhoe work, depending upon the type of equipment available.

*Farming:* This is probably the oldest home business and includes raising field crops and garden products, as well as large and small animals.

*Fence Installation.*

*Financial Advisor:* Workers in this field usually have at least a bachelor's degree in some financially related field, although others have been very successful, having gained their knowledge through experience. For more information, contact the International Association for Financial Planning, 2 Concourse Parkway, Suite 800, Atlanta, GA 30328, (404) 395-1605.

*Fishing, Hunting, Trapping.*

*Fish Farmer:* See *Fish Hatchery Management*, by Robert G. Piper; 1982, U.S. Dept. of the Interior, Fish and Wildlife Service, Washington, D.C.

*Fishing Guide:* If you know where the fish hide, have a knack for catching them, and have contacts for boat and equipment rental, you might enjoy this business. It is easier to pursue if you live near fishing waters and serve visitors to the area, but you can also lead small groups to fishing areas for a few days or weeks of guided fishing.

*Flags and Promotional Supplies:* A home business could be based on distributing state, national, and organization flags, and also special advertising or promotional goods, such as pencils and hats with an organization's name imprinted on them.

*Floral Arrangements:* Because fresh flowers are perishable, silk flowers have increased in popularity. Silk flower arrangements can be made long before they are needed, whenever time is available.

*Furnace Maintenance:* See *Getting Started in Heating and Air Conditioning Service*, by Allen Russell; 1976, Business News Publishing Co., Birmingham, MI.

*Furniture Refinishing, Chair Caning, Upholstering:* This business fits nicely into a home with space in a garage or outbuilding.

*Graphic Design and Illustration:* This service is needed by writers and publishers of all types of printed material.

*Handcrafts for the Disabled:* See *Handcrafts the Handicapped Elderly Can Make and Sell,* by Wiletta Russell; paperback, $14.75 from Charles C. Thomas Publisher, 2600 South First St., Springfield, IL 62717.

*Hauling:* A truck or van and a strong back are all that is needed for this business. A sign in the front yard or a listing in the Yellow Pages will bring customers.

*Hayrides and Sleigh Rides:* This specialty service surely won't provide steady business, but it can be used to supplement another income.

*Health Care:* This field is very large and includes not only doctors and dentists, but also such services as physical therapy and home nurse care.

*Home/Office Cleaning.*

*Home Repairs.*

*House Sitting.*

*Ice Cream Vendor:* They still come when the weather turns warm, and the bells bring children scampering from their homes. Vendors can sell their goods in neighborhoods and at special events such as fairs and sporting events.

*Image Consultant:* Contact the Association of Fashion and Image Consultants, 7655 Old Springhouse Rd., Suite 211, McLean, VA, (703) 848-2664. Ask for a copy of the association's magazine, *Fashion News and Views.*

*Importer and Distributor:* See *How to Make a Fortune in Import/ Export,* by Howard R. Goldsmith; Reston Publishing Company, 17340 Boswell Place, Granada Hills, CA 91344. For further information write to the American Importers Association, 420 Lexington Avenue, NY 10017. Also see *Asian Imports,* a monthly tabloid for importers, distributors, and mass merchandisers (write to 1414 Merchandise Mart, Chicago, IL 60654, and ask for a free copy).

*Income Tax Preparation.*

*Information Detective:* The world's knowledge is doubling every eight years, according to United Technologies, but thanks to the database explosion much of this information can be tracked. Information detectives dig up whatever facts their clients need, primarily searching through computerized data bases. For more information contact the Information Industry Association, 555 New Jersey Ave. NW, Suite 800, Washington, DC 20009, (202) 639-8262.

*Insurance Agent.*

*Interior Decorator:* See the newsletter of the American Society of Interior Designers, 1430 Broadway, New York, NY 10018.

*Inventor:* See *Can You Make Money with Your Idea or Invention?* Free from the Small Business Administration, P.O. Box 15434, Ft. Worth, TX 76119. Also see *Inventors Guidebook—A Step-by-Step*

*Guide to Success*, by Melvin L. Fuller; $7.50 from Inventors Workshop International, P.O. Box 251, Tarzana, CA 91356.

*Investment Counseling:* You might offer this service if you are knowledgable about portfolio management and income opportunities and risks.

*Investigative and Protection Services.*

*Janitorial Services.*

*Jewelry Fabrication:* Much of the exquisite costume jewelry now being sold in America is designed and made by home workers who sell it either at art fairs or through retail gift shops.

*Language Instruction and Translation:* People traveling to foreign lands are anxious to learn a little of the language of the countries they will visit before they depart. Translations are needed by scholars engaged in studies with international workers, and work can be solicited by posting notices at universities, research facilities, and the like. Also, people often want old letters and printed materials translated.

*Lawn Care and Landscaping:* See *How to Make Big Money Mowing Small Lawns*, by Robert Bunch; Brick House Publishing, Andover, MA 01810.

*Legal Services (Lawyer):* This business requires a law degree and a license to practice.

*Limousine Service:* Many kids still splurge on prom night and ride in a limousine to their big party, but this service is also needed by the business and entertainment communities. See *Limousine and Chauffeur Magazine*, 2512 Artesia Blvd., Redondo Beach, CA 90278, (213) 376-8788. For more information contact the National Limousine Association, 1625 1 St. NW, Suite 625A, Washington, DC 20006, (202) 223-5466.

*Literary Agent:* For the cost of a postage stamp you can be listed as an agent in *Writer's Market*. This is where writers locate agents to represent them. Of course, you need to know a little about the market and how to go about selling a manuscript before attempting to get into this business.

*Livestock Breeding:* See *Applied Animal Reproduction*, by H. Joe Bearden; 1980, Reston Publishing Co., Reston, VA.

*Locksmithing:* There is only one qualified locksmith for every 17,000 people in the United States. This business adapts nicely to a home business and can be started with a modest investment. The skills needed for this business can be learned from another locksmith or from mail-order classes that teach the basic procedures (ads for these courses often appear in men's magazines).

*Logging and Timber Cutting:* See *Timber Cutting Practices*, by Steve Conway; 1978, Miller Freeman Publications, San Francisco, CA.

*Luncheon Room:* If your home is located near an office building or factory you might offer home-cooked lunches for the hamburger-weary crowd.

*Machine and Equipment Repair.*

*Mail-Order Business:* See Chapter 2. Also see *How to Start and Operate a Mail Order Business,* by Julian L. Simon; McGraw-Hill, New York, NY 10020.

*Manicurist:* See *West's Textbook of Manicures,* by Jerry Ahern; 1986, West Publishing Co., St. Paul, MN.

*Manufacturing:* The kinds of products one might manufacture are too numerous to mention here, but they include products made of wood, leather, textiles, metal, stone, clay, rubber, plastic, and foods.

*Martial Arts and Self-Defense School:* See *Handbook of the Martial Arts and Self-Defense,* by Christopher Keane; 1975, Barnes and Noble, New York, NY.

*Masonry, Dry Wall, Stone, Tile Installation:* See *Basic Masonry Techniques;* 1985, Ortho Books, San Francisco, CA. Also see *Setting Ceramic Tile,* by Michael Byrne; 1987, Tarrenton Press, Newtown, CT.

*Masseur/Masseuse.*

*Meals for Shut-ins.*

*Messenger Service:* When overnight is not fast enough, people are willing to pay for messenger service. For more information contact the Association of Messenger Services, Inc., 270 Madison Ave., New York, NY 10016, (212) 532-8980.

*Metalworking:* This service is needed by many other businesses. See *Tools of Our Metalworking Trade: Machine Shop Basics;* 1986, McGraw-Hill, New York, NY.

*Modeling School.*

*Monograms:* See *Monogram Business Booklet,* free from Meistergram, Inc., S. R. Gluskin, 5501 Cass Ave., Cleveland, OH 44113.

*Move Organizer:* Yes, there is a need for move organizers. Young couples are pressed for time when both work, and older people need help as they prepare to break up housekeeping and move their possessions to an apartment or retirement home. Many are willing to pay for help to oversee the packing, movement, and sometimes the selling of their possessions. (A fair rate is $20 to $35 per hour for this service.)

*Music Writing, Instruction, Performing:* See *Songwriter's Market,* published annually by Writer's Digest; $19.95 in bookstores. Also see *Making Money Making Music (No Matter Where You Live),* by James Dearing; Writer's Digest, Cincinnati, OH 45242.

*Newsletter Publisher:* See *Publishing Newsletters,* by Howard Hudson; 1988, Scribner's, New York, NY.

*Newspaper Delivery.*

*Notereader-scopist:* An expanding field for home workers, this business entails converting court-recorded stenotype into a typed transcript. For information contact At-Home Professions, 12383 Lewis St., Suite 103, Garden Grove, CA 92640.

*Nursing:* There is a growing need for home health care as hospitals are releasing patients earlier due to changes in the Medicare/Medicaid benefits and people are electing to stay home during illnesses and as they age. See *Homecare Magazine,* 2048 Cotner Ave., Los Angeles, CA 90025, (213) 477-1033.

*Office and Shop Equipment Repair.*

*Optometry:* Requires special education and a license to practice.

*Painting, Exterior and Interior.*

*Parking Lot.*

*Party Planner:* Many parents are now hiring professionals to plan parties for their children. A total package that includes entertainment, favors, and refreshments is attractive to busy people.

*Personal and Household Services:* Too little time is the bane of modern life. Help clients create free time by assuming some of their everyday tasks.

*Pet Boarding (Kennel):* See *Pet Sitting.*

*Pet Grooming:* This occupation can be easily adapted to a home business. A former teacher in my networking group grooms dogs and claims they have less bark and bite than her former students.

*Pet Sitting:* Critter-Sitters Inc. is the name of one home business that cares for animals while their masters are away. The business personnel make periodic visits to the customer's home to feed, play with, and care for pets. This service also waters plants and brings in the mail for clients. See *Pet Sitting For Profit,* by Patti Moran; 1987, New Beginnings, Pinnacle, NC.

*Pet Training.*

*Pest Control:* A single roach spotted on a grocery shelf or on a restaurant wall will send customers elsewhere. Insects and rodents are a problem in many homes and businesses, and people willingly pay to keep these pests under control.

*Photography (Weddings, Special Events, and Portraits):* See *The Professional Photographer—Developing a Successful Career,* by Larry Goldman; 1983, paperback, $12.95 from Doubleday, New York, NY 10167.

*Physical Fitness Facility:* A big gym isn't a prerequisite for this service. Some home operators house equipment in their basements, and customers can pump iron without disturbing the household. Aerobics classes can also be taught in a basement or family room.

*Piano Tuning:* A good ear but little equipment is needed for this occupation.

*Plant and Garden Maintenance:* This includes not only the obvious flower and garden care, but also "plant sitting" (care of indoor plants when customers are out of town).

*Plant Grower, Gardener, Truck Farmer:* Many successful gardeners have developed a home business by growing African violets and other specialty plants in their home/garden and selling them to florists or directly to customers. See *Plants for Profit—A Complete Guide to Growing and Selling Greenhouse Crops,* by Dr. Francis Jozwik; 1984, hardcover, $41.90 from Andmar Press, P.O. Box 217, Mill, WY 82644. Herbs can be grown and sold in small packages in fine grocery stores. See *Growing and Using Herbs Successfully,* by Betty E. M. Jacobs; 1981, paperback, $7.95 from Garden Way, 3599 Ferry Road, Charlotte, VT 05445. Herbs can also be used to develop a potpourri business. See *Potpourri From Herbal Acres* (newsletter), Garden Way Publishing, Charlotte, VT 05445. Ask to see Garden Way's extraordinary book list.

*Postal and Advertisement Delivery Service:* Brochures stuffed under windshield wipers and into mailboxes and samples hung over door handles have usually been distributed by people who work from their homes.

*Printer and Quick Printer:* We are in the "Information Age," and it is estimated that 4 *trillion* pieces of paper were used by businesses in 1989. Many of these were copies, and that is the reason printing businesses are springing up across the country. See *How to Set Yourself Up in Business as a Printing Broker,* by Jack Erbe; paperback, $15.00 from Publishers Services, 6318 Vesper Avenue, Van Nuys, CA 91411. Also see *Quick Printing Magazine,* 3255 S. U.S. 1, Fort Pierce, FL 33482, (305) 465-9450. For more information write to The National Association of Quick Printers, 1 Illinois Center, 111 E. Wacker Dr., Chicago, IL, (312) 644-6610.

*Professional Services:* Doctors, dentists, psychologists, psychiatrists, and lawyers all are in service professions that require special education. Such professionals often require supporting employees, such as secretarial and/or nursing services.

*Psychological Testing and Counseling.*

*Public Relations (PR) Agent:* A PR agent has two types of clients: those who seek to have a specific project promoted and those with whom there is a long-lasting relationship (the agent is kept on a retainer). See *Public Relations News,* 127 E. 80th St., New York, NY 10021, (212) 879-7090. For more information contact The Public Relations Society of America Inc., 33 Irving Place, New York, NY 10003, (212) 861-0630.

*Publisher:* Many of the books in this country are published by small home businesses who use the distribution network of other publishers or distributorships. See *Literary Market Place* (available in most libraries) for a list of distributors.

*Quilting, Knitting, Weaving:* See *Knitting Machine News/Views* (periodical); Alles Knitting Publications, 18 Marymont Dr., Penn Hills, PA 15235.

*Real Estate Agent:* Most realtors work from their homes for a parent company. Many housewives discover they make good realtors because they know what homemakers are looking for and can relate to women. This is often the key to making a sale. See *Real Estate Today,* 430 N. Michigan Ave., Chicago, IL 60611, (312) 329-8900. For further information contact the National Association of Realtors at the same address.

*Refuse Removal.*

*Remodeling.*

*Rental Equipment:* This service could include the rental of air compressors, generators, backhoes, chain saws, construction equipment, sewer cleaners, sump pumps, hand tools, carpet and floor cleaners, lawn equipment, log splitters, and so on.

*Researcher.*

*Résumé Writing Service:* A typewriter or computer is all the equipment needed for this business. It is helpful to be located in a college town or in a community where there is a large turnover in the population, such as near a military base.

*Roofing and Siding:* See *Complete Roofing Handbook*, by James Brumbaugh; 1986, Collier Macmillan, New York, NY. Also see *How to Replace and Install Roofing and Siding*, by T. Jeff Williams; 1984, Ortho Books, San Francisco, CA.

*Sales Representative:* See Chapter 17. Also see *Selling Power of a Woman*, by Dottie Walters; hardcover (now in its 13th edition), $17.95 from Royal Publishing, Inc. P.O. Box 1120, Glendora, CA 91740. Also see *How to Become a Successful Manufacturers' Representative*, by Marvin Leffler; Prentice Hall, 1 Gulf and Western Plaza, New York, NY 10023.

*Saw Sharpening:* This business requires a modest investment in sharpening equipment. Some of the companies that sell this type of equipment also offer an instructional videotape or even a mail-order course. Ads for the equipment are often found in magazines such as *Popular Mechanics, Woodcraft,* and *Popular Science.*

*Schoolbus Driving:* Contact your local school board to learn about this occupation; ask about the qualifications of drivers and also find out who owns and maintains the buses.

*Seamstress:* See *Sewing for Profit*, by Judith and Allan Smith; paperback, $11.00 from Success Publications, P.O. Box 6302, Louisville, KY 40206. Also ask to see Success Publications' list of related books.

*Secretary:* See *Starting Your Own Secretarial Business*, by Betty Loogren and Gloria Shoff; Contemporary Books, Chicago, IL 60601.

*Security and Protection Services.*

*Shoe Repair and Shoe Shine Services.*

*Shopping Service:* This is an invaluable service for the home-bound and the elderly; works nicely as a home business.

*Sign Fabrication and Installation:* See *Ralph Gregory's Sign Painting Techniques,* by Ralph Gregory; 1973, Signs of the Times Publishing Co., Cincinnati, OH.

*Small Animal Breeding:* There are markets for a diversity of small animals, from earthworms and bees to rabbits, gerbils, goats, and chickens. Contact Garden Way Publishing, Charlotte, VT 05445 for a list of the many books it publishes on raising small animals.

*Small Engine Service and Repair:* There are more than 65 million small engines in use throughout the United States, and each one of them will eventually need service and repair. Lawn mowers and gardening equipment use 80 to 90 percent of these engines, and you can build a business repairing and tuning up these engines.

*Snacks:* A portable booth or trailer outfitted with equipment to prepare snacks from pronto pups to cotton candy can be taken to sports events and community affairs, or the owners can follow the fair circuit during the summer months. Also, portable booths can be pulled up outside factories to pick up lunch business. Most of these are home-based operations.

*Snow Removal.*

*Soil Preparation (Rototilling, Plowing).*

*Sports Equipment Rental.*

*Sports Training Schools and Camps.*

*Swimming Pool Maintenance and Winterizing.*

*Talent Agent:* Most people think agents for big-time entertainers live in big cities near their clients, but they can also be effective working from a home office in Middle America.

*Taxi Service.*

*Taxidermy:* See *Practical Taxidermy,* by John Moyer; 1979, Wiley, New York, NY.

*Telemarketer:* Selling by telephone is inexpensive, and for that reason more and more businesses are using telephone solicitors to sell their products. See *Telemarketing Magazine,* 17 Park St., Norwalk, CT 06851.

*Telephone Answering Service.*

*Telephone Wake-up Service:* Hotels and motels, as well as individuals who have a tendency to oversleep, are willing to pay for this service. This service could be combined with a daily telephone check of elderly people who live alone.

*Television and Audio Equipment Repair.*

*Theatrical Performers, Musicians, Agents, Producers, and Related Services:* Nightclubs, entertainment centers, and special events are always in need of performers. Depending on your role in the entertainment industry, you can attract business by being listed in the Yellow Pages under "Entertainment Bureau" or under a specific appropriate heading, such as "Musicians."

*Tourist Home (Bed and Breakfast) Operator.*

*Transporting Children:* With both parents working in many families there is a growing need for this service to transport children to sitters, games, parties, and so forth.

*Transporting the Disabled:* A van with a platform that can raise and lower wheelchair patients is helpful for this type of business. This would be a welcome service in many communities.

*Travel Agent:* See *Guide to Starting and Operating a Successful Travel Agency*, by Laurence Stevens; 1983, Meeton House and Travel Publications, Wheaton, IL.

*Tutor:* With parents anxious about their children's development, tutoring has become a viable business. Slow, advanced, and average students can all benefit from tutoring.

*Typing:* See *How to Start a Profitable Typing Service at Home*, by Nicki Montaperto; 1981, Barnes and Noble, 10 E. 53rd St., New York, NY 10022.

*Vending Machine Selling:* For information contact the National Automatic Merchandising Association, 20 N. Wacker Dr., Chicago, IL 60606, (312) 346-0370. Also see *American Automatic Blue Book* for a listing of companies that make vending machines (same address as above). And see *Vending Times* (a monthly) 545 8th Ave., New York, NY 10018.

*Veterinarian:* This occupation requires extensive schooling and a license to practice.

*Video Editing Service:* The videocassette recorder has created a whole set of new career opportunities. Besides videographers, a cadre of professionals edit video and add sound and special effects to videotapes. See *Videography Magazine*, 50 W. 23rd St., New York, NY 10011.

*Videography:* Video cameras can be used to capture on tape such diverse things as homes for sale (used by real estate agents as a selling technique) and weddings and family gatherings.

*Video Rental.*

*Wallpapering:* Most wallpaper hangers operate from their homes. This business requires little equipment (ladders, pails, brushes, and knives) and a minimum of training. The quality of the work performed varies, and the really skilled find customers seeking their services through word-of-mouth referrals. This business can be adapted to fit family life. It can be slowed to a near stop in summer when kids are home from school, or it can go at full speed throughout the year. Since much of the work is done away from home, an answering machine can be used to pick up new business leads.

*Water Conditioning:* The deterioration in the quality of drinking water is causing this to become a growth industry. For information contact the Water Quality Association, 4151 Naperville Rd., Lisle, IL 60532.

*Well Drilling (Water or Oil):* The proper equipment and some knowledge of geology can make this a profitable business. Some oil drillers drill for a percentage of the profit from a well (rather than for a drilling fee) to encourage land owners to take a cost-free chance and to enable the driller to tap into a long-term pool of income.

*Wheelchair/Hospital Bed/Health Care Supplies Rental:* This much-needed service requires an investment in equipment, a truck for transporting the items, and adequate storage space for equipment that is not in use.

*Wholesaling and Retailing:* See *Selling on the Fast Track*, by Kathy Aaronson; 1989, Putnam, New York, NY. Also see *Opportunities in Sales Careers*, by Ralph Dahm; 1988, VGM Career Horizons, Lincolnwood, IL.

*Window Washing:* There is more to window washing than meets the eye. This business can include not only storefronts, but windows on high-rise buildings as well. It can also be limited to washing home windows. This is hard work, and prices should reflect the labor involved.

*Wood for Home Heating:* With the number of wood stoves and fireplaces being used today, there is an ongoing need for firewood. A chain saw, a pickup truck, and a strong back are needed for this occupation. A sign in the front yard or on a delivery truck, fliers stuffed in mail boxes, or small classified advertisements are all the advertising needed to make this business go.

*Woodcrafting and Custom Furniture:* Woodcrafters can make items either on commission or to sell through shops. See *Workbench*, a monthly magazine with tips on the newest tools, methods for building and repairing furniture, and general how-to information for woodworkers (available in bookstores).

*Writer:* Freelance writers can earn money by writing books, magazine and newspaper articles, brochures for organizations, and newsletters. Aggressive marketing is the key to making a living in this business. See *Writer's Market* (annual), $22.95, in bookstores everywhere; and *Literary Market Place*, available in most libraries.

*Yoga Instructor:* A good friend of mine does this and has built her business through physicians who recommend her services to patients who seem to be uptight and under stress. She offers classes and private lessons as well as stress therapy sessions.

# Part Three

## *Some Important Preliminary Issues*

# 4    Surveying the Market

Now that you have tentatively selected a type of business that interests you, it is time to determine if there are enough potential customers to allow your business plan to materialize.

## *Survey the Market You Intend to Serve*

The first question you must ask after deciding on a product or service is, "Who will buy my product or service?" The answer to this question will help determine if there are enough potential customers to support the business you envision. The size of the market can be ascertained through a little research. If, for instance, you plan to offer child care, the birthrate in the immediate area would be a valuable piece of information. You might do very well attracting customers near a military base, where young couples are concentrated, but this type of service wouldn't be needed in a community of retired couples. If you intend to cater weddings, then you should learn how many weddings occur in a given time period in your business zone. If your goal is to fit hearing aids, you should determine if there is an aging population in the immediate area. Whatever your proposed business, the question you need to answer is, "Are there enough potential customers available to produce a profit large enough to meet my goals?"

Your marketing survey should include the demographics of your business zone, and your chamber of commerce can help you gather this information. The chamber of commerce's job is to encourage the development of new businesses in the community, and it can supply population information that includes income characteristics, payrolls, industrial development, and so forth. Don't hesitate to ask this organization for help. The chamber of commerce may also be able to provide you with information about the competition you can expect. Another source of information is the United States Census Report, which is a national demographic survey taken every 10 years. The report, available in most libraries, contains statistical profiles compiled for each community in America, covering such items as age, sex, race, religion, educational level, and the occupation of the citizens. These surveys often prove to be difficult to read and understand, and it's sometimes difficult to ferret out the information you need. Fortunately, there is a much more available source of information, and that is your own experience. Perhaps you already know something about the market in your area. If you have been a part of the community for awhile you probably know better than any census or survey can possibly tell you how the people live, their preferences, their allegiences, their political and religious composition, their age, education, and other subtle factors that could be of value as you plot your business strategy.

Maybe you have already done a little business "on the side" or in your spare time and found that customers exist, and you think it's just a matter of cashing in on already-established contacts. Be careful about this approach. There is a big difference between fixing lawn mowers for neighbors, painting pictures and crafting items to give as gifts, or helping a few friends figure income taxes and actually converting these activities into profit-making ventures. It takes more contacts, more effort, more financial investment—in fact, more of everything—in order to turn a hobby into a paying business. Still, building a long-time hobby, with already-established contacts, into a profit-making venture is an attractive way to start a business.

Use everything at your disposal—surveys, census data, and your firsthand knowledge of the community—to determine if there are enough potential customers to support your business. And don't overlook networking. This is an excellent way to learn more about the community. Talk with friends, and then expand to businesses and local government people to gather information to complete your market analysis. It is amazing how much people know about your local area and are willing to share with you. They just have to be asked!

If people will be visiting your home as you operate your business, the market analysis should consider such things as the location of your home, the ease of access, and the availability of parking facilities. Of course, customers never visit the offices of some businesses, and for these operations location or ease of access is not a factor. For example, telephone answering services operate almost exclusively out of homes, and this type of service can be conducted from a remote location or in an area where congestion would rule out any business where customers come to the home. In contrast, a beautician relies on customers coming to the place of business, and it must be located in an area that is easily accessible and has adequate parking nearby.

If your business does not depend on customers from the immediate area, but your products or services are sold through the mail, then your market survey must be conducted differently from the survey described above. You could refer to the United States Census of Business, which is a huge compilation of information on the total volume of business generated in specific fields, or you could see if your State Census of Business could provide you with worthwhile information. But again, in addition to any information gathered from surveys, you should depend on your own awareness to define and understand the market that interest you. If, for example, you plan a mail-order business to sell consumables, such as vitamins and health foods, you need to know who buys such products. Do they have much expendable income? Can they be reached or targeted for advertising? How many other companies are selling similar products, and at what price? Answers to these questions will help you determine if there is an adequate number of customers to buy your products.

A manufacturing business needs still other types of market analyses. Will the product being considered for production be a necessity, and thus not dependent on economic good times, or will it be a luxury item? A luxury item may survive bad economic conditions if it is inexpensive, but if it is costly, it may not. Will the product be caught on the wave of already-established products, or will it be a totally new concept? Generally, it's safer to produce goods that are similar to those already on the market if the market isn't flooded. Introducing something totally new is very risky. Certainly pet rocks, hula hoops, and Cabbage Patch dolls made a killing, but they are the exceptions. As you look for a product to manufacture, be aware of the aging population in this country. This aging segment represents a huge market, and manufacturing products designed for this group is well worth considering.

As you can see, doing a market analysis means taking into consideration many facets of your community and its population and product preferences. In summary, some specific questions your research should address include:

- From what geographical area will you draw customers?
- Is the population in the area large enough to yield the customers needed to make a profit?
- What is the age distribution of the designated population—is it a young, mixed, or retirement community?
- What is the median income of the population?
- Is the population growing or getting smaller?
- What comprises the typical family unit in the population?

## What Kind of Competition Can You Expect?

Another aspect of a market analysis is identifying and evaluating the competition. Who are your competitors? Although there may be an adequate number of customers for the product or service you intend to deliver, you need to determine whether somebody else has already claimed them and whether these claimed customers are satisfied or would they be willing—even anxious—to take their business elsewhere.

Identify and study your competitors. Look up the service or product you intend to offer in the telephone directory, call the chamber of commerce, and watch newspaper advertisements and fliers to learn which companies are engaging in a business similar to the one you are considering. Using a map, mark your business location and then mark the location of each of your competitors. Will you be competing with a nearby business? This can be an important factor affecting your ability to attract customers. There is a tendency for people to patronize a nearby business, and for certain businesses neighbors and residents in the surrounding area could be the prime source of customers unless somebody down the street is already offering the same service.

Phone each competitor to learn about their services and prices. Obviously, you shouldn't tell them that you are the new kid on the block and that you intend to give them some stiff competition. Play the role of a customer trying to find out about services or products, and ask if they will send a brochure or give a free estimate. If a competitor is very close to your location, try to learn if the business is growing or declining, if workers have been added or laid off, and if extra space has been added. Does the place look busy and organized or does it seem to be mismanaged? Is the service or product appealing or is it lacking in quality? Can you do a better job than your competitors?

Several years ago a small home business started making cedar clothing hangers, which sold for a significant amount through gift catalogs. Other small businesses noticed how well these hangers were selling and quickly picked up the cedar idea, turning out small cedar blocks to place in drawers, heart-shaped pieces to put in coat pockets, shaved cedar in lace bags to hang in closets, and on and on. The market was soon glutted with cedar products, and several of the small, single-product companies folded because the competition forced the prices too low to make a profit. A small manufacturer in New Jersey was getting squeezed out of the cedar market until the proprietor thought of a new way to use cedar. Chemicals released from the heartwood of red cedar kills insects, and the reason cedar is used among clothing is

### PHOTOGRAPHER FINDS PROFITABLE COMBINATION BUT EQUIPMENT NEEDS CHANGE

Mike has always been fascinated with photography. When video cameras hit the market, he became interested in this new technology and acquired the skills to tape and edit video films. It wasn't long before he started a business producing videos of weddings. To get under way, Mike bought two quality video cameras, an editing board, and a few other pieces of equipment. Then he started marketing his business, only to discover some unsettling problems.

Competition from inexperienced friends and relatives was his first difficulty. We have come to accept the fact that wedding photographs and bridal portraits cost a bundle ($300 to $600, sometimes more), and even though practically everybody owns a camera and can take pictures, the wedding couple still prefers to hire a professional photographer to capture their special event. The same doesn't hold true for videotapes. For some reason, people are unwilling to spend much for a videotape of their wedding, and they are delighted when a family member or friend offers to tape it for free, even though the amateur may scamper about the church making a nuisance of himself or herself during the ceremony. Often the lighting is poor, the filming is unsteady and badly focused, and the resulting tape is of poor quality.

But there was another problem. Producing a quality video film is more difficult than Mike had realized. Taping the wedding and reception is but a small part of the job. A great deal of time and effort is required to edit the films from the two cameras in order to produce a smooth, artistic re-creation of the wedding. Time spent editing cut into the time he could devote to other work, and Mike decided the profit margin for edited videos just wasn't large enough to warrant his trying to develop a video wedding business, especially since he was having to compete with friends and relatives who were anxious to get in on the action.

Mike decided to change his service to meet consumer demands. He sold most of his video equipment and used the money to purchase a rather complete line of quality photographic equipment. He now offers a wedding photography package that has proven to be a winning combination. Mike does traditional photography but also offers a one-camera videotape which requires no editing and therefore costs very little to produce—it's a matter of aiming and shooting. Since he can operate only one camera at a time, Mike hires a photography student from a local college when clients want both traditional photography and a video of their wedding. With this change in place, and with a striking advertisement in the Yellow Pages, his business now shows a profit.

We can learn two important things from Mike's experience. First, check the market before investing in equipment, and don't invest too much before you test the viability of your idea; and secondly, be flexible and willing to change business plans in order to be successful.

to destroy moth larvae. Cedar also kills fleas, and this small New Jersey business, operating out of a basement, began manufacturing pillows filled with cedar shavings to be used as pet beds. These pet pillows are now being sold through gift catalogs, and sales representatives sell them to pet stores. Finding a new way to package cedar allowed this small manufacturer to sidestep the competition, stay in business, and turn a nice profit.

By investigating the competition, you place yourself in a position of strength. The more you learn about your competition, the better you'll be able to position your business and carve out a market niche for yourself. Your goal is to find a corner in the marketplace that your competitor has missed or else one that is not being adequately filled. If you go after the same market being serviced by a competitor, you will need to create a competitive edge. In order to attract customers, your product or service will have to be different from your major competitor's in some significant way. Your product or service may be higher priced and appeal to an exclusive market, or it may be lower priced to pick up the mass market. You could have different hours, perhaps doing business late in the day after your competitor has closed shop, or you might offer emergency service (of course, an emergency service would keep you on call, but that may be what it takes to build a clientele).

In summary, some important questions to answer concerning the competition include:

• Who are your major competitors?
• How will each competitor's location, pricing, promotional activities, and image affect your business?
• Can you compete effectively?
• Have your competitors expanded their operations lately?
• Have any firms similar to the one you are considering gone out of business lately? Why?
• What is the approximate sales volume in your market area?
• What percent of the sales volume can you expect to attract?
• Can you create a competitive advantage to attract that volume?

After surveying the market and the competition you may conclude that a niche is waiting to be filled and your plans have a good chance to materialize. Or you may conclude that the market can't support another business such as the one you had in mind, in which case it would be in your best interest to change plans and pursue a business that has a greater chance for success.

## *Before Your Plans Go Any Further*

If you've been following this book through from the beginning, by now you probably have a relatively firm idea of what business would be a workable one for you, based on self-analysis, location, home life, market analysis, and the various other factors discussed so far. Before you get more deeply involved in implementing a plan for your business, *think about the actual work you'll be doing.* Is it the kind of work you want to do? Think about the daily chores, the bookkeeping, and the extra work that will be demanded of you. Are your family members willing to share their living space with your business? Can you handle the pressures of being boss, the uncertainty of when and whether customers will pay their bills, and the stress of running short of cash when bills keep piling up? Are you in good health and feel you have the will and perseverance required to succeed? Do you have the skills and expertise to succeed? Think deeply about the specific business adventure you are about to undertake.

This is the time to be realistic and make sure you understand just what it is you are getting involved in. You need to acknowledge the risks associated with the work you are about to begin—statistics indicate there is less than a 50–50 chance that a new business will survive for five years. Are you the type of person who uses those kinds of odds to strengthen your determination? Of course, the probability of being successful improves the more thoroughly you plan your business, so if you're determined to go ahead with your plans, then keep asking questions and looking for the answers that can give your business the best possible chance to succeed.

Starting a business is a big job, and the work never seems to end. You need to understand that clearly before you proceed. At the same time, you should also understand that making a business work and being responsible for its success is a wonderfully rewarding experience. Just be certain that you are pursuing the right business dream before your plans get so far along that they take on a life of their own and you find yourself caught up in a project that will change your life forever.

# 5    Zoning Laws and Legal Issues

Is it legal to operate a business from your home, to craft and sell things, to meet with clients, to have employees—in short, to do what you want in your own home? Both public zoning laws and private covenants address the issue of a business within the home, and there are laws directed to home businesses on the local, state, and federal level that both restrict and protect you. It is important that you have at least a modest acquaintance with these laws and an understanding of how they may affect your proposed business before too many plans are made.

Sometimes people start a home business without learning about zoning restrictions and how other laws can affect them, only to discover that the workshop and promotional material they have developed cannot be used. This more frequently happens to an individual whose enterprise begins more as a hobby than a business. When you stop painting, cooking, building, or doing whatever you do just for fun and plan to convert it into a business, you should also make it your business to find out how laws can affect your plans.

## Zoning Laws

The use of property is controlled by zoning laws. Property is classified according to the activities and types of structures permitted. There are four types of zones: residential, commercial, industrial, and agricultural. Most people interested in setting up a home business live in either residential or agricultural zones.

Theoretically, residential zones are areas where people live but don't work, and to the untrained eye, that is exactly what seems to be the case. Actually, however, today's residential neighborhoods are buzzing with home businesses, but many of them are undetected because they are conducted over the phone, in front of a computer or sewing machine, or in the kitchen between mixing bowls and ovens. These kinds of businesses do not adversely affect neighborhoods and therefore do not draw the attention or the complaints of neighbors.

The family farm is the most prevalent home business in agricultural zones. These zones are usually sparsely populated and are generally nonrestrictive regarding home businesses. Virtually any business can operate within an agricultural zone, partly because there are few neighbors to be inconvenienced or annoyed by the activity.

## LEARN THE ZONING LAWS THAT AFFECT YOU

Zoning laws affecting home businesses vary from city to city. Some cities have no residential zoning laws, while others are very restrictive of business activity. Many of the laws were written long ago in an effort to protect neighborhoods from changes that might detract from the quality of life, but some of these early laws are thwarting the development of certain types of home businesses that would not be a detriment to their neighborhoods. In fact, most home-based entrepreneurs add to the neighborhood and the economy and take nothing away. Nonetheless, many zoning laws are very restrictive. According to a report from the National Center for Policy Analysis in Dallas, nine out of ten localities have regulations on home-based work. Some forbid outdoor signs and Yellow Pages advertising. Others restrict the storage of materials or inventory in a garage. In Arlington, Virginia, a home-based employer may not hire anyone who does not live in the home. In Southern Pines, North Carolina, no retail sales are permitted in a residence. Forest Grove, Oregon, prohibits on-street parking by any client or customer of a home-based worker. And in Chicago, the city attempts, but fails, to ban virtually all home-based work, even going so far as to ban connecting a home computer to an office computer. Some of these restrictions are insensitive to the home-business phenomenon, and the surge of home workers and their vocal dismay at this unfair treatment is causing some communities to reassess their inhibiting rules. As a result, a growing number of communities have begun to develop zoning regulations that allow quiet, nonpolluting, low-traffic kinds of home businesses to operate.

Zoning laws in your town or city are probably handled through a local planning commission that may be a county or city office (or these laws may be under the jurisdiction of a city or county zoning board). Call the various offices and ask about zoning restrictions (look under city or county offices in the Yellow Pages). Ask them to send you a list of the zoning restrictions that apply to your area. The list you receive may not contain the exact restrictions listed below (which are in effect in my home town), but these are representative of restrictions found in many urban areas:

1. A zoning use permit must be issued by the zoning commission for each occupation.
2. The home occupation must be conducted entirely within the dwelling by a person who is a resident member of the family residing on the premises and with no additional employees.
3. The floor area devoted to the business may not exceed 25 percent of the floor area of the dwelling.
4. No manufacturing is permitted.
5. A display of goods or services relating to the home occupation must not be visible from the exterior of the home.
6. An outside entrance may not be provided solely for the home occupation.

Some of these restrictions are unrealistic and are rarely enforced. After talking with personnel in several municipal offices in the city where I reside, I have learned that these laws remain on the books, but they are inconsistent with other regulations. For instance, number 2 above states that only a resident can work in a home business, but the zoning law for the city allows for occupations that require a second working person. An example would be a lawyer who needs a secretary and maybe a legal assistant to gather information. The same rule says the work must be conducted *entirely* within the residence. Would that prevent a potpourri manufacturer from drying plant stems and leaves in the backyard? But then, according to number 4 above, manufacturing is prohibited, so making potpourri is out of the question. However, this restriction is so loosely worded that it could even prohibit making original art since the word *manufacture* originally meant to "make by hand." The zoning officer with whom I spoke wasn't sure if original art could or could not be made at home. And number 5 declares that a display of goods or services is prohibited; however, you can display a business sign if you pay a small fee for a zoning use permit. When asked about rule number 6, the zoning officer said an outside entrance into the business part of a home is permissible only if it was there *before* the business was started, but an entrance cannot be legally added just to facilitate business activity. Yet, it's very common for a person to work at home in an office or shop that was once a side porch or room without an outside door, and an entrance was added when the business was established. I have never heard of an instance where this added entrance has become an issue.

These out-of-date and rarely enforced rules leave the home business operator caught in a quagmire of ambiguities. What you do about zoning restrictions depends on where you live. In some cities the zoning laws are strictly enforced, but in many areas zoning commissioners rarely go looking for trouble because they realize the laws governing home work are archaic and in some cases unenforceable. Through the years the rules have been inconsistently interpreted, and there is a lot of leeway. Zoning commissioners do encourage home business operators to apply for a zoning use permit or license but admit that only a very low percentage of home business operators actually do this.

Permits cost a minimal sum, usually from $10 to $100. If you are found to be operating a home business without a permit, you will most likely need to apply for one but probably will not be penalized. The usual reason a home business is notified that it needs a permit is because a disgruntled neighbor has called the zoning board to protest an objectionable business activity. And why shouldn't they? Neighbors *should* protest if a business has a negative impact on the neighborhood. That is the reason for zoning laws in the first place.

A complaint about a home business is usually investigated by an agent who will drive past the business-residence or park on the street for awhile to observe how the business affects the neighborhood and to determine if the complaint is valid. A letter is then sent to the offending party indicating a specific time period in which to respond to the complaint. If the matter is not resolved, a cease and desist order is issued. In this case the owner can file an appeal with the appeals board or request a change in the regulation. The business may continue to operate while the proposed change is being considered. Of course, the zoning board may reject the proposal and force compliance with the zoning restrictions. As a last resort, a court could close the business.

You will probably not have any problems with neighbors if you are sensitive to how your business affects the neighborhood. Keep a low profile, operate your business in an unobtrusive manner, and never blatantly flaunt your business adventures before your neighbors.

## A SPECIAL-USE PERMIT MAY BE NECESSARY

You can apply to the zoning board for a special-use permit if your business cannot operate within the restrictions set by the zoning code. Since the issuance of this permit could affect the neighborhood, a public hearing is held during which those who are concerned have an opportunity to present their points of view.

There are two ways to approach the zoning board for a special-use permit. You can quietly seek permission for the permit and hope that the neighbors don't object enough to protest, or you can actively solicit neighbor support. You can be sure the zoning board will be alert for activities that would change the neighborhood. If your proposal would bring about such a change, then it would be wise to talk to your neighbors and find out how they feel about your proposed venture. Ask for their support, if they are not opposed to your business, because neighborhood support will greatly enhance your chance of winning approval.

### REZONING MIGHT BE THE ANSWER

You can request to have your property rezoned if your business requirements are different from those allowed in a special-use permit. The zoning office will supply you with an information packet that explains the procedure. Filing for rezoning is time-consuming, and it costs several hundred dollars and requires a public hearing. The fee includes a filing fee, the cost of publishing a description of the intended rezoning, a legal advertisement, and the cost of sending a notice to anyone who owns property that borders the property under question. Some communities frequently grant rezoning requests, while others are very protective of the integrity of their neighborhoods and resist any change in the zoning status. If you fail in your quest for rezoning, you have no recourse other than to change your business plans or move to a zone where your business would be permitted.

## Other Restrictions

A private homeowner's covenant could also affect your home-business plans. Homeowners' Associations have been formed to control certain activities in condominiums, apartments, and housing developments. The restrictions are defined in the property deed, but many of them are not legal and some are downright unconstitutional. It might be wise to seek legal counsel if you have unresolved questions about private restrictions that affect where you live and hope to work.

State governments also have guidelines and rules directed toward home businesses. State laws vary, but you can learn about the restrictions that apply to you by contacting the office of the secretary of state in your state or your local chamber of commerce. From these sources you can learn what can and cannot be manufactured in a home business in your state and also whether you need a license to operate. Some businesses are subject to close scrutiny by local and state officials. Generally, businesses based on food preparation are obligated to work under special restrictions and must allow periodic and unscheduled inspections of the work area by local and state health officials. Some states prohibit the preparation of food to be served in commercial establishments, while others have no such restriction. Most states prohibit home businesses from making drugs, poisons, explosives, sanitary products, children's toys, and children's clothing. If you are planning a manufacturing business, be sure to check the restrictions that apply in your state (see sidebar entitled "State Restrictions on Home Work" for an overview).

The federal government also has a few things to say about home work. As recently as November 1988, a major restriction against home work was lifted. At long last, the Labor Department rescinded the ban against piecework done in homes for commercial companies. This law was passed by Congress in 1943, when it bowed to the pressure of a powerful labor lobby and banned home workers from knitting gloves and mittens, doing embroideries, and making buttons, buckles, handkerchiefs, and certain kinds of jewelry. In 1981 the Reagan administration sought to revoke the regulations, and after prolonged litigation brought by the garment workers' union, the Labor Department won a revocation only on knitted outerwear. Thus, the ladies of Vermont were permitted to knit sweaters at home, but they had to be paid at least the minimum wage by their employers. It took another seven years for the regulations, which had been so vigorously supported by the garment workers' union, to be totally banned.

Dissenting labor unions would have us believe that federally sanctioned home work will enable companies using home workers to evade the minimum-wage and child-labor laws. What really bothers Big Labor, of course, is that home workers will not become dues-paying members of unions. And why should they? After all, they are semi-independent contractors, and working conditions pose no problem inasmuch as these people enjoy the comfort of their own homes. How can the unions hold sway over such individuals, much less exhort them to strike?

Nor does the unions' anxiety end there. They are worried about the proliferation of home work in such industries as telecommunications and information processing, and, just as they feared, opportunities are expanding for a large, home-based, clerical work force. No wonder Big Labor wants a total ban on all clerical work at home.

Several labor unions are threatening to mount a legal challenge against the Labor Department's home work decision. We must hope that the courts will reject any litigation that would restrict budding enterprises whose efforts would benefit the economy and enable families to have more control over their lives.

It is important to keep up to date with zoning legislation, home work laws, and other legalities relating to the home-based entrepreneur. Get into the habit of reading the business section of your local paper. You may also consider joining a local chapter of a business group, such as the Rotary Club, chamber of commerce, or a business

## STATE RESTRICTIONS ON HOME WORK

Many states restrict what can be produced in the home. Most states prohibit the home manufacture or crafting of the following items: cigars and other tobacco products, drugs, poisons, bandages, sanitary goods, explosives, and fireworks. The states listed below have further restrictions. If you have questions about the work you will be doing, contact either the department of labor, the department of industry, or the industrial commission in your state. The information below was provided by the Center on National Labor Policy, Inc.

| State | Articles that are prohibited or restricted for home manufacture |
|---|---|
| California | Food, drink, wearing apparel, toys, and dolls (prohibited) |
| Hawaii | Garments (special permit needed) |
| Illinois | Food, drink, toys, and dolls (prohibited) |
| Indiana | Coats, vests, trousers, cloaks, furs, shirts, purses, feathers, overalls, knee-pants (!) (prohibited) |
| Maryland | Apparel, feathers, fur, artificial flowers (prohibited) |
| Massachusetts | Apparel (prohibited, except hosiery and women's millinery) |
| Michigan | Apparel and purses (permit required, special restrictions apply) |
| Missouri | Apparel, purses, feathers, and artificial flowers (limited to three persons per room) |
| New Jersey | Food, drink, toys, dolls, infant's and children's apparel (prohibited) |
| New York | All home work (prohibited in all industries except where the industrial commissioner determines that such work may be performed without unduly jeopardizing the jobs of factory workers). |
| Ohio | Apparel (prohibited) |
| Pennsylvania | Food, drink, toys, and dolls (prohibited) |
| Puerto Rico | Food, drink, toys, dolls, cosmetics, pipes, and articles used by smokers (prohibited) |
| Tennessee | Dwellings (restrictions apply; Board of Health must be notified). |
| Texas | Any work deemed injurious to the health of workers or the general public (prohibited). |
| Wisconsin | Any activity injurious to workers (prohibited). |

council. These groups will keep you informed of business issues through newsletters and meetings, and they provide an opportunity to network and develop friends who have interests similar to your own. They also conduct informative seminars through which you can learn business skills and make useful contacts with other business people.

# 6   How Should Your Business Be Organized?

Plan to give some serious thought to the legal structure you choose for your new business. Each type of organization has advantages and disadvantages, and it is important to understand how the organization you select can influence business opportunities. A comparison of each type of organization follows.

A home business can be organized as a sole proprietorship, a partnership, or a corporation. The sole proprietorship is preferred by most home business operators because they are seeking independence, they need relatively little capital to get started, and the chance of liability claims are minimal. Partnerships are formed when more money or extra workers are needed to run the operation but when liability is not considered a threat. A business is incorporated when several people are interested in working together, when larger amounts of capital are needed, when the intention is for the company to grow into a larger firm, and/or when the owners feel the liability for lawsuits or business debts could be a threat to their personal property.

If your business does not easily fall into one of the categories and you question which would be best for you, perhaps you should seek legal assistance. This advice should not cost too much, and it may save you a lot of other problems and fees in the long run.

## The Sole Proprietorship

A sole proprietorship is a business owned and operated by one person who is responsible for its debts and losses and assumes all its risks. At least 85 percent of the home businesses in America are organized in this manner, which means, essentially, that the owners are self-employed. While a sole proprietorship is owned by an individual, hired workers can help in the operation, and, although capital is provided by the owner, loans can be acquired to supplement the owner's investment.

The main advantages of a sole proprietorship are that the formation is easy (no special form of organization or legal paraphernalia are required), the profits are not shared, the owner is free to make independent decisions, and there is an important tax advantage. The sole proprietor can start business by putting out a sign, gathering supplies, and going to work—he or she can stop business by closing the front door. Decisions can be made quickly in response to changing circumstances because there are no co-owners or partners to consult.

There is little governmental control and no special taxation of this type of organization. In fact, the IRS allows business losses to be deducted from the owner's other earned income before taxes are figured. This is a very important point, because as a business is getting started it will usually lose money, and it's a common practice for the owner or the owner's spouse to keep working at another job until their business starts to show a profit. This advantage is also available to partnerships and S corporations (discussed later), but not regular corporations.

There are a couple of disadvantages to organizing a business as a sole proprietorship. The biggest is the liability the owner must assume for all business debts, taxes, and lawsuits that might be filed against the business. The liability for business debts becomes a problem in the event of business failure, but this is not an overwhelming problem since large sums of money are not usually borrowed to start a home business. The possibility of a lawsuit is much more worrisome. Liability can threaten not only the business investment, but also all the proprietor's personal holdings, including cars, house, livestock, and other possessions. Business owners should make every effort to protect themselves against this eventuality (a discussion of insurance and protection against risks appears in Chapter 19).

Another disadvantage of the sole proprietorship is that less capital is available to contribute to the business since there is but a single investor; however, this may not be a serious problem since many home businesses don't require much capital to get under way. Also, a sole proprietorship has only one person contributing ideas, but you may consider this to be an advantage instead of a disadvantage, depending on your point of view. Sometimes a home business is started by the take-charge type of individual who is excited about trying new ideas and does not want to share decision making. Less adventurous souls may need the support and ideas of a partner. It's for you to decide whether you need someone to help with financing and decisions or if you would rather go it alone.

## Partnerships

A partnership is similar to a sole proprietorship except that it involves two or more people sharing a business. Each shares in the profits and each is responsible for liabilities incurred by the business. A partnership is formed in order to share responsibility for the management, the work load, and/or the financial investment in the business. The roles of the partners are usually defined in an Articles of Partnership document and should never be based on a handshake. If you select this type of organization you must be very careful, because a partner can legitimately influence business decisions that you might prefer to have under your control. Also, there is always a danger of serious disagreement that could put a partnership in jeopardy. Partnerships are very easy to form, and there is little governmental control or special taxation. In fact, they are granted the same tax break as sole proprietorships, with business losses deducted from other income before figuring taxes.

A partnership can be tailored to suit the needs of a particular business. Some partners are active and share in the day-to-day responsibilities of running the business, while others are limited partners who financially subsidize the business but do not become involved in its operations. (If the partnership association is not known to the public, the uninvolved partner is called a "silent partner.")

Like the sole proprietor, partners who operate a business are burdened with unlimited liability. If one partner absconds with company funds, the remaining partners are personally liable for the debts of the partnership. However, a limited partner who does not participate in the management or conduct of the business is not subject to the same liability as general partners, and he or she risks only the agreed investment in the business.

Many people who work at home are reluctant to share the making of business decisions, and that is the main reason partnerships are rare among home-based businesses. Of course, there are always exceptions. A couple of friends might start a home business because they enjoy each other and share a common goal, and in these cases a partnership is the natural form of organization. But if you plan to do this, you might heed the warning of John D. Rockefeller who said, "A friendship founded on business is better than a business founded on friendship." Of course, there are often informal partnerships in home businesses, as when parents subsidize a business venture of their offspring (whether the offspring is a child trying to set up a lemonade stand or an adult trying to find a niche in the business world).

If you form a partnership, make some arrangement in the event of the death of one of the partners. This should be done through a Buy and Sell Agreement at the time the partnership is formed. It might be wise to consult a lawyer when setting up a partnership, especially in the preparation of this agreement. The Buy and Sell Agreement requires the surviving partner to buy, and the heirs to sell, the deceased partner's interest. The surviving partner of a two-partner operation would then become the sole owner, and the heirs of the deceased partner would receive cash for their share of the business.

## Corporations and S Corporations

A corporation is a legal entity that is distinct from the individuals or the personal worth of the people who own it. There is the misconception that incorporating is of value only to large firms, but small operations can also gain some advantages (and disadvantages) through this legal structure. In many states, a corporation may be formed with as little as $500 in stock, as compared to large corporations that issue millions of dollars worth of stock.

Being incorporated has several inherent advantages. Two, in particular, are worth special notice. In the first place, it is easier to attract investors and secure large amounts of capital if a business is incorporated. The two main sources of capital are stock issues and long-term bonds. A home business that is incorporated can sell shares of stock and use the proceeds to finance the business. Usually shareholders in home businesses are limited to family members, but others may be invited to buy into the company if more money is needed. Another source of capital available to corporations is bank loans. Corporations can obtain long-term financing from lending institutions by taking advantage of corporate assets, while sole proprietors and partnerships are less successful in acquiring this type of financing.

The second big advantage of incorporation is that liability is limited to the assets of the corporation, which means the personal assets of shareholders are not threatened in the event of liability claims against the corporation or even bankruptcy. In other words, rather than risking all of their assets in a venture, business owners and investors buy shares of stock in the incorporated firm, and this investment is the total liability to which they can be subjected.

Another characteristic of incorporated businesses is that they usually delegate authority and rely on more than one person for ideas, skills, and expertise, although this is not always the case. Many home businesses are incorporated to put structure into the organization, to acquire capital, and as a protection from unlimited liability, but the business is actually operated by a single person.

An incorporated business has perpetual life and survives the demise of its shareholders. When shareholders die, their stock is passed to their heirs. A corporation remains a business until it is dissolved by its board of directors.

One of the biggest problems with being incorporated is that the government imposes numerous regulations on corporations and requires the filing of a variety of reports throughout the year. Also, it costs more to form a corporation if you hire a lawyer to do the paperwork, although you can do your own legal work and the cost is minimal. See *How to Form Your Own Corporation Without a Lawyer for Under Fifty Dollars*, by Ted Nicholas; 1987, Enterprise Publishing, 725 N. Market Street, Wilmington, DE 19801. Also see *Incorporating a Small Business*, available at no cost from the Small Business Association, P. O. Box 15434, Fort Worth, TX 76119. If, after reading these publications, you still feel uneasy about the legal ramifications of incorporating, consult a lawyer for guidance.

There are two types of corporations: the regular corporation and the S corporation. An incorporated business qualifies for S corporation status if (1) there are no more than 10 employees, (2) there is only one class of stock and no more than 35 shareholders, and (3) there are no nonresident alien shareholders. The size of the corporation's income and assets is not a factor.

Corporations are taxed differently than unincorporated businesses, but an incorporated business classified as an S corporation pays taxes as if the shareholders are partners. Any profit or loss from the corporation passes directly to the shareholders as though it were ordinary income.

When a business is organized as a regular corporation, profits and losses accrue to the corporation itself. The corporation pays tax on all profits, and the shareholders pay tax on the dividends they receive, on the capital gains they receive from the sale of their stock, and on any capital gains realized upon the sale or liquidation of the business.

A corporation must have a minimum of three officers, who form the board of directors, but the board can be larger. The board of directors for a small home business might consist of Mom, Dad, and their child; a married couple and one of their parents; a couple and a friend; or various other combinations. A few states require only one director to start a corporation.

Should you incorporate? That depends. If you plan a small home business and do not foresee it growing into a large operation, and the probability of overwhelming liability is very slight, then you probably would not gain much by incorporating. However, if you expect your business to grow and you anticipate an eventual move to a larger location, it might be wise to incorporate early so as to take advantage of the

---

***ADVANTAGES AND DISADVANTAGES OF DIFFERENT BUSINESS STRUCTURES***

| Structure | Advantages | Disadvantages |
|---|---|---|
| Sole proprietorship | Ease of starting<br>Freedom to make decisions<br>Profits not shared<br>Few legal restrictions<br>Tax advantages | Unlimited liability<br>Limited input of ideas and labor<br>Capital more difficult to raise |
| Partnership | Ease of starting<br>Help in planning and working<br>More sources of capital<br>Tax advantages | Decision sharing<br>Unlimited liability<br>Potential for unreliable partner to endanger business |
| S corporation | Limited liability<br>Perpetual life<br>Ease of transferring owner-ship<br>Ease of expansion<br>Tax advantages | Government regulations<br>Expense to get started<br>Extra paperwork<br>Shared decisions |
| Regular corporation | A regular corporation has the same advantages and disadvantages as an S corporation, except that it does not get the tax advantage explained in the chapter. | |

---

more readily available financing, the limited liability, and the input of funds, expertise, and ideas from members of the board and the shareholders. Or you might begin your business as a sole proprietorship or partnership and change to a corporation as the business grows and gets to a point at which its needs are better met by incorporating. See the accompanying table for a comparison of the various business organization structures discussed in this chapter.

# 7    Finding Space for a Business in Your Home

You may live in a small apartment in the midst of a metropolitan zone or in a huge farmhouse far removed from populated areas, but wherever you live, there probably isn't a totally empty room or garage waiting for your business to fill it. Your task is to find a place to house your business. There may be space in a corner of the laundry room, or in the breakfast nook, garage, barn, or guest room. You might not find the necessary room, in which case you will need to create new space for your business (or change your plans). Whether using existing space or building new space, it is unwise to make drastic changes before you get a good feel for what is required. As you are getting under way, try to *just* get under way—just enough so you can start functioning as a business. It takes time to discover what type of space and how much space is actually needed, so it's best to let the space evolve as your business grows.

## Designing Work Space to Meet IRS Requirements and Gain Tax Benefits

One way to save money by working at home is by taking advantage of the tax deduction allowed for home work space. By learning what is required to make work space tax-deductible, you can plan your space to fulfill the requirements. This effort is worthwhile because these deductions can amount to a significant savings. The items that are tax-deductible are listed in Chapter 18, but it's worth mentioning here that the list is extensive and includes a percent of the utility expenses, mortgage interest, and repair costs, and the total amount of money spent developing the business area.

In order to qualify for a deduction, the part of your home used for business purposes must meet certain qualifications. It must be

1. Clearly *separated* from family living space
2. Used *exclusively* for business purposes
3. Used on a *regular* basis
4. Used as your *principal* place of business *or* used as a *meeting place* for you to interact with clients or patients

All of these requirements must be met. Each of the requirements is explained below, as is the additional issue of freestanding structures.

***Separation from Family Space.*** The easiest way to separate business space from family space is to confine it to a room behind a door or in a separate building, but that isn't always practical or possible. Separation can also be accomplished through the use of screens, partitions, and furniture arrangement. A desk used only for business purposes that sits within a room used by the family will not meet the separation requirement.

***Exclusive Use.*** Exclusive use means the designated area is used *only* for the purpose of carrying on your trade or business. The following example illustrates this rule. If your spouse takes the family car from the garage each morning and drives to work, and you set up a work station in the area where the car had been, you cannot claim a deduction for the garage because the garage is not used exclusively for business purposes. If, however, the car were parked outside of the garage and you left your work station permanently set up, this arrangement would meet the exclusive-use provision.

There are two exceptions to this rule. One applies to the storage of inventory, and the other applies to the use of the home as a day-care facility. The space used to store inventory can be tax-deductible if *all* of the following qualifications are met:

1. Your business or trade is wholesaling or retailing products.
2. The inventory is needed for use in your trade or business.
3. The storage space is used on a regular basis.
4. The space is identifiable as storage space.

If all the above tests are met, business items can be stored in areas within the parts of the home used for family purposes—such as kitchen cabinets, under beds, on shelves in the garage, or in closets that contain family clothing—and still be claimed as tax-deductible space.

The other exception to the exclusive-use rule is space used for day care. In this case, deductions are based on the percent of time and the percent of area used as a day-care facility. If a child care, elderly care, or mentally or physically impaired care facility operates for 12 hours each day (or 50 percent of the 24-hour day) in a family room which is used by the family after the clients leave, and if the family room is 50 percent of the floor area of the home, the allowable deduction is calculated as 50 percent (portion of day the area is used) multiplied by 50 percent (percent of home area used), yielding a 25 percent home-use tax deduction. However, a 50 percent home-use deduction could be claimed if the area used for day care is *not* used by the family after clients leave.

*Regular Use.*  Regular use means the business part of the home is used on a continuing basis. It does not need to be used each day, but it must be used regularly, perhaps each weekday morning or every weekend. Even if a part of a home is used exclusively for business purposes, but it is used only occasionally, it does not meet the requirement and cannot be claimed as a deduction.

*Principal Place of Business or Place to Meet with Patients or Clients.*  The part of a home claimed for a business deduction must be the principal place of business. If you work outside your home during the day, but work at home in the evenings or on weekends on a different business, then your home work space would be the principal place of business for your home business. The area also qualifies if it is not your principal place of business but is used as a place to meet or deal with patients, students, clients, or customers in the normal course of your trade, business, or profession. For example, a lawyer may have an office away from home but use a home office to interview clients in the evening. The home office would satisfy the meeting place requirement, and expenses would be tax-deductible if the office were used exclusively and regularly to meet with clients. However, a university professor cannot claim a tax deduction for a home office that is used to study and to prepare lecture notes, even though the office is used regularly for this purpose, because the principal place of business is the university.

*Freestanding Structures.*  A separate, freestanding structure is tax-deductible if the structure is used *exclusively* and *regularly* for business purposes, but it does *not* need to be the principal place of business or to be used to meet clients. A freestanding structure could be a trailer, shop, studio, barn, chicken coop, garage, or the like. Many people use barns and outbuildings to store inventory, or they do work in these buildings that is not a suitable indoor activity. I had an acquaintance who covered a barn floor with compost several feet deep and then raised mushrooms on the compost. The mushrooms were then taken into the house where they were pickled, canned, and sold to delicatessens. She claimed business use and received tax deductions on both the barn and a designated portion of her kitchen.

## Recognizing Potential Business Space

As you look for possible places to set up shop, think about the amount and kind of space needed, keeping in mind your other home needs and your responsibilities. Will you need to work where you can see customers or shipments arriving at the door, or will you be looking after a child while tending to business? Will you need a separate entrance for clients? What about toilet facilities and a waiting room? Also take into consideration the kind of work site that appeals to you. Do you prefer to get away from household activities and noises, or do you want to be within ear and eye range of the household? Do you like being surrounded by light, or would you object to working in the basement or in areas without windows? Windowless areas are very depressing to some people, while others seem unaffected by the lack of natural light.

As you search the premises for a business location, keep in mind the exclusive-use requirement needed to qualify for a tax deduction. Remember that a part of a room can qualify if it is clearly defined and separated from the nonbusiness portion. Of course, if you can't find space that will qualify for deductions, but it is the only space available to you, it may in your best interest to pass up the deduction in order to get a business under way.

It's time to take an in-depth look around your house to find some unused or underused space. At first it may appear that there isn't any available space that is suitable, but if you keep looking you will probably recognize some potential business space. Is there extra space in your kitchen? A business that involves food preparation needs to be centered in the kitchen area, but a kitchen can also be used as an office or a place where you can sew, paint, or do some other business activity. A business built on food preparation will place a burden on a home kitchen since the kitchen must double for both business and home cooking, but a well-organized operation can accomodate both needs. Of course, it will not meet the exclusive-use test and therefore will not qualify for the tax deduction if it is used for both business and home cooking. Extra storage space will surely be required for supplies and equipment, but this could be set up in another area of the house or in the garage.

What about the kitchen or dining room table? You can make the dining room table your center of operation if you don't have other choices. If necessary, set up shop each morning and put things away in time for the evening meal. Where there's a will, there's a way, so do what you must to make it work.

A breakfast nook can be converted into a nice, off-the-beaten-path office or work room. Breakfast nooks are usually set apart from the rest of the kitchen and have lots of windows which makes them especially pleasant work areas.

Is your living room used very often? Some families fly past the living room on their way to the family room, and it sits empty most of the time. This could be a good place for an office, especially if you have clients calling on you and you want to meet them in a formal setting. The desk and other furnishings should be selected to complement the decor of the room. After a few pieces of equipment have been moved in, the room may appear to be more of an office than a living room, but a little reshuffling will allow the family to reclaim it for special occasions. Since the area would be used for both a living room and an office, it would not be tax-deductible because it would not meet the exclusive-use test.

A guest room or extra bedroom might be an excellent space choice. This type of room works nicely for a home office because there is usually a bathroom nearby and the room can be shut off from the rest of the house simply by closing the door. You can still have the room function as a guest room by replacing the bed with a sofa bed, although you should have some way to lock up private business files when guests use the room. Your own bedroom might be another possibility for a small office because it is probably rarely seen by guests in your home. The beauty of using such a private place is that you don't need to be so particular about keeping it tidy and can leave papers and projects on your desk from one work day to the next. Normally, a bedroom isn't a good choice if clients visit your office, because it is usually located in the inner sanctum of the house and clients would need to pass through family living space. If at all possible, don't allow clients access to the part of your home used by the family.

It's easy to overlook an attic as a possible work area, especially if it is unfinished. Even if your attic has no flooring, the walls are bare studs, and the only access is a hole in the ceiling, you may still be able to convert it into your business home. An attic that has at least seven feet of head room can be converted into work space. It would be wise to add outside stairs if clients will be visiting, but indoor steps will be handier if you plan to work alone in the area.

Do you have a basement in your house? Many types of businesses can be housed in a basement. It's an ideal location for a manufacturing business for which unsightly equipment and large amounts of supplies are needed. But a basement can also be used for an office and even for a business that has clients visiting, although a separate entrance would make it more effective for this purpose. If you plan to use a basement setting to meet with clients, make an effort to give the illusion that it is above ground. This can be done by using drapes on the walls, an abundance of lights and mirrors, and shades of green in the decor. Also, a dehumidifier and heater might be needed to ward off dampness and coolness, and carpeting could be used to soften the harshness of a concrete floor.

A porch makes a wonderful office or workroom. With the ceiling, floor, and at least one wall already in place, it is usually not difficult or terribly expensive to make a porch into a room. A side porch is preferred to a front porch if your business will have clients or customers coming and going, because family visitors would not need to pass through the office to get into your home.

A breezeway can also be converted into convenient business space. These little areas usually have a lot of windows, which makes them light and pleasant to work in, and most of them have an outside entrance.

And finally, don't overlook outbuildings and other freestanding structures. A garage, barn, shed, shop, guest house, trailer, or any other separate structure on the lot might be a good location for your business. As mentioned earlier, a separate structure is tax-deductible if it is used exclusively and regularly for business purposes, even if it isn't your primary place of business and/or isn't used to meet with clients.

While you may be able to find work space, it may not be appropriate for meeting with clients and you may be unable to convert it into an appropriate setting. One way to get around this problem is to meet with clients in *their* offices or homes. Of course, this arrangement isn't as convenient, but it's better than exposing clients to barking dogs, crying kids, and rooms stacked to the ceiling with supplies. There is no reason for customers to ever know why you are willing to do business on their turf. In fact, you can use housecalls as a selling point—you'll come to them for their convenience.

If, during your search for a work area, you fail to find any space to convert to business use, you may feel that it's necessary to make new space by adding to your home or garage. Building new space is expensive, and I caution you, again, not to make expensive changes until you are sure your business will support this type of development. There is another reason for not rushing into a big building project. A business costs more to start than you might suspect, and you will probably need all the money you can gather just to purchase supplies and equipment and to keep up with home and family expenses until customers start paying their bills. Also, you won't have time to oversee a building project while you are getting a business started. Therefore, if at all possible, squeeze your business into existing space, make due with minor remodeling, and put off extensive building and remodeling until your business is under way and the future looks promising.

## Turning Space into a Place for Business

You can probably get started in much less than optimal work conditions, so don't spend much time and money creating the perfect home workshop or office before you have tested the market. Still, there is a minimum amount of space, supplies, and equipment needed to get under way. It's true, you can save a little money by using the ironing board as a bookshelf and an old trunk as a filing cabinet, but the stress and strain of operating without proper space and supplies will be reflected in your work attitude. And you can't expect clients to flock to your office if it's a dreary hole in the basement. So, as you start, make your space workable, but plan to do any extensive remodeling and decorating as your business grows.

### RESHAPING SPACE

After you locate a spot for your business, the next task is to reshape it. Space can be reshaped and rooms can be divided into defined areas very inexpensively through the use of screens, drapes, bookcases, and furniture.

Maybe all you need is a room divider to separate living and business space. Such dividers are used in modern office complexes to dissociate one office from another, and the same principle can be applied in your home to separate an office or work area from a family-used part of the room. Strategically placed drapes are also effective room dividers. Space can also be partitioned into different shapes with nothing more than the placement of office furniture and equipment; if the area used for business is obviously defined, then even though part of the room is used for family purposes, the business portion of the room would meet the IRS separation rule and qualify for a tax deduction.

The space you have found might require structural remodeling rather than reshaping with screens, drapes, or furniture, but try to make relatively minor changes until you know just what kind of space you really need.

### DECORATING WITH YOU AND YOUR CUSTOMERS IN MIND

You will spend a lot of time in your office or work zone, so make it as pleasant as possible. It should also look inviting and be comfortable to all who visit your office. I never cease to be amazed at the offices and work stations of most people in the business world. People spend at least one-third of the day in these work settings, but many never bother to make the settings pleasing—unless you count putting a plastic flower on the corner of the desk and hanging a poor-quality picture on the wall. Why not make your work area as delightful as possible? My husband, a university professor, has an office that has become a stop on university campus tours because he has taken the time to decorate it with exciting art and interesting artifacts. Maybe he has gone beyond the call of duty with unusual stained glass panels, wall murals, and a profusion of plants, but his office is inviting to his students and colleagues, and it contributes to his enjoyment of his workday.

There are several decorating elements you might use as you plan your decorating scheme, including color, wall and window treatment, floor covering, and furniture.

**Walls.**  The colors you select will influence the "feel" of the area. If your workroom is located on the north side of the house, it can be made to feel warmer and sunnier with warm colors (yellow, beige, brown, tan, peach, or orange); if it's on the south side, then you can cool it off by using light blues or greens.

If you work alone, you can put anything you please on the walls, from family pictures to Playboy centerfolds, but the walls should be decorated more discreetly if clients visit your work area. In this case, don't display a bunch of family photos or personal items; an interesting collection of artworks might be more appropriate. Display your license to practice if you are a professional or if you pursue an occupation based on special education that requires licensing.

**Windows.**  Leave windows bare or use blinds that can be fully opened if you want to bring the outside in; however, the outside world can be a source of distraction, and sometimes the view is less than desirable, especially if houses are close together. Drapes are powerful decorating tools and can be used to either control the outside light and noise, create a more intimate feeling, or create an illusion of windows where no windows exist.

**Floors.**  Appropriate floor treatment will depend upon where in the house you work and the type of work you are pursuing. It is easier to keep a linoleum or resilient tile floor clean and tidy, but carpeting has several advantages. Carpeting is sound-absorbent, which may be important if your work area is located in a busy or noisy section of the house. Also, carpeting will make a floor feel warmer, it usually looks better than linoleum or tile, and it prevents slipping. The disadvantages of carpeting are that it traps dirt, which can be a serious problem if it is used in high-traffic areas, and it sometimes creates static electricity.

***Furniture and Equipment.***   Arrange the furniture and equipment in your work area so there is a minimum of wasted space and motion. Many people work more efficiently if the basic equipment is arranged in a U-shape. Be sure to provide enough places for everything—enough bookshelves, filing cabinets, and drawers—and clearly label drawers and cabinets so you can quickly locate things when they are needed.

## CONTROLLING YOUR WORK ENVIRONMENT

More work will be accomplished if you feel comfortable and have a minimum of environmental distractions. Three factors that should be carefully controlled in your work area are temperature, lighting, and sound.

***Temperature Control.***   The goal is to keep the temperature at a level that is conducive to work and comfort. Most people prefer a temperature between 70°F and 74°F in the colder months and between 74°F and 78°F during the warmer months. Relative humidity also affects comfort level, and the amount of water vapor in the air can be controlled with a dehumidifier or humidifier.

***Lighting.***   It has been shown that light exerts a powerful psychological influence on some people, with more light causing them to feel better and to be more productive. What is especially fascinating is that this characteristic is genetic, just as eye color is genetic. If you feel "blue" when the sky is overcast and the light level is reduced, you may be susceptible to the psychological influence of light. If you think this is the case, increase the amount of light in your environment, either by working near windows or by increasing illumination through electrical fixtures.

***Sound Control.***   Sounds in home offices need to be controlled as carefully as those in commercial settings. This is necessary because noise is fatiguing and can reduce efficiency. Irritating sounds can be either masked with less offensive sounds or eliminated through insulation and sound-absorbing materials. The goal of sound control is to isolate the work area from street and household sounds and from sounds created by business equipment.

Bare walls, hard floors, and nonabsorptive ceilings reflect sound, but noise bouncing from these surfaces can be reduced if the surfaces are covered with sound-absorbing materials, such as acoustical tile on the ceiling; carpeting rather than hard tiles on the floor; and drapes, cloth hangings, or decorative rugs on the walls.

Street sounds can be reduced by using storm windows and drapes. In fact, the same measures that insulate against severe weather are also often effective against sound. Household sounds seem to carry through air ducts, and it is difficult to stop these noises other than by going to the source. That is why children must understand that they must be quiet when clients are present. Some types of business equipment also produce irritating sounds, but a few strategically placed noise-absorbing pads can bring most of these sounds down to a tolerable level. Undesirable sounds that cannot be eliminated can be masked with different sounds. Music is sometimes used for this purpose, although it is important to select the right kind of music so it will not be more irritating than the original noise. Also, a fish tank bubbling in the background or a ticking clock can be used to mask unpleasant sounds.

# 8    Funding Your Business

## *How Much Money Do You Need to Get Started?*

A home business means different things to different people. Some of you are planning an operation that will support yourself and your family, while others of you intend to use your business to supplement another income. Whether your home business will be large or small it will get *started* in much the same way, and it will probably require less capital than you might suspect. You won't need to rent space or pay much extra for utilities, since you'll be working at home. And, as far as equipment and supplies are concerned, it's wise to start with the minimum amount needed and buy items as the demand develops. Too often people make unrealistic plans and spend too much money for space renovation, equipment, and supplies before they test the market or their business acumen. They end up paying for expensive equipment that is of no use to them if the plans fail to materialize.

It is safer and more prudent to start your business as a part-time operation that allows you to test the waters. As you find a market and customers, then you can fine-tune your business goals and add equipment and space as needed. During this start-up phase, it may be in your best interest to keep your current job to ensure a steady income that can support both your family and your business. You will feel more secure in letting go of a regular paycheck and devoting all of your energies to the new enterprise after you have ironed out the start-up problems and found a niche in the market.

There is another advantage to this part-time approach. It is very difficult to get a loan for start-from-scratch expenses, but if you can show lenders that your business is up and running and that you need money not to get started but for expansion, they will be much more willing to consider your proposal.

Some kinds of businesses can get under way with very little capital and just a few customers. The service industry is generally characterized as being labor-intensive, and service enterprises usually require comparatively little capital to get started. Also, since many service businesses are based on a skill, hobby, or interest of the proprietor, the basic equipment is often already available. For example, a seamstress may start a business with nothing more than a sign in the front yard, advertisements in the local media, and her old familiar sewing machine. A secretary, baker, music teacher, or furniture refinisher, to name just a few, can often start a business just as easily.

Product-oriented businesses, especially those based on crafted items, can also get under way with a modest investment. For several years I have watched a lady turn cloth remnants into lovely puffed baskets that she sells at craft fairs and on consignment in retail shops. These baskets sell as fast as she can make them, yet she has never needed to make a substantial investment in her business. Of course, if she ever decided to go national and sell through catalogs or retailers, with a corps of sales representatives selling her products, then her financial needs would be quite different, as she would need to build up inventory and hire helpers to meet the increased demand.

Equipment and supplies must be in place before work can begin in some types of businesses. A very popular home business is carpet

## GREETING CARDS AND DIAPER BOXES

You've probably seen them, chuckled, and felt somebody else knows about the world you inhabit. "Working Woman" greeting cards, memos, and calendars celebrate such occasions as TV Dinner Day and Permanent Press Day. They are produced by Barbara and Jim Dale and are nationally distributed to some 25,000 retail outlets across the country. The Dales hadn't thought their witty greetings would go big time. They just made them for friends and, as Barbara tells it, "had them printed on typing paper at the speedy print place just down the street." Soon, the manager of one of the local gift shops wanted some of the cards, and 18 months later the Dales were in business. Barbara said, "I delivered our first local orders in empty Huggies Diaper boxes." Demand for their product grew so quickly that the Dale's could not create the cards and also manage the business end of the operation. Consequently, they turned over part of the business to Recycled Paper Products Inc. of Chicago, which now handles the publishing, marketing, and distribution of the line while the Dales continue to sketch and quip about their own experiences from a studio in their home. This is a perfect example of testing the market before remodeling to make space, filling the house with supplies, and making financial commitments. While you might need more than a diaper box to ship goods, the word is, *go minimal*—get enough in place to get started and let your business dictate your future needs.

cleaning (it operates *from* the home, not *in* the home), but basic cleaning tools and supplies are needed before any work can be done, and they are quite expensive. I know of a cleaning company that started with rented equipment—the type that is rented by the hour. When a cleaning call came in, the owner simply stopped by the rental shop on the way to the job. He now owns several fully equipped vans and has seven workers on the payroll, and he is still operating out of an addition to his garage. Manufacturing is another business that often requires a significant investment before production begins, but start-up costs can be kept to a minimum if used equipment can be located for sale.

If you are planning a business that requires a substantial outlay of capital before you can start, you should be aware that commercial lenders probably won't consider your loan proposal if you cannot provide at least 50 percent of the start-up funds. A lender will be more inclined to consider your request seriously when you show this degree of personal financial commitment.

Money is needed for different phases of a business. Start-up costs are usually covered by personal funds or money borrowed from family or friends, with a lending institution loaning not more than 50 percent of the total. As a business grows and expands, funding may be needed for space renovation, equipment, and an expanded inventory. Funding for expansion is usually acquired through a long-term loan from a lending institution or by selling a part of the business (equity). Short-term loans are sometimes needed to meet operating expenses and to circumvent a cash-flow crisis, which is something many novice business people fail to anticipate. Cash flow is an important matter that will be discussed shortly (and again in Chapter 17).

## FIGURING FINANCIAL NEEDS

A detailed budget should be prepared to determine your financial needs. You already know the importance of a budget for personal financial planning; a business also needs a financial blueprint for success. As you make a budget, consider not only the needs of your business, but also what it will take to keep your family and home intact until your business starts to earn a profit.

***Business Start-Up Expenses.*** Start-up expenses will depend, of course, on the kind of business you are planning. Many of them are one-time, nonrecurring expenses, while others are ongoing expenses. Start-up expenses include some or all of the following:

Tools, equipment, and supplies needed to manufacture a product or to provide a service

Inventory-related furnishings and hardware, such as storage bins, cabinets, and shelves

Fixtures

Installation of fixtures and hardware

Remodeling and decorating

Utilities (gas, electricity, water)

Legal, accounting, and secretarial fees

Insurance

Property rent

Taxes

Salaries for helpers

Commissions for sales representatives

Banking fees

Vehicle maintenance and fuel costs

Shipping supplies and fees

Telephone deposit, listing, and calling costs

Office supplies, including stationery, purchase orders, invoice forms, and a myriad of miscellaneous items

Shop supplies

Office furnishings and equipment, including desk, chair, filing cabinets, typewriter and/or computer or word processor, shelving, lighting fixtures, and maybe a copier

Marketing and promotional items

Licenses and permits

Dues and subscriptions to trade associations and magazines

Debt interest

Petty cash

Each of these expenses should be subdivided, and each subdivision researched or estimated, to yield a detailed list of start-up costs. For instance, under marketing and promotional items you might list and estimate costs for the following specifics:

Business logo design

Signs and posters

Business cards

Mailers

Advertisements

Carefully calculate the cost of each item to determine the total amount of money needed to get your business under way. Equipment manufacturers, builders, and suppliers of raw materials can supply you with cost estimates and price lists that will help you determine your financial needs accurately.

*Cost-of-Living Budget.* The cost-of-living budget is an estimate of the money you will need to support your household from the time your business is launched until it starts to earn a profit that is sufficient to support your family. Figure a cost-of-living budget if you, alone, are responsible for the support of your family; if your spouse or someone else will provide all or most of the support for your family while your business is growing to profitability, you can skip or modify this part of the financial plan. (Needless to say, every effort should be made to be thrifty during this period.) Your budget should include some or all of the following items:

Food
Household expenses: maintenance, utilities, telephone
Personal expenses: clothing, medical care, entertainment, gifts, spending money
Vehicle and transportation expenses
Monthly payments: car, insurance, rent or mortgage, loans, credit cards
Taxes: property, county, state, and federal

---

## BUDGET PLAN

A budget plan should include the items listed below to enable you to project your financial needs accurately.

Expected cash receipts for a given time period (one, three, or six months):
    Cash sales
    Collections on accounts receivable
    Other income
Expected cash disbursements for the same period of time:
    Supplies
    Advertising
    Other marketing expenses
    Salary
    New equipment
    Payments on loans, taxes, interest, etc.
    Maintenance expenses
    Utilities (gas, electric, telephone, water, etc.)
Expected cash balance at the end of the time interval:
    Cash receipts less cash disbursements

Using past records, calculate the cost of the above expenses for an average month and multiply that figure by the number of months you anticipate it will take to start earning enough profit to support your family. Be realistic. It usually takes longer than you might expect to generate profit that can be taken from a young business without jeopardizing its financial stability.

### FUNDING FOR EXPANSION AND OPERATING EXPENSES

After your business has begun to grow, you may want to expand. You will probably need to borrow money for remodeling or creating new space, for more equipment and supplies, or for the research and development of new products. Funding for expansion can be acquired through a long-term loan from a lending institution or by selling a part of your business to investors.

Even though a business is doing very well, a short-term loan might be needed to ease a cash-flow crisis, which is a very common phenomenon among young, small businesses. A number of circumstances can cause a cash shortage, but it frequently results from having too many outstanding accounts receivable or from not recognizing and anticipating the natural time interval between when supplies are bought to produce a product and the actual delivery of and payment for that product. I am reminded of a very successful home business that was nearly brought to its knees as a result of a cash-flow problem. This business produced a clever "kitchen witch" that was sold locally for many years. In an effort to expand, the owner courted the Japanese market and was ecstatic when the product attracted the fancy of a Japanese importer who placed a huge order. In spite of the promise of money and profit, the first order resulted in a cash-flow crisis. Bills for the supplies that went into the product were coming due while the items were still on a ship steaming its way to Japan. Since the goods had been sold and a profit was anticipated, the owner was able to find a bank to bail her company out of the bind, but it took a long time to build up sufficient cash reserve to handle the time interval between producing an item and being paid for it by a foreign buyer. Now, her company regularly sells to foreign markets. She is very proud of her healthy and profitable business that is helping to reduce our nation's trade deficit.

## Ways to Fund Your Business

Many people automatically think of borrowing money from a bank when they need money to start a business, but that's not always the best approach. You may eventually need a bank loan, but it might be to your advantage to start with money gathered from other sources. Personal savings or inherited money are ideal, but if these aren't available then you might get a loan from family members or perhaps from friends who would be willing to loan you something to get started. But just a word about these kinds of loans. Don't expect your friends and relatives to loan you money if you aren't contributing financially to the project. You must show them that you are committed to the success of your venture, not just through your enthusiasm and reputation but with some of your money as well. In other words, you will be more convincing if you "put your money where your mouth is." If you borrow money from family or friends, it is imperative that you have a written agreement detailing the terms of the loan and how it will be repaid. Also, you should be sensitive to the strain a loan can create between you and your family or friends. If you think this may be a problem, getting money from them may not be worth jeopardizing the relationship.

Equity capital is another way to fund a business. This is money acquired by selling a part interest in the business to another party. The money is not repaid as a loan, but instead any business profit earned must be divided among the parties who hold equity in the business.

You may be able to accumulate all the money you need to get started from these various sources. However, if you still need more money, and have gathered at least 50 percent of the money needed to get started, then you are in a position to approach a bank, savings and loan institution, credit union, or the Small Business Administration (SBA) for a business loan.

### LOANS FROM BANKS AND OTHER PRIVATE LENDERS

Banks are in the business of loaning money to make money. For this reason, they are looking for prospects who have the potential to be successful and who can repay, with interest, the money they have borrowed. Banks are also looking for customers who have collateral to back up the money the banks have loaned in the event that a business fails and there is no money available for repayment. In this case, the bank will take possession of the collateral. Each loan a bank makes represents a risk to the bank, so banks are looking for qualified borrowers who make the risks worth taking. There are differences between banks and other lending institutions, each having their own requirements, rates, and repayment plans. It is in your best interest to make a chart listing all of the lenders in your community and the terms they offer as you try to determine where you can get the best deal.

By the way, when considering collateral, don't overlook your life insurance policy. When an insurance policy (except term insurance) has been in effect for a few years it builds up a loan value. The interest rate charged by the insurance company is lower than that charged by most lending institutions, and the loan value of an insurance policy can be counted on as a reliable source of cash (whereas a bank might refuse a loan application). The face value of the life insurance policy remains in effect during the loan period subject to the outstanding loan. A life insurance policy can also be used as collateral for a loan from a lending institution with the lender becoming the beneficiary of the policy for the amount of the loan. When the loan is repaid, the policy reverts to the original beneficiary.

## SBA LOANS

The SBA, which is associated with the federal government, makes loans to new businesses started by minorities (including women), veterans, and disadvantaged persons *if they have been turned down by private lenders.* The rate of interest is slightly higher than that charged by a bank or a savings and loan institution because the risk is considered to be greater. Also, there is a painfully long wait between application for and receipt of the loan; but still, it's a possible way to get the money needed to launch a business. If you can't get a loan elsewhere, an SBA loan is well worth pursuing. For further information about SBA loans, read the SBA booklet *Business Loans From the SBA*, available from the Small Business Administration, P.O. Box 15434, Ft. Worth, TX 76119.

---

### FUNDING SOURCES FOR YOUR BUSINESS

1. Personal savings and inheritance.
2. Loans from family and friends.
3. Loans from banks and commercial lending institutions (credit unions, savings and loans, etc.) secured by personal assets (savings, stocks, bonds, real estate) or business assets (accounts receivable, inventory, equipment, real estate).
4. Loans from the Small Business Administration (SBA) secured by personal assets or business assets.
5. Loans from a life insurance company secured by a policy's cash value.
6. Equity. (This is money received from the sale of part of a business. It is not a loan, so the money is not repaid, but the buyer shares in the profit generated by the business.) Equity can be sold to family, friends, and venture capitalists.

---

## Going After a Loan

Knowing how to apply for a loan and being familiar with basic banking procedures will increase your chances for loan approval. It might even be worth your effort to "practice" on one bank in anticipation of applying at another (of course, you may be approved by the first). A loan application consists of two basic parts: the written proposal and the interview or oral presentation. While a friend can help you write a proposal, you will be better prepared for the interview if you prepare the written proposal yourself. In the process you will learn enough about banking terms and expectations to have the confidence and background to convince a loan officer that your proposal is sound and worthy of funding.

The terms listed below are used regularly by funding organizations. Familiarize yourself with them and integrate them into your loan application.

*Balance Sheet:* A financial statement that describes the financial status of a business on a given date. It lists all assets and liabilities of the business.

*Collateral:* Property of worth that can be held by a lending institution to be claimed in the event the loan is not repaid. Collateral can include real property, stocks (up to 75 percent of their market value), bonds (up to 90 percent of face value), savings accounts (the bank keeps the passbook), life insurance policies, and business assets.

*Asset:* Anything that can generate cash. Accounts receivable, inventory, and equipment are considered assets if you are already in business. If you are not yet in business, your assets are your personal property (see also definition of *Personal Financial History and Statement,* below).

*Liabilities:* The monies and obligations that you owe at the moment. If you are not in business, these would be your personal debts.

*Cash-Flow Projection:* The amount of income anticipated minus the amount of cash needed to cover expenses during a given time period. Sometimes a short-term loan is required to bridge the interval between the time money is required to cover expenses and the time it is received for goods sold or services rendered. The goal is to keep enough money on hand to cover the cash requirements, but not much excess.

*Personal Financial History and Statement:* A record of your borrowings and repayments and a list of personal assets and liabilities. Your assets are made up of your savings accounts, and the market value of stocks, bonds, and real estate that you own. Your liabilities include personal debts, such as life insurance premiums, mortgages, and installment credit payments. When a bank is reviewing your personal history, it will consider your potential for earning income from salary and investments.

*Short-term Loan:* Money borrowed for a period generally no longer than 12 months. Short-term loans are easier to obtain than long-term loans because they are usually used for a special purpose which in turn generates income for the business (such as paying for supplies needed to produce goods).

*Long-term Loan:* Money borrowed for more than a year, usually used for such expenditures as equipment and building expansion. Repayment is from accumulated profits.

Pick up an application form at a bank and fill it in. This will usually entail writing a detailed description of the business you are planning (or planning to expand) and providing the following information:

1. Your name, address, and telephone number.
2. A description of the business you presently operate or want to start.
3. A résumé of your past business experiences.
4. The amount of money you need to borrow. Be realistic in your forecast, and ask for the total amount required for a given period so you won't need to ask the bank for an additional loan within a short time.
5. An itemization of each proposed expenditure and an explanation of how the money will be used to benefit the business operation.
6. Proposed repayment terms and payback schedule. (The bank may not accept your terms, but this gives you some input.)
7. Financial documentation. Describe how the repayment money will be acquired by submitting records of past business performance if the loan is for business expansion. If you are applying for a new business loan, predict the business earnings for the first year.
8. A personal financial statement. List all personal assets and liabilities and describe any collateral you intend to offer to secure the loan. Indicate the current market value of all securities.
9. Other information. Include reference letters, letters of intent for buy/sell agreements, and any evidence of business activity or the prospect of your business making a profit.

After you have completed the application form, make an appointment with a loan officer of a lending institution and go prepared to sell your idea. As you prepare your case, think about some of the questions a lender might ask and plan how you will respond. You can expect these kinds of questions:

- What kind of business do you have in mind?
- Why are you planning this type of business?
- Have you looked into the competition?
- What skills and background do you have that have prepared you for this undertaking?
- How much business do you expect the first year?
- How much money can you contribute to the business?
- What collateral do you have to back up a loan?
- When do you expect the business to start making a profit?
- Why do you need a loan, and exactly how do you intend to use the money?
- How and when can you repay the loan?

Of course, you will have answered most of these questions on the written proposal, but nonetheless, expect to answer them again during your interview. You will be questioned less rigorously if you convince your interviewers right away that you are knowledgeable about the proposed business and that you have the ability to make it work. This convincing is effected both by your demeanor (do you seem confident and competent?) and by the thoroughness with which you prepare your application and your oral presentation.

Bankers are looking for success waiting to happen, and you will probably get a loan if you convince them that you and your business are worth the risk. The following main points are considered when the processing officer evaluates the application:

- The debt-paying record of the borrower
- The debt-to-net-worth ratio of the borrower
- The value of the collateral offered for security
- The borrower's character
- The prospect of business success

If your loan request is turned down, be sure to find out why, and use the information to improve your plans and your future loan applications. Do what is necessary to make your plan feasible. The bank may have detected a weak link, and it may be necessary to change your plans in order to garner a loan. It could be that you don't have enough collateral or enough experience and the loan officers are uneasy about your ability to succeed and repay the money you borrow. Maybe you are applying for a loan prematurely. If this is the case, you should work to accumulate both experience and personal funds before reapplying for a loan.

When you find a lender willing to support your plan, proceed carefully. Ask to see the papers you will be signing *before the loan is closed*. Ralph Waldo Emerson wrote, "Money often costs too much." You must be certain that the loan you are being offered doesn't cost too much, and for that reason you should take the time to carefully study the terms of the loan. If you are apprehensive about the loan contract or don't understand exactly what it means, it would be prudent to have it examined by an accountant or legal advisor who can interpret it for you.

# Part Four

## *Setting Up a Business*

# 9     Naming Your Business, Designing a Logo, and Getting Into Print

## *A Descriptive Name Is Like Money in the Bank*

Selecting an appropriate name for your business is important because it will have an impact throughout the life of your business. There are several characteristics you should strive to include in the name you choose. It should be *descriptive,* yet still be a bit *ambiguous* in order to accommodate any shift in the direction of your business. This ambiguity is necessary because as you get started you may not know exactly how your business will fit into the scheme of things. You may need to readjust your plans, perhaps changing direction somewhat as you focus on a specific market or refine your business goals.

A name with a ring of familiarity is of value because it's easy to remember and it might catch the attention of potential customers as they glance over the businesses listed in the Yellow Pages of the telephone directory. Any name that will make a customer pause at the listing of your business is worth considering. I'm reminded of a horticulturist who planned to offer a class on the care of house plants. He advertised in the local paper, calling the class "Learning to Grow Houseplants." Very few people enrolled. He advertised again, but this time he titled the class "Plant Parenthood"—and was startled by the huge response. Similarly, the "Wish Upon a Star" organization, a group that grants wishes to ill children, also has a name that conjures up a memory and catches people's fancy.

A business name should convey a message. How many businesses have you seen with names like The John Lamport Company or Jerry's Corner? Such names waste an opportunity to inform. Names such as John Lamport's Insurance Company and Jerry's Korner Kitchen are much more descriptive.

Finally, try to incorporate your own name into your business name, especially if you are known in the community. This is frequently done by athletes who have had their names splashed over the sports pages. When their playing days are over, they can use the years of public exposure to their advantage by incorporating their names into their business names. Examples that come to mind are Mattingly's 21 Restaurant (named for Don Mattingly, who wears uniform number 21 for the New York Yankees) and Joe Montana's Men's Wear. But you don't need to be an athlete to cash in on name recognition. If you've been a teacher, principal, or coach, or been active in politics or in any highly visible position, you should certainly make your name a part of your business name. A young friend operates a music business from her home where she writes and produces radio and TV commercials. She named her business Commercial Productions. To supplement her income from the commercials, and because she has a beautiful voice and likes to perform, she began singing for functions around town and became a well-known personality. While her singing career blossomed, her commercial business languished. Now she has tagged her own name onto her business name, calling it Susie Jackson's Commercial Productions, and this has allowed her to take advantage of success in one field and extend it to another. As a result, the commercial business has begun to grow because customers recognize Susie's name, and this sets her business apart from competing businesses.

On the other hand, there are times when using one's name isn't such a good idea. A local doctor specializes in testing nerve damage and nerve impulses by shock, which is a painful procedure. This man's name is Paine, and the name of his practice is *The Paine Neurological Center*! Either the name was intended as a bad joke or else someone just wasn't thinking.

Before having promotional material printed, register the name you select both with the secretary of state in your state and with the local county clerk. You will not be permitted to use the name if it is already being used by another business, but the probability of its being in use is reduced if it includes your personal name (unless you have a very common name).

Registering your name is simple and inexpensive. It's a matter of filling in a form provided by your state or local government. Be *sure* to date the registration form and keep a copy of it in your files in case at some future date you need to verify when you started using the name. You may not want to bother with this registration, but the name of your business becomes valuable property after you put money and energy into making it known in your community. Take the time to protect it by registering it. This must be done prior to having anything printed with your business name on it.

## Designing Your Logo to Convey a Message

Many of the same characteristics you incorporate into your business name should be brought to your business logo. It should be just as

## EXAMPLES OF NAMES AND LOGOS

The following business cards illustrate both some good and poor features commonly found on business cards, with a few words of explanation.

BUS. (812) 536-3157

### NALLEY LOGGING

*Buyers of High Quality Saw Timber*
*Export Veneer Logs & Timber Land*

RT. 1
BRETT NALLEY                    STENDAL, IN 47585

**GILLES SCHWINN CYCLERY**

39 W. COLUMBIA ST. / EVANSVILLE, IN 47710 / (812) 422-6800
2346 WASHINGTON AVE. / EVANSVILLE, IN 47714 / (812) 479-6021
200D S. GREEN RIVER RD. / EVANSVILLE, IN 47715 / (812) 477-8828

(812) 425-9142

**APPLE  VIDEO  PRODUCTIONS**

1001 JEFFERSON
EVANSVILLE, IN

MICHAEL & JANET CRAWLEY, OWNERS

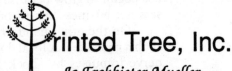

# rinted Tree, Inc.

*Jo Frohbieter-Mueller*
*Author · Consultant · Speaker*

*2357 Trail Drive*
*Evansville, IN 47711*            (812) 476-9015

*MUSIC FOR EVERY OCCASION*

*RICK WHITEHOUSE        BRIAN DEMPSEY*
*423-2644               479-7120*

*Confidential Writing Services*

Business · Personal · Creative · Technical
"Wording Is So Important"

(812) 473-4958
DAVID H. DAVIDSON
Evansville Manager

644 Chateau Drive
Evansville, Indiana 47715

- Advertising Copy
- Reports/Manuals
- Descriptions
- Speeches
- Resumes

*Examples of business cards with good and bad features.*

1. *Nalley Logging:* This is an excellent business name and logo because it contains both the name of the owner and the type of business. The drawing of a logging truck emphasizes the type of business.
2. *Apple Video Productions:* This name and logo is effective for several reasons. "Video Productions" explains the type of business, and "Apple" was used

for two reasons: because the apple is a recognizable symbol that is easy to remember and, just as importantly, because the name starts with an *A*. Because the name starts with *A*, in the telephone business directory the business's name is listed first in a long list of other video production businesses. The chance of attracting customers increases the closer to the beginning of the list a business name appears.

3. *PandA Sounds* (P and A Sounds or Panda Sounds): This name and logo are ineffective. The name does not explain what this business offers, and the logo, a panda head, is not descriptive of a disk jockey business that spins records for wedding receptions, school parties, and other gatherings.

4. *Gilles Schwinn Cyclery:* This symbol catches the eye and cleverly uses the initials of the owner to illustrate a bicycle and rider. Because it is used extensively in the company's marketing, GSC has registered this trademark so it cannot be used by another business.

5. *Printed Tree, Inc.:* This symbol suggests writing, alludes to printed matter, and is easy to remember. It has been used for both a manufacturing business that produced paper products and for a freelance writing business.

6. *Confidential Writing Services:* This name and logo are descriptive of the type of business it represents. The owner's name was not used in the business name because he is new in the area and not well known. (Still, it is often a good idea to include one's personal name so it will become known as the business grows.) This business card wisely lists the various services performed, but the card would be more attractive if the name and logo were centered, rather than skewed to one side.

descriptive as your business name. It should inform, be built on a recognizable symbol, or include a phrase that is catchy and easy to remember. Some of the more famous logos include NBC's peacock, used in the early days of color TV because it was so colorful; MGM's lion; the stylized letters of IBM; the swirl of Whirlpool Corporation; and the camel of Camel cigarettes. You can design a logo that is just as effective as the ones used by the big corporations. See the illustrations in the nearby sidebar for a few samples of logos being used by home businesses. Sometimes, instead of a logo, a business uses a motto. An insurance agency could use something like "Being Insured Is a Good Policy," and a wallpaper hanger might use a saying like "Paper Hangers Like Wall Flowers." Another possibility is to combine a logo with a saying. For instance, a chimney sweep might use a drawing of a top hat and the saying "We Make a Clean Sweep of Things."

Designing a logo may require original artwork, but it could be as simple as selecting an illustration from a sheet of "press-ons" that are available in most art supply shops. These sheets have a wide variety of styles and subjects from which to choose. If you cannot find an appropriate illustration and are unable to make you own, contract the services of a freelance artist. Art supply shops can provide you with names of artists, or look in your telephone directory under the heading "Artists, Commercial" or "Artists, Freelance."

Your logo may also be used as a trademark. According to the Trademark Act of 1946, a trademark "includes any word, name, symbol, or device, or any combination thereof adopted and used by a manufacturer or merchant to identify his goods and distinguish them from those manufactured or sold by others." You can protect your name, logo, and trademark on the national level by filing an application for trademark with the Patent and Trademark Office in Washington. This costs around $175 and may not be worth the time and money since you can claim a trademark by placing the letters "TM" near it, even though it is not registered.

Although logos are desirable, they are not absolutely necessary. If funds are hard to come by, a well-designed letterhead and business card can suffice as you get started, and then you can do a logo at a later date when funds are more readily available. To learn more about registering names, logos, and trademarks nationally, order the booklet *General Information Concerning Trademarks* from the Superintendent of Documents, Government Printing Office, Washington, DC 20402.

## Getting Your Name and Logo Into Print

After choosing a good name and a clever logo, you will need to put them to use. Advertising and promotional strategies are discussed in Chapter 16, and your name and logo will figure prominently in these. However, the first use of your name and logo probably will be on letterhead stationery, envelopes, bank checks, and calling cards, because these are needed to make initial contacts as you develop your business.

After checking that the name you selected is not registered by another business, have stationery printed. First, you will need to prepare "copy"—the original from which the stationery will be printed. You can save money by making your own copy, or you can have it done by the printer.

Some computer-printer combinations have the capacity to produce professional-looking letterheads, while others yield poor-quality graphics. If you have the equipment to produce professional-quality printing at your fingertips, it's a snap to put together a letterhead or any of the many forms you will need in the course of doing business. If you do not have this equipment and must do the work manually, then use transfer lettering sheets, available from art supply shops. Create the original on white paper using only black ink (India ink is not necessary) to make lines and designs. Errors can be covered with white correction fluid and no trace will appear on the copies.

Your business must look good on paper, and it's worth skimping on other items in order to purchase good-quality stationery. Have your letterhead printed on 24-pound paper stock. Again, try to find a way to set your business apart from others. For instance, you might consider having your stationery printed on colored paper—maybe green if you are a florist, a more sophisticated buff color if you are a lawyer or some other professional, pink for any business catering to beauty care, and so forth. Calling cards should match your stationery with the same color and style so people will associate your business with a certain look.

Be sure to ask the printer for the originals when you have the materials printed so you will have them for subsequent printings. Some printers will keep them on file for you, but they will be more secure and you will be in a better position to change printers if you keep them on file in your own office.

The cost of printing is determined by the number of pages printed; the cost per page decreases as the number of copies printed increases. Therefore, while you don't want to spend too much on printed material as you get under way, you will save money in the long run (you will hear that often) if you have 500 or 1,000 pages of station-ery and matching envelopes printed at once. Of course, use business-size envelopes. With stationery and calling cards in hand, you are ready to start making the contacts needed to acquire the necessary supplies and equipment to make your enterprise fly.

# 10  Keeping Track of Your Business Finances

## Bookkeeping and Financial Records

You need accurate and easy-to-understand records for several reasons. They will be used to (1) evaluate your business success, (2) make business decisions, (3) apply for loans, and (4) prepare and document tax returns.

Keeping accurate and up-to-date business records is essential to the effective operation of a business. Poor records lead to poor financial management, which is a major contributor to many business failures. Records should provide answers to questions such as: Is there enough cash to keep the business operational, to make loan payments, and to pay taxes? Are accounts receivable being collected promptly? Is too much capital tied up in inventory?

Bookkeeping seems to be a mystery to people who are unfamiliar with financial records, but those who keep books know there is no mystery involved—it's just a matter of systematically recording daily business transactions. Most home business financial records can be adequately maintained by someone who has had no experience with bookkeeping other than maintaining a record of their personal and home income and expenses. If you are apprehensive about this aspect of a business, determine to learn to keep accurate records right from the start lest you find yourself totally confused and without substantiating information when tax time comes around or when you want to diagnose your business's financial strengths and weaknesses.

If your business is based on an activity that is sometimes considered a hobby (such as crafts, photography, or art), it is very important to keep detailed records; these kinds of businesses are sometimes questioned by the IRS, which may claim you are doing little more than pursuing a hobby. (This subject is discussed further in Chapter 18.) The IRS could even disallow certain expenses or losses on your tax return unless you keep good records and give every indication that you are seriously in business to make a profit.

Make an effort to select a bookkeeping system that will best meet your needs. It should be one you understand, one that is easy to use, and one that will help you see how your business is performing. Any system that verifies the pertinent information concerning your business operation is acceptable to the IRS. The IRS's only requirement is that you maintain permanent books which can be used to identify your income, expenses, and deductions.

Your records should tell you, at a glance, three vital bits of information:

• Cash on hand
• What is owed to you
• What you owe to others

There are many types of prepackaged record-keeping systems available from office supply stores that are appropriate for a home business. Also, a simple-to-use bookkeeping system built into a checkbook is now on the market. For a free brochure about this excellent system, call Deluxe Business Forms at (800) 843-4294 and ask for material on the One-Write system. You may prefer to use a system of your own design and keep it on lined paper in a three-ring notebook in which extra pages can be added when and where they are needed.

Most small businesses can get by with a very simple bookkeeping system consisting of a checkbook, a cash receipts journal, an accounts receivable record, a voucher register, a sales journal, and a petty cash fund. Each of these elements is described below:

*Checkbook:* Listed here should be each check written, its number and date, to whom it is disbursed, and the amount, along with a notation explaining the purpose of the payment.

*Cash receipts journal:* This shows the amount of money received, the date of receipt, from whom the cash was received, and the reason for the payment to you.

*Accounts receivable record:* This is a record of the money owed to you, the date it is due, who owes it, and for what it is owed.

*Voucher register or accounts payable:* This is a record of the money you owe, noting the amount of each bill, the date it is due, and to whom and for what it is owed.

*Sales journal:* This describes each business transaction, the date it took place, the customer's name, the amount of the sale, and the sales tax (if any).

*Petty cash fund:*  This is usually a box containing currency and coins used to pay for the small incidentals needed during the course of doing business; however, it may be nothing more than a listing of those items you purchase for the business with out-of-pocket money which must be reimbursed from your business account.

The following is a time schedule and checklist for record keeping that will help you keep a finger on the pulse of your business.

Each day you should

1. Determine the cash on hand.
2. Summarize sales and cash receipts.
3. Record monies paid out.

Each week you should

1. Send notices for past-due accounts receivable.
2. Pay accounts payable as they come due (or earlier if there is a discount advantage).
3. Figure payroll and taxes if you have employees.

Each month or quarter you should

1. Prepare an income statement (see sidebar entitled "Income Statement Example").
2. Prepare a balance sheet (see sidebar entitled "The Balance Sheet").
3. Check that the bank statement listing deposits and checks written agrees with your checkbook.
4. Check that the total amount of the receipts for miscellaneous expenditures equals the amount of money removed from the petty cash fund. Tally the receipts and reimburse the petty cash fund with business money. You may prefer not to have a petty cash fund and instead make petty cash payments out of your own pocket and then reimburse yourself each month with a business check.
5. Check that tax payments are up to date. If you collect sales tax you will probably need to forward this money to your state revenue department every three months. Also, when you begin showing a significant profit, you will be required to make quarterly estimated income tax payments to the state and federal government.
6. Study inventory records and make adjustments to keep it at optimum levels by either ordering more or fewer supplies, or by increasing or reducing production.

## INCOME STATEMENT EXAMPLE

Also called a profit and loss statement or an earnings report, an income statement shows how a business performed over a given period of time, such as a month, quarter, or year. It shows the total income from sales and the cost of producing the product or rendering the service. The difference between sales income and costs is the gross profit. Expenses are deducted from the gross profit to show the net profit (or loss).

| | | |
|---|---|---|
| Net sales | | |
| (gross sales less | | |
| returns and allowances) | | $80,000 |
| Cost of goods sold | | |
| (cost of inventory) | | 40,000 |
| Gross profit on sales | | 40,000 |
| | | |
| Expenses | | |
| Wages | $9,000 | |
| Bad debt allowance | 500 | |
| Depreciation | 400 | |
| Delivery expenses | 200 | |
| Insurance | 800 | |
| Advertising | 1,300 | |
| Interest on loans | 500 | |
| Utilities | 200 | |
| Maintenance | 200 | |
| Taxes | 1,100 | |
| Miscellaneous costs and | 800 | |
| operating expenses | | |
| | | |
| Total expenses | | 15,000 |
| | | |
| Net income | | $25,000 |

If a business operated at a loss during a certain accounting period, the income statement might appear as follows:

| | |
|---|---|
| Net sales | $20,000 |
| Cost of goods sold | 12,000 |
| Gross profit on sales | $ 8,000 |
| Total expenses | 9,000 |
| Net loss | ($1,000) |

It is in your best interest to keep up-to-date records, so plan to set aside some bookkeeping time each day. This is time well spent because it will keep you aware of the progress and financial health of your business and ease the burden of collecting the information necessary for the quarterly and annual tax returns.

Evaluating your business is an essential part of management, but it is of value only if you use the process to improve operations. Information needed to evaluate your financial condition effectively should be available from your business books and records. Plan to study this information with a critical eye and to move to solve any detected problems before they get out of hand. Also, strive to recognize the

## THE BALANCE SHEET

A balance sheet provides a picture of the financial health of a business as of a given date. It lists the assets of a business, arranged in decreasing order of how quickly they can be turned into cash. Liabilities—what the business owes—are listed in the order of how soon they must be repaid. Net worth is the difference between assets and liabilities (assets minus liabilities equals net worth).

Assets include:
    Cash
    Accounts receivable
    Merchandise inventory
    Equipment and machinery
    Furniture
    Land and buildings
    Patents and trademarks
Liabilities include:
    Notes payable (loans)
    Accounts payable
    Accrued wages payable to employees
    Taxes owed

The *liquidity* of a business is determined by the amount of cash on hand and the value of any assets that can be converted quickly and readily into cash. A business's total liquid assets would be the sum of cash, accounts receivable, and the portion of merchandise or inventory that could be easily sold.

*Working capital* is the difference between current assets and current liabilities.

The *proprietorship ratio* shows the relationship between the owner's investment and the total assets of the business. It is determined by dividing the owner's investment in the business by the total assets of the business.

strengths of your operation and try to capitalize on them. Keep in mind that good money management won't *make* a business grow, but it will *allow* it to grow. Your job is to decide how to use your money for optimum results.

## Do You Need a Bookkeeper and/or an Accountant?

If you know anything about bookkeeping, then doing your own book-keeping for the first year is probably a good idea. It is very easy to get caught up in doing the actual business and yet not know if your work is yielding a profit—unless you handle the paperwork (the daily business records) that clearly show in black and white (or red!) the results of your labor.

If you are unfamiliar with basic bookkeeping procedures then it might be prudent to have professional assistance in setting up the books. This can be done in as little as a single half-hour session with an accountant and/or tax adviser, who can point out proper and improper bookkeeping techniques. After that you can do the books yourself and use an accountant only at tax time. Many business owners hire a Certified Public Accountant (CPA) to set up their accounting system, but a bookkeeper should be capable of doing this, and for a much lower fee. However, you may want to hire an accountant at least once or twice each year to analyze the books, prepare and analyze financial statements, and help with tax returns. This accountant can also render a valuable service by advising on financial decisions and helping to chart the future course of the business based on an analysis of the financial records. An accountant can function as a financial adviser, alerting you to potential danger areas and advising you on how to handle growth spurts, how to plan for slow business times, and how to nurture and protect your business future. Most businesses fail, not for lack of good ideas or goodwill, but for lack of financial expertise and planning. It's worth paying for the knowledgeable service a professional provides.

You can expect an accountant to spend at least some time ex-plaining complex concepts, but don't expect him or her to teach you basic bookkeeping and accounting skills. It might not be a bad idea to take a course in record keeping and taxes to develop more skill in areas where you are inexperienced. Elementary business courses are offered at many community colleges, often in the evening after regular school hours.

Perhaps you plan to hire a tax preparer and not bother with an accountant. That could cost you money. Tax preparers work with the numbers you provide and do not dig through records in pursuit of the elusive tax break, whereas an accountant, who should be familiar with your business, will be alert to tax advantages and can suggest business moves to capitalize on them. By providing this advice, an accountant will probably save you more money than the service costs.

When selecting a bookkeeper and an accountant, ask around to learn whom others recommend. Get referrals from trusted friends, business associates, or professional organizations. Your bookkeeper and accountant should have experience working with small businesses. Their reputations should be impeccable, because they will know more about your business and financial dealings than anyone else. For this reason, you will want trustworthy people who are close-mouthed, especially if you live in a small community. When contracting for bookkeeping or accounting services, discuss fees in advance so there are no unpleasant surprises.

## Keep Personal and Business Checking Accounts Separate

Open a separate banking account for your business before the first deal is struck, even though a business account is more expensive and has different charges than a personal account. There are three important reasons for this. First, you will have a complete record of your income and expenditures for tax purposes, and you won't need to ponder each check, trying to remember whether it was written for business or personal purposes. Also, in the event of an audit, you may need to reveal your books to the IRS. An audit is usually confined to a specific area of financial dealings, but if your personal and business records are intertwined, the IRS auditor will be able to look into your personal finances when the audit is directed to your business, and vice versa. Second, the checks you write for your business carry a message, and if you use personal checks for business expenses the message is, "This is a little one-horse operation"; the message is quite different if the check carries the name and logo of your business. Third, it is much more difficult to unravel your personal and business finances if they are kept in the same account, but it's just a matter of looking at the bottom lines when they are kept in separate accounts.

One final word about your business checking account. When you open the account, ask that your check numbers start at 300 or above so it is not so obvious to your creditors that you are just getting started. Some suppliers are reluctant to extend credit to a new business that has no track record of reliability or success. Having check numbers start at 300 rather than 1 helps convey the impression that you've been around for awhile.

## *Record Keeping Also Means Keeping Records*

A lot of papers will accumulate in your office, and the trick is to determine which ones should be saved and how to file them so they can be retrieved when needed. Save anything containing information you may need again. This certainly includes all accounting records, selected correspondence, sales and purchase agreements, tax returns, originals or copy masters for printed matter, and records relating to insurance, personnel, shipping, and freight.

Some of these papers could be vital for future operations and should be protected in a safe deposit box or a personal safe, while others can be organized in ordinary filing cabinets. As records become outdated, but still need to be saved, they can be stored in boxes in less valuable space, such as under stairs or even under beds.

All expense records and receipts should be kept for tax purposes. Expenses include the cost of supplies and materials used in the business, leased or purchased equipment, and any other costs needed to maintain the business. Accurate records are required by the IRS to document the miles traveled if you use your own car for business purposes. (This is discussed further in Chapter 18.)

You will also need to be diligent in documenting the numerous miscellaneous expenditures you make. During the course of doing business you will purchase untold numbers of items that are too insignificant to pay for by check. Pay for these items with out-of-pocket cash, and at the end of each month (or week, if they are numerous) reimburse yourself from the petty cash fund or with a check drawn against the business. Again, it is important to keep all receipts, noting on the back of each the item purchased. Stash these receipts in a large manila envelope, using one envelope for each month. Write the month, the year, and the dollar total for the receipts on the outside of the envelope, and file it with other tax records in the event the IRS wants you to verify the expenses.

For more information see *Step-by-Step Bookkeeping*, by Robert C. Ragan (1987), available from Sterling Publishing Co., Inc., Two Park Avenue, New York, NY 10016, for $6.95.

# 11 Computers and the Entrepreneur

This chapter is directed to those of you who are apprehensive about computers. Some of us grew up before computer usage was taught in schools, and we're not sure if our efforts to learn about the contraption will really benefit our personal and business lives. Do they really think? Do they talk back? Can you trust one with business secrets? Actually, a personal computer is somewhat like a pet. If you train it (put in the right programs), and give it the proper care (maintain it), it will provide faithful service and add a new dimension to your life. But, like pets, not everybody likes having one around, and many people do very well without this added responsibility.

*Skip or skim this chapter if you already use a computer;* however, if you have decided that a computer will not benefit your business, this chapter is for you because you may not know enough about computers to make that judgment. A computer may help maximize your personal management skills and help direct your company's growth. It's true that the management and bookkeeping systems of some businesses are so simple and straightforward, and the need for computer-generated information is so small, that there is little advantage to computerizing. Many small business owners already have their fingers on the pulses of their businesses and do not need a computer system. But other small business owners have seen the computer open whole new avenues of business for exploitation, and their computers have removed the tedium from such procedures as report preparation, record keeping, information retrieval, and mailings.

Should you computerize your business? To answer that question you need to learn what a computer can do and what its limitations are, and also to determine if using one is cost-effective for your business. The following discussion is limited to the less expensive, yet capable, microcomputers (personal computers), with a few comments about the exciting new workstations that are being introduced into the business world.

## What Is a Microcomputer (Personal Computer)?

A microcomputer, or personal computer (PC), is an inexpensive, small, lightweight piece of electronic data-processing equipment. Some PCs are portable, while others are designed to remain in position on a desk. All run programs that do an amazing array of tasks, and they can be operated by personnel who haven't the slightest notion *how* they work because the "brains" are built into the system. Prices continue to drop, and PCs with minimal capabilities can be bought for as low as $500, although a small business owner would probably be better satisfied with the performance of a more expensive system.

## A Few Words about Workstations

While the PC has held center stage in the electronics world for nearly two decades, a new and more dazzling electronic system is beginning to displace it in some work environments. The workstation looks like a personal computer and is small enough to fit on a desktop, but it acts like a powerful mainframe, with some workstations having 60 times the computing power of a personal computer. The workstation is the second-generation PC and is currently the fastest growing segment of the computer industry.

Until recently, workstations were very expensive and difficult to use. They were tools used mainly by engineers and scientists, but price reductions and technological advances have made them more accessible for business use. In particular, with their extraordinary graphics they are becoming the workhorse for desktop publishing. From a practical standpoint, only a very few home businesses need a workstation, but it is good to know of their availability.

Workstation prices range from $7,500 to over $20,000, and software has been developed that makes them as simple to use as a PC. Information about these systems can be obtained at computer outlets, which always welcome inquiries.

## Is Computerization for You?

Computers can give you answers, but they cannot figure out the right questions. If you know what you want to accomplish, have an organized record-keeping system, and have a clear understanding of your goals, a computer can probably help you with your business.

Generally, a business will benefit from computerization if a large amount of repetitive information must be handled. For example, a computer system can perform the following tasks:

- Organize and store mailing lists and other information that is similarly structured
- Retrieve a single piece of information, such as an address, invoice, or employee's wage rate
- Print information, such as a sales report or a balance sheet
- Print multiple copies of a letter or document
- Perform complicated mathematical computations, such as the repayment schedule of a long-term loan

Information is fed to the computer through programs called *software*, and it is through these programs that the business applications of computers are realized. You can select from a huge assortment of software programs and in this way can personalize your computer's operation to fit your needs. Software programs enable the user to enter, manipulate, and process huge quantities of data with unbelievable speed and accuracy. Here are a few business applications of a computer:

- Transactions can be recorded, and records, such as cash receipts and accounts receivable, can be maintained and printed on demand.
- Word processing enables the user to write, edit, and store letters and documents—that is, to do anything that might be done on a typewriter and a whole lot more, with much greater ease and efficiency. The written material can be printed on demand and as frequently as desired.
- Financial modeling programs can prepare and analyze financial statements and project a business's future financial position.
- Record-keeping, statement, and report software programs enable the user to maintain cash receipts accounts and a receivables ledger and to prepare a balance sheet and income statement.
- Payroll programs maintain payroll records; calculate pay, benefits, and taxes; and prepare paychecks.
- File management programs enable the user to create and design forms, and then store and retrieve the information placed on them.
- Inventory control programs enable easy maintenance of accurate inventory records.

Computers are sometimes expected to do more than their design allows. Don't expect a computer to clean up a mess of records. Records must be organized before they can be computerized, but thereafter, the computer will do the work. Also, don't expect a computer to start cranking out information as soon as you plug it in. While you are learning to operate the system, it will take longer to perform tasks on the computer than it would to do them manually, but once you get through this initial start-up period a computer will save you time, energy, and frustration. You will discover that the computer is an indispensable tool that can help you accomplish numerous tasks.

## Selecting the Right System

To computerize your business you will need to (1) choose the right software (programs), (2) select the right hardware (equipment), and (3) interface the various components to make a functioning system. The most direct approach to selecting a computer system is to talk to other business people who have computerized their operations and get them to show you their systems. After seeing a demonstration of the main features of a computer and some of the tasks it can perform, you will quickly grasp the benefits of computerization. Visit computer stores for further demonstrations of the capability of various systems. Before purchasing anything, do a lot of asking, looking, and comparing. Also, refer to the *Computer Buyers Guide and Handbook* that is available in libraries and bookstores. Also, a large selection of books and magazines are on the market that can help guide you as you wander through and wonder about the myriad of options available to you. The more you learn before you buy, the greater your chance of selecting the system that will best serve your business needs.

### SELECTING SOFTWARE

Begin your search for a computer system by asking yourself, "What do I want a computer to do?" The answer to this question will determine what kind of *software* you will need, and your software needs will narrow your equipment (hardware) choices. A program, or software, is a set of instructions that tells the computer how to do a particular task. *Hardware* is the equipment that enables software to be used and includes a processor, memory, storage, terminal or keyboard, disk drives, and printer.

To help determine software needs, prepare a list of your business functions that require the quick and accurate handling of information. Include such items as reports you produce and the kinds of information you would like to see displayed on the computer video screen, such as time cards, mailing lists, work orders, receipts, customer and employee files, and inventory. Determine the approximate number of each created in a given time period. Include inventory control on your list, as well.

Next, visit several computer stores and describe your needs. Most likely the salespeople will be able to select and supply the software to fulfill your exact requirements. You should check the following features of the software or programs you might purchase:

- Is the manual that accompanies the software written for the beginner? Is it organized so you can easily find information?
- Is the program easy to use—is it user-friendly?
- Can information be easily added and deleted from the program?
- Does the instruction manual describe in detail the operation of the program and its capabilities?
- Does the program have security features, such as a password?
- Is the program widely used in the business community?
- Is there a "help" number you can call if you have a problem or question?

## SELECTING HARDWARE

Finding the best software for your business is the most difficult part of selecting a computer system. Since software is written to be used with one or several specific computers, you will have narrowed your equipment choices down by selecting the software that meets your needs.

There are several pieces of equipment that make up a computer. They include:

*Terminal:* A terminal (see illustration) consists of a typewriter-like keyboard and a display screen, or CRT (cathode ray tube). Look for a screen that will display at least 24 lines of 80 characters each. Some display screens have a color and graphics capability. Decide if you need or might enjoy this feature. Otherwise, the screen display is limited to letters, numbers, punctuation marks, and symbols.

*Processor (also called the central processing unit or CPU):* This unit executes software instructions, performs calculations, controls the flow of data to and from memory, and controls other hardware components. It is located within the terminal.

*Computer memory:* This part of the system stores information. One type of memory, ROM (read only memory), is a fixed part of the computer system and cannot be changed by the user or an externally entered program. Another type of memory, RAM (random access memory), contains information provided to the computer by the operator via the keyboard or the software. Its capacity is measured in "Ks" (one K equals 1,000 characters or bits of information). Approximately 64,000 (64K) characters (letters, numbers, punctuation marks, and

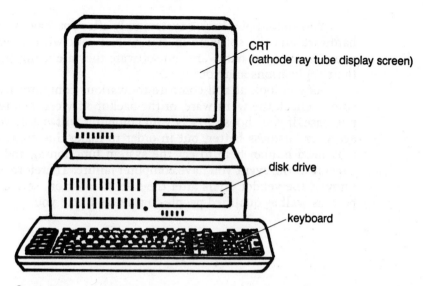

*Components of a computer terminal. Disk drive may be part of the terminal or it may be separate.*

symbols), or about 32 typed pages of information, can be stored in a computer with a 64K memory. Information stored in RAM lasts only as long as the power is on. In order to keep information for later call-back it must be transferred (saved) to disks for storage.

*Storage:* Most small business computers store information on disks which resemble small phonograph records. They serve as the file cabinet for information that is used by the computer. There are two kinds of disks. The floppy disk, as its name implies, is thin and floppy and is usually enclosed in a stiff paper envelope. Hard disks are more expensive than floppies, but they can store more information and provide faster access to information. Floppy disks are usually used by small business owners, but, as the technology improves, more computerized small businesses are moving to hard disks.

*Disk drive:* A disk is inserted into the component called the disk drive so that the disk can be read or information added to it.

*Printer:* The output of a computer is directed either to the video screen or to a printer (or to both). The quality and the cost of printers varies. Two main factors influence the cost: the speed of the printer (some print material much faster than others) and the quality of the print generated. Characters are produced by either the dot-matrix method, in which each letter or number is composed of many tiny dots, or by a printing (daisy) wheel, which produces print of typewriter quality. Laser printers are also available, but they are considerably more expensive than the dot-matrix and daisy wheel printers.

You should purchase a system only after you have seen both the hardware and the software in action. Network with other entrepreneurs to see what hardware and software they are using and compare their applications and your needs.

As you look at and compare the various computer packages, be sure to check the warmware, or the backup services, before making a purchase. If you choose wisely your computer will enable you to manage your business better, but in order to make this come about you may need human help to get the system functioning and continued support in the event you have computer failure. Therefore, you should know if the vendor offers after-the-sale installation, service, and support, as well as qualified people to train and help you.

# 12    Purchasing and Inventory

## Locating and Buying Supplies

Many of you will be starting a business by further developing an existing hobby, interest, or on-the-side business. In this case you may think you already know where to buy supplies, but you will probably pay too much for them. While pursuing an activity for fun you probably bought your supplies and materials from retailers, but the prices you paid as a hobbyist are certainly not the same as those you should pay when operating a business. Some of the retailers from whom you have bought in the past may offer significantly better prices when you start ordering larger quantities, but these prices will still not be as low as those you can get if you go to *the retailers' suppliers*. In other words, the cost will be lower the closer you can get to the originating source. This source may be a manufacturer or an importer, although you may have to settle for a wholesaler, because some manufacturers will sell only to wholesalers, who then distribute the goods.

Finding suppliers and acquiring their goods can be both time-consuming and expensive. While some types of businesses require very few supplies, others require quite a lot. Supplies may be one of your larger investments as you start business. Try to buy them on credit if the supplier seems willing. If a $10,000 supply of inventory can be purchased with a 50 percent down payment and the balance payable in 30 days, the wholesaler will be providing $5,000 toward the opening of your business. A deal like this is sweet, but in most cases credit and good terms are only extended to customers after they have shown that they are reliable and pay their bills on time. Most likely, your first batch of supplies will be delivered cash on delivery (COD), but you can expect better terms on subsequent orders. Be sure to ask for a credit application when you place your first order. Filling in a credit application is a real problem for a beginning business because the application asks for a list of businesses with whom you have dealt. You may not have any to list, or maybe only a few, since you are just beginning, so ask friends and relatives if you can use their businesses as references.

Where should you look for supplies and suppliers? With the exception of office supplies, which can often be purchased less expensively through a catalog, you should look for supplies and suppliers in your area. As compared with long-distance suppliers, local suppliers are handier, orders can be filled and delivered more quickly, and shipping charges are kept to a minimum. So start your search locally, referring to the Yellow Pages of your telephone directory. Of course, you probably won't be able to find everything nearby and will need to look far beyond your immediate area. You can locate suppliers by referring to the Yellow Pages in the phone directories of large cities, to trade journals and directories such as the *Craft Supply Directory* and *Gifts and Decorative Accessories Directory*, and to the multivolumed *Thomas Register*. This last publication contains an extensive list of manufacturers in the United States. These publications are available in libraries. Also, don't overlook the most obvious source, and that is on products in stores and shops. Take names and addresses off the boxes or containers that contain the products in stores and get in touch with the source. It may be a manufacturer, importer, or wholesaler. Ask for catalogs and price lists. Be sure to use letterhead stationery when making these contacts. Also, there is no reason to inform a potential supplier that you are just starting a business or that your operation is home-based. Some manufacturers and distributors are reluctant to sell to home businesses because they don't want to bother with low-volume orders, but others are glad for the business. Just keep looking for suppliers who are willing to deal with you. Many manufacturers and importers have several price lists, and they reserve the best (lowest) prices for customers who purchase large volumes. The bigger and more established your business appears, the lower the prices you will be asked to pay for supplies. It may not be fair, but that's the way it is. You will quickly discover that most suppliers require a minimum order that sometimes isn't so "minimum" to you, and you may be forced to tie up more money than you might like, but this is still better than paying retail prices. Always keep in mind that the cost of supplies must be included in the price your customer pays, and your product will be overpriced and uncompetitive if you pay too much for supplies.

Locate suppliers, get price quotes, and prepare orders, but do not order supplies until everything is in place and you are ready to open shop. This will shorten the time between buying and selling, which, as you will quickly discover, is very important in preventing cash-flow problems caused by having money tied up in inventory.

## SALES TAX NUMBER

In those states that collect a sales tax, each business is issued a sales tax number. The businesses must then contend with both sides of the sales tax issue. The first is the requirement to *collect* the tax from consumers and forward it to the state, and the second is the obligation to *pay* the tax on purchases that are not resold but are used in the business.

State regulations vary, but usually a business is required to pay a sales tax on purchased items that are used in the operation of the business. This includes such purchases as equipment, office furniture, and supplies. This expense will be deducted from income at the time taxes are figured. However, a sales tax is *not* paid on supplies and goods in inventory that are resold to customers. Instead, a business is required to *collect* the tax on items sold to the final consumer and turn it over to their state government. For example, an auto mechanic would pay taxes on equipment used to repair cars, but not on the new parts that go into the cars. The owner of the car must pay taxes on the new parts installed by the mechanic. It is the mechanic's responsibility to collect the taxes on the new parts used in the repair of the car and turn them over to the government.

Before you start buying supplies, apply to your state's department of revenue for a sales tax or tax exemption number, also known by a variety of other names in different states. When you are issued a number you will receive instructions for collecting and forwarding the sales tax. This number will also be kept on file by your suppliers and used to identify goods you purchase from them but that you will resell. It is through this system that the government keeps tabs on businesses. The biggest misuse of this number is when a business purchases supplies and equipment that will not be resold, but it nonetheless uses the number to avoid paying the tax.

It is handy to make multiple copies of your sales tax number (they are usually *very* long), printed on a sheet containing your business name and address to provide to your suppliers. Always carry some in your business vehicle so they are available if you happen to purchase from a business you haven't dealt with previously. Most businesses will keep these numbers on file, but some may ask for the number each time a purchase is made.

## TAKING ADVANTAGE OF DISCOUNTS

Assume that the *list price* of practically everything you buy for your business is the price someone else must pay. Your goal should be to pay a lower price. Don't pay list price without at least attempting to get a better deal. There are many ways to get a reduced price, and good management dictates that you aggressively look for and take advantage of every legitimate way open to you. Two possibilities are quantity discounts and purchase discounts.

***Lot-Size or Quantity Discounts.*** Many items are packaged in large quantities—a gross of this, 100 gallons of that—and the cost of the product is often considerably less if you buy in quantity. The more you purchase, the less you will pay per item. Sometimes the total order amount determines the discount; for example, a certain supplier may give a 10 percent discount on orders totaling $200 or more. If you can foresee using the larger amount in the not-too-distant future, you should surely take advantage of the lot-size or order-size discount. However, it's no bargain if you buy more than you can use in a reasonable period of time, because you tie up cash and the product may be out of date before you get to the end of it.

***Purchase Discount.*** A purchase discount is a reduction in the price of an order in return for prompt payment. The most common discount offered by suppliers is "2/10, n/30," which means that 2 percent of the gross amount can be deducted if the invoice is paid within 10 days, but the entire amount (net) is due in 30 days (that is, if the discount is not taken, the entire amount must be paid sometime between 10 and 30 days.) Thus, $20,000 worth of supplies can be acquired for $19,600 if paid for within 10 days, and this amounts to a savings at an annual rate of 36 percent. The purchase discount on a large purchase should always be taken, even though you may not actually have the cash to take advantage of it. If you lack the cash on hand, but have a good line of credit at your bank, then you can borrow the money needed to pay the bill. A loan for 20 days (the number of days between the end of the discount period and the time the bill must be paid—at which time, presumably, you would have the money to pay the bill or repay the bank loan) at a rate of 9 percent would cost $98.60. Deducting this amount from the $400 that would be saved by early payment leaves a total savings of $301.40. As you can see, this is one of the easier ways to save money.

## Acquiring Equipment

### PURCHASING

Buy less rather than more; buy used rather than new. How often I have seen people spend themselves poor as they gather equipment to start a business, only to learn after being in business awhile that their equipment needs were quite different than they had expected. Buy only the equipment that is absolutely essential to get your business in operation. You included a budget for equipment as you developed your business plan and forecast your financial needs. You may or may not need all that money as you get started. If possible, buy used equipment if it is in good shape and will do the job for you. You can often find used office equipment for sale at business closings. These are listed in the newspaper classified ads. What you can't find there, buy reconditioned, rather than new. The money you save can be used in business development, and you can always trade up as your business shows some success. You will probably have to buy new equipment and pay the full price if your business requires specialized or unusual items. Another option is to lease the more expensive and less available equipment.

## LEASING

The cost of equipment required to operate your business will clearly depend on the type of business you undertake. If the needed equipment would cost too much to purchase, you might consider leasing as an alternative, although it might be wise to seek your accountant's advice on the wisdom of leasing versus buying versus renting.

Leasing is a long-term agreement to rent equipment, land, buildings, or any other asset. The lease payment covers the original cost of the asset and provides a profit to the grantor of the lease. Almost anything can be leased, including manufacturing equipment, office furniture, vehicles, and computers.

There are several advantages to leasing as compared to buying. Perhaps the most persuasive reason for the small business low on cash is that equipment, land, or buildings can be acquired without making a large cash outlay, while a loan to purchase the same would require a down payment of approximately 25 percent of the cost. Also, lease payments are usually lower than loan payments and are spread over a longer period of time.

The most common type of lease is the financial lease. This is usually written for a term not to exceed the economic life of the equipment. Payments are made throughout the period of the lease, but at the end of the leasing period the lessee has several options, depending on how the leasing agreement was written. The leased equipment can be purchased at fair market value by the lessee, or the lease can be renewed and the old equipment still used. Another possibility is for the lease to be renewed, but the leased equipment replaced with a newer model. (Considering the rapid technological changes and the speed at which equipment becomes obsolete, there is a big advantage to the latter arrangement.)

There are several disadvantages to leasing. First, the equipment doesn't belong to you—it is not an asset—and, therefore you are not building equity when you make lease payments. Another disadvantage is that the long-term obligation continues even though you may decide you no longer need the equipment before the lease contract period expires.

Be careful. A lease agreement is a legal contract that is binding. Remember: "Before investing—*investigate!*" Before signing an agreement, be sure that you are dealing with a reputable lessor, that the lease arrangements are the best you can reasonably get, and that the equipment is the best suited for your purpose. The lease document agreement or contract should specify the following:

- A full description of the item, including model and serial number
- The age or condition of the item and date of manufacture
- Terms of the agreement, including the payment amount and due dates
- Location of the item during the lease period
- Party responsible for maintenance and taxes
- Party that receives the investment tax credit
- Disposition of the item at the end of the lease period
- Renewal options
- Cancellation penalties

## Inventory

Inventory refers to the stock needed to do business. It represents a large portion of the business investment and must be carefully managed in order to maximize profits.

Inventory for a manufacturer is composed of raw materials, products being produced, and finished products; inventory for a retail store consists of merchandise to be sold; and inventory for a service business includes those items needed to perform the service. Each type of inventory represents money tied up until the inventory is purchased, or in the case of a service business, until the service is performed.

*Balance* is the key word in maintaining inventory. Successful inventory management involves balancing the costs of inventory with its benefits. Inventory costs include the cost of the money invested in goods, as well as the cost of storage, insurance, and taxes; the benefit of inventory is having goods available for use and sale. A small reduction in the amount of inventory can result in a shift in a company's financial situation. If inventory is managed well—delicately balanced between costs and benefits—then working capital will not be tied up unnecessarily, and this could prevent the need to borrow money in order to keep the business functioning.

Inventory management involves knowing where, what, and how much to order, as well as when to order and what price to pay for goods. It also involves making sure the items in inventory are used to make a profit.

## *INVENTORY RECORDS*

Inventory records provide the information a business owner needs to make decisions about buying—when to buy and how much to buy. The kind of records you keep will depend upon the type, diversity, and kinds of goods handled. You may be able to keep a visual record and base new orders on what you see on the shelves, if your business requires just a few supplies. But if you require a diversity of goods, then you need an efficient way to keep apprised of the quantity of the various supplies on hand.

Records can be kept on file cards or on pages in a notebook, if there are a limited number of different items in the inventory. Computers can also be used to maintain inventory records, and there is software specifically designed for use in inventory control. Whichever method you use, its value is based on the accuracy and discipline you bring to maintaining up-to-date records. For each particular type of item your records should include the number of items on hand, the date goods are used or sold, the date a new supply is acquired, the address of the supplier, the time it takes to receive a new supply after you place an order, the name and address of an alternate supplier, and the turnover rate of the item.

## *TURNOVER RATE*

Turnover rate is the length of time an item is a part of inventory, measured from the time it is placed in inventory to the time it is taken from inventory and used to perform a service or actually sold to customers. There are several ways to determine this rate. Large companies have sophisticated formulas they apply, but you probably can determine turnover rate just by keeping track of incoming and outgoing dates.

The goal of inventory control is to keep supplies and merchandise on hand for the least possible amount of time. Inventory costs money, and good inventory management controls the cost by keeping the turnover time as short as possible. Inventory is like money sitting in a bin

## SAMPLE INVENTORY SHEETS

*Sample inventory sheet for supplies:*

A manufacturing business that makes rag baskets would need a sheet such as this for each supply used.

Item: Fabric, wine-color

Supplier: American Fabric Company
  2284 Bankslide
  Houston TX 77135
  1-800-792-8641
Delivery time: 8 to 10 days
Price: $.40/yard; minimum order $25.00
Terms: 2/10, n/30

Alternate supplier: Colonial Weavers Inc.
  400 Gooseneck Road
  Cranbury, NJ 08592
  1-609-566-5221
Delivery time: 2 to 3 weeks
Price: $.45/yard, no minimum order
Terms: net 30

| Date | Amount used | Amount received | Total in inventory |
|---|---|---|---|
| Aug. 1 | | 100 yards | 100 yards |
| Aug. 3 | 20 yards | | 80 |
| Aug. 11 | 15 | | 65 |
| Aug. 20 | 18 | | 47 |
| Sept. 7 | 20 | | 27 |
| Sept. 8 | Ordered 100 yards | | |
| Sept. 12 | 14 | | 13 |
| Sept. 18 | | 100 | 113 |
| Sept. 22 | 18 | | 95 |

*Sample inventory sheet for completed products (16-inch rag basket with wooden handles):*

| Date | Sold | Added | Total in inventory |
|---|---|---|---|
| Aug. 9 | | 9 | 9 |
| Aug. 11 | | 7 | 16 |
| Aug. 12 | 10 | | 6 |
| Aug. 14 | | 8 | 14 |
| Aug. 18 | | 9 | 23 |
| Aug. 20 | 15 | | 8 |

or on a shelf—and that money cannot be used to pay bills. In fact, you might be paying interest on the money used to purchase inventory (or on money to pay bills, because all capital is tied up in inventory). Therefore, it is imperative to keep the inventory as lean as possible without jeopardizing the efficiency of your business. On the other hand, the wisdom of the saying "You can't make money without spending it" certainly applies to inventory. Obviously, a single item required for a manufacturing process, but not available, brings the process to a halt. Therefore, it is essential to determine the minimum amount of each item that should be kept on hand and to know the lead time required to get more.

Some very successful home operators have inventory control down to a science, and they maintain a healthy cash flow by practicing "just-in-time" inventory control. As the name implies, supplies are ordered just in time to do a job. Very few supplies are waiting to be used. Of course, this requires being constantly alert to usage rates and knowing exactly how long it takes to receive an order from suppliers. This technique is an excellent way to keep money working rather tied up in inventory.

Care should be taken to make sure supplies and finished products don't get old in your storeroom. FIFO stands for "first in, first out," meaning the oldest inventory is used first. If something is not moving, you should remove it from stock either by running a sale (if that is appropriate) or by donating the item(s) to a nonprofit organization and taking a tax deduction for the cost.

## INVENTORY AND TAXES

Inventory is an asset, and taxes must be paid on all assets. The amount of taxes owed can be reduced by reducing the amount of inventory. This is what inspires the late-February sales that have become a normal part of the merchandising world. It is to your financial advantage to have inventory at the lowest possible level when its value is determined for tax purposes.

Figuring the cost of the inventory is not as straightforward as you might think. It would appear that valuing inventory would involve a rather simple calculation, but there are different ways to establish inventory value that can dramatically alter your tax bill. For instance, you can use the amount that you paid for the goods as the basis for establishing value, or you can use the amount you would need to pay for the goods at the time inventory is taken. There can be a significant difference between the two, as shown in the following example.

Orders for 20 bolts of cloth, each containing 100 yards, were placed at different times during the year:

| Purchase date | Cost/bolt | Total cost for 20 bolts |
|---|---|---|
| January 15 | $25.00 | $500.00 |
| April 12 | 27.00 | 540.00 |
| July 7 | 28.00 | 560.00 |
| November 10 | 31.00 | 620.00 |

Each bolt is of a different design, and some fabric is left on each bolt at the end of the year.

| Month of purchase | Average yards remaining per 100-yard bolt | Inventory value if value is based on the actual cost | Inventory value if value is based on current or replacement cost (cost of most recent purchase) |
|---|---|---|---|
| January | 12 | 12/100 of $500 = $ 60.00 | 12/100 of $620 = $ 74.40 |
| April | 18 | 18/100 of $540 = 97.20 | 18/100 of $620 = 111.60 |
| July | 28 | 28/100 of $560 = 156.80 | 28/100 of $620 = 173.60 |
| November | 64 | 64/100 of $620 = 396.80 | 64/100 of $620 = 396.80 |
| | | Total $710.80 | Total $756.40 |

The difference between the two calculation methods amounts to $45.60. In this example, it would be to the business owner's advantage to figure the inventory value on the actual cost for tax purposes, because this results in a lower inventory value and, therefore, a lower tax bill. If the cost of the fabric had gone down, rather than up, then it would be advantageous to figure the inventory on current cost for tax purposes. (Either method is acceptable to the IRS.) As you can see, the method of calculation changes the value of inventory. There are times when it is to your advantage to show a higher value, as when showing assets to a bank to garner a loan; however, the lower value is advantageous when figuring taxes.

The pamphlet *Tax Information on Accounting Periods and Methods* (IRS Bulletin 538) includes a section on inventory valuation and accounting. It is available from Department of Treasury, Internal Revenue Service, Washington, DC 20224 or your district IRS publications center.

# 13    Postal Services, Delivery Services, and Packing

## The United States Postal Service

People who don't have businesses for the most part mail only first class letters and cards carried by the U.S. Postal Service. While as a business owner you will still use first class service for some mailings, there are many other services you should consider for your business, including third-class bulk, first-class pre-sort, express mail, certified and registered mail, postage-paid reply envelopes, fourth class for packages, and others. Each of these classifications of mail is designed for a specific purpose, and it would be wise to learn about them. They are explained in a brochure that is available at no charge from your local postmaster.

To ease the preparation of mailings, you'll need a small postal scale to check the weight of envelopes and small packages. Keep different denominations of stamps on hand so you can apply the correct postage without visiting a post office. Also, it is no longer necessary to go to a post office to purchase stamps, as they can be ordered through the mail from your local postmaster and delivered to your home.

## Do You Need a Post Office Box?

You can expect to receive a lot of mail when you start a business, and you should consider the best location for delivery of your mail. If you haven't already, give some thought to using a post office box. A post office box looks more professional than a home address, especially if you live on a street that sounds very neighborhood-like, such as Trail Drive or Oak Lane. A post office box also helps to keep a low business profile in the neighborhood. If your business is a mail-based one, such as a mail-order operation, you may want to work from a postal box so neighbors remain oblivious to your activity. In some cases there is a

137

more compelling reason to use a post office box. If your home is in a zone that does not permit businesses, but the post office is in a commercial zone, a postal box number is all that is needed to allow you to work without the special-use permit required by some communities.

Many home business operators like to use a post office box because it puts space between them and their customers. Customers might be more inclined to drop in rather than communicate through the mail if they know your home address. And there is always the chance that an irate customer could harass you and your family. Another advantage is that you can keep the same business address even if you move your place of residence. This can be very beneficial if you advertise in periodicals, because the lag time between the placing of an ad and its appearance can be several months, and sometimes people respond to an ad many months, or even years, after its publication. For this reason, there are advantages to keeping the same business address year after year.

There are two disadvantages to using a post office box. The first is that the mail isn't delivered to your home, and you must make a special trip to the post office to pick it up. This can be a significant disadvantage if the outing disrupts the flow of your daily activities, although you can plan daily errands around this pickup. Another disadvantage is that shippers, such as United Parcel Service and trucking companies, cannot deliver to a post office box number. If you expect shipments via these carriers you will need to supply the sender with your street address, but also give them your post office box number for first-class envelope mailings. Also, a post office box is another expense, although a minor one.

If you receive parcels that are too large to fit into the postal box, or if occasionally there is too much mail to fit into it, the postal personnel will either slip a note into your box informing you to ask for the excess at the desk or they will place a key in the box that fits a locker in the lobby of the post office where the mail has been deposited.

## Shipping

Inspecting, wrapping, and shipping orders is a daily activity for many small businesses. Besides the U.S. Postal Service, a variety of other shipping services are available through private carriers. These include parcel delivery services, air cargo and package express service, express and transfer services, freight consolidation, and railroad and trucking services. Selecting the best method of shipment will depend on several factors, the most important one being the size and weight of the parcels to be shipped. For a complete list of the types of services available in your area, refer to the Yellow Pages under the heading "Shipping Agents." The three methods of shipping most frequently used by small businesses are United Parcel Service, parcel post, and truck.

### UNITED PARCEL SERVICE

United Parcel Service (UPS) is a private shipping company that offers reliable service for a reasonable price. It is the best buy around. Small to medium-sized parcels with a combined length and girth of no more than 130 inches (see illustration) and weighing no more than 70 pounds can be shipped by UPS. If you expect to use UPS, call and ask for a representative to visit you to explain the company's many services. The representative will provide you with all the supplies and information needed to ship by UPS including:

- A rate or destination sheet used to determine the cost of each shipment
- A log book for keeping track of packages sent
- A book containing the zip codes of all but the smallest towns in America
- Stickers and rubber stamps needed to prepare shipments
- A 130-inch chain to use for checking the length and girth limitations of packages
- Information on the overseas service provided by UPS

UPS will pick up parcels at your home or business for a small weekly charge. One of my neighbors has an arrangement with the UPS driver to stop for packages whenever an old milk crate is sitting near the door, and the driver stops at my home when he sees a small stained

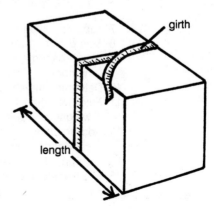

*Critical dimensions of a package to be shipped via UPS. Combined length and girth may be no more than 130 inches.*

glass panel leaning against the window. Packages must be weighed before pickup and the appropriate forms filled out, but this becomes part of the shipping routine, and it's a very simple procedure. UPS insures all packages for $100, but you can purchase more insurance, if you wish. Shipping charges are determined by the weight and distance a parcel will travel, and UPS will bill you monthly.

## PARCEL POST

This is an operation of the U.S. Postal Service. The maximum size and weight that can be shipped is 84 inches (length and girth combined) and 40 pounds.

The rate is determined by package weight and distance shipped, and the postal service will provide you with a chart listing the rates. It's wise to insure packages shipped parcel post, because this will allow them to be traced in the event they are lost in transit.

This method of shipment is not as fast or as reliable as UPS, and since the parcels must be somewhat smaller and lighter than those shipped UPS, many businesses prefer UPS to parcel post.

## A CHECKLIST FOR SHIPPING VIA UPS

1. Arrange for pickup by UPS route man.
2. Gather packing supplies—cartons, tape, labels, packing material.
3. Prepare invoice and packing list.
4. Affix mailing label to carton and cover with clear tape.
5. Pack carton tightly, cushioning the merchandise in the carton with adequate packing material.
6. Insert packing list before sealing the carton, or affix it to the outside of the carton.
7. Tape carton on top and bottom and run tape around it.
8. Stamp carton with UPS shipping number.
9. Weigh carton and write the weight in pounds and ounces by the shipping number.
10. Determine the shipping charges by referring to the UPS rate sheet.
11. Enter into the UPS log book the recipient's name and address, the carton weight, and shipping charges.
12. Add shipping charges to invoice and mail in separate envelope (or don't seal carton until weight is determined, complete the invoice by adding shipping costs, and slip invoice inside the mailing carton).
13. File invoice copy in accounts receivable file.

## TRUCKING SERVICES

Businesses turn to trucking services to ship packages that are very large and bulky or weigh more than 70 pounds. Trucking companies are usually more expensive and much slower than other methods of shipping, and for these reasons they are used only when packages are too large or too heavy to go via UPS or parcel post. Most trucking companies service rather limited areas, but if a parcel is to be shipped beyond a company's range, it is transferred to another trucking company that carries it to its destination. Look in the Yellow Pages under "Trucking—Motor Freight and Local Cartage" to learn rates, routes, and regulations.

# Packing with the Product and the Customer in Mind

The goal of packing is to ensure that the merchandise arrives at its destination undamaged. It is very destructive to your business image to send weak-walled parcels that fall apart en route or arrive with damaged goods. It takes time for the recipient to return the goods and more of your time to prepare another shipment. This is not only an aggravation for everyone concerned, but your customer may look elsewhere for a supplier if the merchandise is needed in a hurry. The supplies needed for packing are durable corrugated cardboard cartons, mailing labels, packing material, sturdy tape, and perhaps a few labels or rubber stamps that give instructions and precautions to the shipper.

Use printed package stuffers. Package enclosures are a good way to pick up new sales. Take advantage of everything that goes out to send a message, whether it's stamping a notice of a sale on the outside of a package of merchandise or inserting extra fliers with a bill. A catalog or special offer gets a free ride in outgoing orders since the postage and packing costs are usually paid by the customer.

To set our business shipments apart from the rest that arrive at our clients' shops, we stick a pack of chewing gum into each package. You would be surprised at the comments we get from that gesture. We believe our customers watch for the arrival of our merchandise and carefully unpack it, looking for the "prize."

*Cartons.* You will probably need to stock several different sizes of cartons. Although it may be hard to believe, some small business owners prowl the waste bins of liquor stores to pick up cartons (liquor boxes are very sturdy)—but having shipments arrive in boxes labeled Jim Beam or something similar detracts from one's business image. Boxes can be purchased from carton and paper suppliers, and a large supply can be stocked in a small area since they fold flat. The cost will depend on size and number purchased. The price per carton drops significantly as the number purchased increases. If possible, purchase cartons locally and in the largest lot that can be used within a reasonable time.

*Packing Material.*   The most economical way to protect goods is to wad up newspaper and stuff it around the merchandise. Or, for a price, there are a variety of packing materials, such as the white plastic foam "peanuts" and "mushrooms." "Bubble paper," the plastic sheets containing trapped air bubbles, can also be used to wrap fragile goods. Except for newspaper, all of these packing materials are another expense—and they are not biodegradable. They also take quite a lot of storage space, so consider all these factors as you plan your packing procedures. Whatever you use, be sure to stuff the cartons tightly so the merchandise cannot rattle around or shift while in transit.

*Tape.*   Don't tie packages together with string. Use strong tape. UPS and the U.S. Postal Service won't accept packages bound with string. Tape dispensers can be purchased at shipping and office supply shops. Use more, rather than less.

*Labels.*   While you can write the pertinent information on the shipping carton, it is better to use a mailing label because it is more obvious. Standard mailing labels can be purchased from office supply stores, or, for a more professional look, you can have labels imprinted with your business name and address. Even though labels have a gummed back and are supposed to stay in position, a piece of clear tape over them will ensure that they don't peel off and get lost in transit. The clear tape cover will also prevent the address from smearing should the label get wet. If a parcel is being shipped COD (cash on delivery) you will need to fill out a label that states the amount to be collected and other pertinent information (see more on COD under "Shipping Charges"). This is placed over, or in place of, the regular mailing label. The shipping service you use will supply the appropriate labels. Parcels shipped by truck require a bill of lading, and this, too, is provided by the shipper.

*Weighing the Shipment.*   Anything shipped UPS must be weighed before it is picked up, and the weight must be indicated on the outside of the carton beside your assigned shipper's number. Your shipper number is provided to you on a rubber stamp when you start using UPS services. You will need an accurate scale, so don't plan to rely on a bathroom scale. Shipping scales come in different sizes. Purchase the

## U.S. POSTAL SERVICE STAMPS

The following stamps are used by the U.S. Postal Service and indicate a few of the services available:

**FIRST CLASS**

**AIR MAIL
PAR AVION**

**1st CL. MAIL
ENCLOSED**

**Return Receipt Requested
Showing Address
Where Delivered**

**THIRD CLASS**

**FRAGILE**

**SPECIAL
4th CL. RATE**

**RESTRICTED
DELIVERY**

**FOR DEPOSIT ONLY
U.S. POSTAL SERVICE**

**RETURN RECEIPT
REQUESTED**

**PRIORITY
MAIL**

**SPECIAL
HANDLING**

DUE SENDER $_____
M.O. FEE _____
TOTAL _____

*Ink stamps used by the U.S. Postal Service.*

size that can accommodate the weight range of the cartons you will be shipping.

Parcel post packages are weighed by the post office personnel, and they figure the cost of shipment. The cost of shipment is based on the package weight and the distance from the shipping point to the destination.

***Packing Slip and Invoice.*** A packing slip, listing the contents of the parcel, should be included with each shipment. This can either be affixed to the outside of the box in a gummed packing-slip envelope or tucked into the top of the carton before sealing. The packing slip should be obvious and immediately available to the recipient so it can be used to check and compare contents as the carton is unpacked. If an order is shipped in more than one box, be sure to mark on the box "this is one of (fill in total number) boxes."

An invoice can be sent with the shipment, or it can be mailed later in a separate envelope. If you are shipping UPS or parcel post, you can calculate the shipping charges before the box is sealed by using the rate cards provided to you. If you wish, you can post these charges on the invoice, total the amount owed, and enclose the invoice with the order. Sometimes this brings an immediate remittance, but you shouldn't count on it. You may prefer to send the invoice through the mail in a separate envelope.

***Shipping Charges.*** Shipping charges should be included in the terms of sale, and they are customarily paid by the buyer. If your shipment is to go by UPS or parcel post, you pay for the delivery and then the charge is added to the invoice; if the shipment goes by truck, the trucking company will collect the shipping charges when the carton is delivered, or you can prepay the charges and bill your customer later. COD service is offered by the postal service, UPS, and other delivery services. The shipper collects from the recipient the money due to you for the delivered merchandise and shipping charge, plus a small service fee. The service fee is deducted and the remainder of the money is forwarded to you. COD is the preferred method for shipping to a customer whose credit history is unknown or questionable (see Chapter 17).

# 14     Do You Need Help?

The largest percentage of home businesses are basically one-person operations, and they use no outside help other than maybe a bookkeeper or an accountant. Some home businesses use part-time workers, while others use one or more full-time employees. Often, family members make up the work force, but another arrangement is to subcontract work to independent contractors who are not, for legal purposes, considered employees.

Whether or not you need help will depend on your goals and the type of business you operate. A business based on the owner-operator's skill, such as dentistry or consulting, cannot use employees except in supporting roles (such as nurse or secretary), but those based on manufacturing or a service that does not require extensive experience or education can very effectively use employees to help the business grow and to increase profits.

What do you need in the way of help? You may plan to keep your business small and handle all the work yourself, but if your business is to grow and expand as a market is developed, you may not be able to do all the work and thus will need to hire outside help.

## Employees

Webster defines an *employee* as "a person who works for another in return for financial compensation," but the U.S. Department of Labor elaborates on the definition as follows: "An employee is one who performs services subject to control by an employer, not only as to the result to be accomplished by the work, but also as to the details and means by which that result is accomplished. That is, an employee is subject to the will and control of the employer not only as to what is to be done, but also as to how and when it shall be done." This means that an employer defines not only the work to be done but also the circumstances, including the time and place, under which it will be performed. As you will learn later in this chapter, this definition can play an important role in determining the kind of help you use.

The question you must ask is "Will employees increase profits?" In answering this you will need to compare the *cost* of employees with the amount of *income* they can generate. When calculating the cost, include not only wages but also the benefits you will be expected to pay and the expense of keeping the employee records required of employers. If the answer to the question is "Yes, employees will increase profits," and there is space to enlarge your business, then proceed to hire helpers; otherwise, there is no real point or advantage in hiring helpers.

An important consideration when adding employees is "When should they be hired?" Hiring help prematurely will threaten your financial well-being, but waiting too long will cause you to lose business. The right time to hire help is when your business is bringing in enough work to keep employees busy and enough money to pay them on an ongoing basis—not for just a month or two. An employee is expected to be a permanent addition to the company. And never overlook the fact that hired help gets paid before you do. Many small business owners constantly fight the cash-flow battle and have difficulty meeting the payroll. While employees usually have the notion that the boss is "rolling in the dough," the truth is that employees often have more in their pockets than the boss because there is little left over for personal use after the many business bills are paid. This is particularly true of the very young business, but it can also be a problem for older ones that have unsteady or fluctuating sales.

Hiring employees is not what it used to be. Before the government got into the act, it was a straightforward procedure: the employers established the guidelines for work and paid the employees. Now, governmental regulations include minimum wage laws and fair employment regulations, and employers must function as agents of the federal government by withholding income taxes and other deductions from employee paychecks.

There are several things you must do to satisfy the government when you hire employees. Federal and state laws require the employer to provide employee benefits in addition to wages or salary. Employers are legally required to pay into Social Security, Workers' Compensation, Unemployment Insurance, and, in a few states, State Temporary Disability Insurance. These benefits can be costly, and they certainly affect operating expenses and profits. Besides these, some of the larger small businesses offer a variety of compensation packages such as pension plans and group insurance. Very few home businesses have enough employees to get involved in these kinds of programs, although some of them do offer vacation, holiday, and severance pay.

Labor laws are discussed in booklets available from the Department of Labor. To receive these booklets contact the Department of Labor, found under U.S. Government Offices in the Blue Pages of the telephone directory.

Even though hiring employees is costly, time-consuming, and beset with governmental regulations, the fact remains that if you intend to expand and do more business than you alone can handle, you will need to find help.

## FINDING THE RIGHT EMPLOYEES

Finding an employee is easy; finding the *right* employee is much more difficult. Some people try to find helpers to whom they feel superior and whom they will feel comfortable "bossing around," but as R. H. Grant observed, "When you employ people who are smarter than you are, you prove you are smarter than they are." Look for qualified people who want to serve both themselves and your business. The employee of a small business usually needs to wear many hats, cleaning up shop one moment, putting together an order the next, and sorting out customer problems after that. There are motivated workers, who do whatever must be done to keep the ball rolling, and then there are those who aren't willing to look for things to do but are more inclined to do only the specific job for which they were hired. The latter is not the type of worker a home business needs.

You will have a much greater chance of finding the right person if you define precisely what you need before beginning your search. The following guidelines should help you.

1. Write a job description that includes the work to be done, the skills needed to perform the work, and the salary offered.

2. Actively recruit applicants. Advertising in newspaper classifieds is an effective way to attract applicants. Also, job openings can be listed with high schools and colleges that have job placement bureaus and with local government employment agencies. Some people find employees through friends and family, but this approach can put you in the awkward position of being unable to reject someone because of a relationship you are unwilling to imperil.

3. Have the applicants fill in application forms and provide references. Studying the responses and the manner in which the forms are completed (handwriting, neatness, grammar, and spelling) can give you some insight into applicants' abilities and attention to detail. It is of the utmost importance that you check references and other personal data. If an applicant says he or she graduated from a certain school or

worked somewhere, check it out. Application forms are available from office supply stores, or you may prefer to write your own in order to include questions you consider pertinent.

4. After studying the completed form, schedule an interview if the applicant seems to possess the qualifications you need. Discuss the position to be filled, along with past work experiences. Try to get a feel for the whole person—personality, likes and dislikes, hobbies, habits, family responsibilities, and so forth. This whole-person approach is very important, because you will probably work very closely with your employees, especially if your business and its physical space are small. You might as well look for a person who can not only do the job but also will be pleasant and interesting to work with. You might find someone who has all the qualifications you seek and yet you detect something in the interview that causes you to have reservations. Let's say, for instance, that the individual mentions that his or her family lives 60 miles away. Will the person commute daily? Why is he or she looking for work so far away from home? As another example, if an applicant has worked at many jobs the issue is worth investigating. Is there an acceptable reason for the job-hopping? Watch for unaccounted periods in an applicant's work history (was the person in jail, ill, or doing something he or she doesn't want you to know about?), and be alert for unusual circumstances that could affect an employee's effectiveness.

5. Hire a new employee for a trial period of a stated duration. During this time you can judge the person's job performance, and he or she can ascertain if the job is a good match, too. Have an understanding with the trainee that at the end of the period you will decide if the trainee will be retained. Do not hesitate to release someone who does not fit into your organization or does not perform satisfactorily.

### DO YOU NEED PART-TIME OR FULL-TIME HELP?

As you consider hired help, you might think about the advantages of hiring part-time workers instead of full-time help. A part-time employee can be hired to do a specific job and only when that job needs to be done, whereas a full-time worker expects to be on the job and paid even when business is slow. You are not required to provide the benefits to part-time workers that are normally expected by full-time help. Of course, people who work for you only occasionally will not feel the same commitment to your business that an individual who works steadily feels, but it may be a fair trade-off because you can hire people with specific skills for specific jobs. It can be very frustrating trying to keep an employee busy when there simply isn't much work to be done.

For the cost of a single full-time employee who works 40 hours each week, you could employ many people with different skills. For example, you could employ:

| | |
|---|---|
| A cleaning person, ½ day, once each week | 4 hours |
| A delivery person, 1 hour, four times each week | 4 hours |
| A secretary, ½ day, once each week | 4 hours |
| A bookkeeper, ½ day, twice each week | 8 hours |
| A fabricator or service person, ½ day, five days each week | 20 hours |
| | 40 hours |

Of course, when business increases it may be necessary to hire one or more people for each of the above jobs, but until that time, part-time workers may better fulfill your needs.

Some part-time workers may want to be paid "under the table," but it is important to pay all employees, whether part-time or full-time, with payroll checks from which taxes are withheld. Uncle Sam has sophisticated computers watching for numbers that don't add up, and you would be risking IRS attention if you attempted to circumvent the tax collection system.

## ESTABLISHING A PERSONNEL POLICY

Establish a personnel policy as soon as you decide to hire employees. Good workers are a valuable business asset, and it is important to attract and *keep* them.

As you contemplate how to deal with employees, take into consideration their needs and expectations. You can assume they are interested in fair wages, continuous employment, reasonable work hours, safe and pleasant working conditions, a sense of improving status, and a feeling they are contributing to the well-being of the business.

The following ideas might be a guide in developing a personnel policy.

1. Give employees the opportunity to contribute ideas to your business and take their suggestions seriously.
2. Give employees adequate training, either on the job or through special training sessions.
3. Review worker job performance at specific intervals (semiannually or annually), and discuss the evaluation with the worker.
4. Try to keep salaries in line with those offered by competitors.
5. Keep employees apprised of the health of your business. You might be surprised at how they will help if they know what is needed or if they realize that there are difficulties.

## Subcontractors (Independent Contractors)

Subcontractors, sometimes called independent contractors, are not employees in the legal sense. That is to say they work independently, on their own schedules and at locations of their own choosing. They are responsible for paying their own taxes and handling their own insurance and other benefits normally supplied by employers. The IRS and the Department of Labor continue to raise questions about the use of independent contractors because they feel that people are being taken advantage of—that they do work for a business but do not receive the benefits due them. The guidelines offered by the Supreme Court to distinguish employees from subcontractors are presented in the sidebar nearby entitled "Characteristics of Employees and Subcontractors."

Many home businesses use subcontractors instead of employees for several reasons. In the first place, subcontractors are easier to hire

---

### CHARACTERISTICS OF EMPLOYEES AND SUBCONTRACTORS

Guidelines offered by the U.S. Supreme Court:

| *Employee* | *Subcontractor* |
|---|---|
| Work is an integral part of the business | Work is not such a large part of the business |
| Permanent relationship | Not a permanent relationship |
| Little or no investment in equipment | Larger investment in equipment |
| Place and time of work controlled by employer | Place and time of work not controlled by employer |
| Little opportunity for profit or loss | Greater opportunity to gain profit and sustain loss |

Guidelines used by most small businesses:

| *Employee* | *Subcontractor* |
|---|---|
| Steady work | Intermittent work |
| Equipment supplied by employer | Not all equipment supplied by contractor |
| Place and time of work determined by employer | Place and time of work determined by worker |
| Employer must pay benefits | Contractor not responsible for benefits |
| Employer must collect and forward taxes to government | Contractor doesn't collect taxes |

for limited work. They can be contracted for a specific task and nothing more. Also, by using the services of a subcontractor, rather than an employee, there is no requirement for the employer to collect taxes, contribute to the fund for FICA (Federal Insurance Contributions Act), or provide other benefits for employees. The only responsibility to the government is to file a 1099 form for each individual who was paid at least $600 during the year. Another big benefit of subcontracting is that the work is done somewhere other than on the employer's property. This is especially important to the home business where space is at a premium and where outside workers could interfere with the functioning, security, or serenity of the household.

Various kinds of work can be subcontracted, but one of the most common instances is the home manufacturer who uses subcontractors to fabricate inventory. Workers (subcontractors) are located by advertising in the classifieds for people who want to work in their own homes. The ad specifies if special equipment is needed, such as a sewing machine or a band saw (or the necessary equipment might be supplied to the worker if it is unusual and not readily available). The manufacturer supplies the materials and teaches the subcontractor the process for making the item, and the two agree on a price for the finished items. Each subcontractor may be contracted to do just one step in the manufacturing process. For instance, one worker might cut out and sand wooden objects that are then turned over to another subcontractor for painting and still another for assembling.

In most subcontracting situations the worker is not paid for the amount of time worked, but rather for the number of pieces produced (this arrangement is called *piecework*). Obviously, those who work quickly make more money per time unit than those who are slower. It is important to incorporate strict quality control measures into the process because most workers doing piecework will try to turn out items as quickly as possible to earn a better hourly wage, which could lead to sloppy work.

My family has used subcontractors in our home business with very good results. Workers picked up supplies we had prepared in units that would yield a specific number of items, and they returned them to our home when the items were completed and were paid immediately for their work. The only record keeping required was a running total of the amount paid to each worker, which was reported to the government.

Another type of help you might need, if you are a manufacturer or an importer of goods, is that of a sales representative, who can either be a subcontractor or an employee. Sales representatives are discussed in Chapter 17.

## Family Workers

Home is where the heart is, and it may also be where the help is. Some home businesses are built on the labor of family members, including the very young and the very old. Some families grow stronger as a result of working together, but other families are incapable of this type of arrangement, and working together results in arguing, strife, ill feelings, and shoddy work. Before you solicit the help of family members, consider the personalities involved and how they might contribute to the health of your business—and how your business will affect family relationships. Remember the following couplet as you consider hiring friends and relatives:

> Think once, then twice before you hire
> Family or friends you're reluctant to fire.

Let's assume you *do* hire family members. You will need a personnel policy for them just as you do for outside workers. Maybe you can be a little more flexible in order to accommodate their other schedules, but if your spouse or children are working with you, and you are depending on their help, they must understand their obligation. Depending on age, a child might operate a computer, do clerical work, answer the telephone, clean the office, pack products, and so forth. And your spouse might contribute any number of skills and perform many tasks as you work together to make your business a success. But you need to give some thought to how you will resolve disagreements concerning the management of the business. Does accepting spousal help mean sharing business decisions, and if so, are you willing to share them?

Will you pay family members for their help? The IRS has ruled that a parent can deduct, as a business expense, payments to a child for services rendered if such services would be deductible if performed by someone else. A dependent child can earn up to the amount of the standard deduction before any tax is due, and thereafter the wages are taxed at the rate for the child's tax bracket. This is one way to shift income and reduce the amount of taxable income. Also, wages earned by dependent children are exempt from social security taxes. Wages paid to your spouse must be included in your joint income, so they will not alter your tax liability; however, a tax advantage can be gained from payments to a spouse, as explained in Chapter 18.

## Other Hired Help

As your business develops you will be beset with questions about how to proceed. This is the time to look for help from people who have the knowledge or skills your business needs. Almost all businesses can benefit from the knowledge and expertise of an accountant, as mentioned in Chapter 10.

Do you need a lawyer? A struggling home business is seldom in a position to pay legal fees, and most home businesses do just fine without ever asking a lawyer for advice, but that is not to say you can plow through the legal issues associated with your business without guidance. Contracts and legalese can be very confusing, but good accountants often know the legal language and can advise you as to the significance of the small print. In most cases an accountant's advice is much less expensive than a lawyer's. Be aware, however, that some contracts, especially those that deal with long-term agreements including such issues as partnerships, distributorships, franchises, and royalty contracts, can have such a large impact on your business life that you have no choice but to hire a lawyer when these types of contracts are being negotiated.

If you decide it is in your best interest to hire a lawyer to oversee business matters, go shopping. Ask friends and other business owners whom they use and if they are pleased with the work. Also, ask about fees before you get too involved with this type of relationship.

# Part Five

## *Sales: Pricing and Marketing*

# 15    Pricing Formulas

The price you charge for your product or service will determine if you make a profit, break even, or lose money. "What is the right price?" is the wrong question, because there isn't any specific "right" price—although there are wrong ones. A price is wrong if it's so high that few people will buy the product or service, or so low that, even though you make a lot of sales, you don't make much profit. There is a price *range* that will attract buyers and still enable you to make a profit, and your goal is to determine that range.

There are several formulas and different approaches to guide you as you establish prices. It is wise to calculate the costs in different ways before making a firm pricing decision.

The price of your service or product should be based on formulas that incorporate the following factors:

1. Costs, both direct and indirect
2. Competitor's prices
3. Supply and demand
4. The profit factor

Each of these is discussed below and then used in several formulas and examples.

## Direct and Indirect Costs

### DIRECT COSTS (LABOR AND MATERIALS)

*Materials.* The cost of the materials that go into your product or the cost of supplies needed in a service business is determined by the prices in the marketplace. Every effort should be made to find the best prices available (see Chapter 12). Calculate the cost of the raw material and supplies needed to make a single item or to perform a service a single time.

*Labor.*  How much should/can you charge for your time and skill? If special education, skills, and experience are needed to perform your work, you should charge more than if they are not. Generally, professionals and other highly educated or specialized people earn more than members of the work force that support them. A physician earns more than the assisting nurse, and the nurse earns more than the secretary who schedules appointments. An engineer who designs automobiles is paid more than the assembly line workers who make them, but an assembly line worker earns more than the mechanic who repairs them. Society usually pays more for "brain" than "brawn," although there are exceptions, as in the case of professional athletes.

Where does your labor fit into the pay scale? Many home workers, especially those who have not worked at another job outside of the home, underestimate the value of their time and end up working for a pittance. Don't allow this to happen as you figure labor costs.

After deciding on an hourly wage, decide how long it will take to make an item or perform a service, then multiply the hourly wage by the time needed to complete the job, and this will be the labor cost for a single product or service job. More about determining labor costs is presented below.

## INDIRECT COSTS (OVERHEAD)

The many expenses of operating a business belong in the indirect cost category, including packing and shipping supplies, business telephone calls, interest on loans, rent or mortgage payment (in proportion to the work space and storage areas in your home), gas and electricity, repairs, maintenance, delivery and freight charges, cleaning, taxes, insurance, and the many other expenses associated with maintaining your business. Don't forget to include the cost of advertising and marketing. Calculate each expense for a single month (or year), then add them together to determine the cost of operating your business for one month (or year). Next, divide the total overhead figure by the number of items you plan to produce or the number of service jobs you plan to perform each month (or year). This is your overhead cost per item or job.

So far, the cost formula per product unit or single service job looks like this:

*Formula 1:*

Materials for a single product or service
+ Hourly wage × hours to make product or perform service
+ Overhead per single product or service
_____

Total cost of a single product or service job

## LABOR AND OVERHEAD CAN BE FIGURED TOGETHER

Another, perhaps easier, way to figure costs is to combine labor and overhead and then add materials or supplies to arrive at the cost for a single product or service. The rule of thumb is to multiply the hourly wage you would receive while working for someone else by a factor of 2.3 to 2.8 to arrive at the amount to charge for your labor and overhead. Thus, if your hourly wage is $12.00 per hour in the business world, then you would charge at least $12.00 × 2.3 ($27.60) per hour when you work at your home business. You may think this wage is too much, but that hourly rate factor is what is needed to cover both wages and overhead expenses (depending on your business, of course). To this figure you would add the cost of materials and supplies, as shown:

*Formula 2:*

Hours to make one product or perform one service × hourly rate factor
+ Materials for a single product or service
_____

Total cost of a single product or service job

Still another way to figure labor and overhead costs together to determine price is to divide the yearly salary you intend to take by the number of working hours in a year, and then multiply that number by the 2.3 to 2.8 factor to yield the hourly cost of labor and overhead. For example, if you work 2,000 hours each year (50 weeks at 40 hours each week) and you intend to take a yearly salary of $20,000, that comes to $10 per hour for your labor ($20,000 per year divided by 2,000 hours worked per year equals $10 per hour). That $10 per-hour wage multiplied by the 2.3 factor (minimum) needed to cover overhead yields an hourly rate of $23 per hour for labor and overhead. If it takes 3 hours to make an item or to perform a service, the labor and overhead charge would be $69.00 (3 hours × $23.00 per hour). To this figure is added the cost of materials to arrive at the *total cost* of a product or service. (Remember that in order to make the $20,000 per year you would need to keep busy eight hours each day, which is most likely an overly optimistic assessment of your early business activity.)

*Formula 3:*

(Salary ÷ working hours) × overhead factor = hourly cost of labor
and overhead

($20,000 ÷ 2000)  ×  (2.3 to 2.8)  =  $23 to $28

And, to complete the calculation:

Hours to make a product or perform a service × hourly
labor and overhead charge
+ Materials for a single product or service

Total cost of a single product or service job

***Break-Even Point.*** If you charged the amount calculated using Formulas 1, 2, or 3 you would make a living (because you figured in salary) but you would not make a profit that would provide money for business development and expansion. The above calculations give the *break-even point* for your business efforts—the point where income covers costs. There is no profit or loss. In order to make a profit the break-even point must be surpassed.

## The Profit Margin

One of the main reasons for operating a business is to make a profit, so a profit margin should be included in the pricing formula. We'd all like to make a large profit, but several outside influences play a role in determining profit.

Competition is a major factor that affects the amount of profit you can add to the cost of a product or service. Is there a business down the street trying to attract your customers, or are you trying to woo their customers? Is your product or service a little better or a bit inferior to those of your competitors? Do you intend to advertise more or less than your competitors? If you intend to advertise, you will need to increase the product's price to reflect the cost of advertising. However, the extra advertising will probably increase the amount of business so you might not need quite as much profit per sale. You can arbitrarily establish a profit margin if you don't have direct competitors, but don't go to either extreme. If you charge too little you will give the impression that your product or service is of little value, while customers will look elsewhere for a better deal if you overcharge.

What will the market bear? Supply and demand is obviously influenced by competitors—if you are the only business that offers a service or product you can charge more than if others are offering it. But there is another aspect to supply and demand that needs to be considered. Do you need to create a demand for your product or service, or will you be filling an already established need? For example, an air-conditioning repair business is needed in an area where air-conditioners are commonly used because there is an already established need; however, bicycle rental along a beach isn't a needed service so the bicycle entrepreneur would need to create a demand for it. Demand could be created by hiring several beautiful girls to ride along the beach with instructions to laugh a lot, to stop for soft drinks, to chat—and in general to create in the mind of the observer that riding on the beach is fun. The cost of creating this demand would be added to overhead costs (marketing), but by establishing a demand, an increase in the profit margin will be realized.

Now, let's put everything together:

Materials
+ Labor and overhead
_____
Break-even point or total costs

And continuing—

Break-even point
+ Profit
_____
Price to charge per item or service

Materials and overhead cannot be altered much because they reflect costs over which you have only limited control. Of course, you must find the best prices available as you seek out supplies and materials, and you could lower overhead by turning out lights and dropping the shop temperature a degree of two, but basically you are tied into these costs. However, the cost of labor and the profit margin are more flexible and more subject to the influence of the market (as you will see in the examples below).

## Examples of Pricing Formula Applications

Each of the following examples has taken into account:

• Cost of materials
• Cost of labor
• Overhead expenses
• Profit
• Competitors
• Special circumstances relevant to the business

### PRICING A SERVICE: A BEAUTICIAN'S PRICING PLAN

Beauticians frequently work at home. To simplify calculations, we will assume that the beautician in our example only gives permanents.

She works on her front porch, which has been enclosed and outfitted with two beauty-care stations. She works 8 hours a day, 5 days a week (40 hours each week), and gives 6 perms each day for a total of 30 perms each week. She takes a salary of only $180 each week ($4.50 per hour). The cost of supplies needed to give a perm is $8. Overhead costs are very low because (1) the floor area used for her business is a small percentage of her total home, (2) she doesn't advertise but gets customers by word of mouth and through a sign in her front yard, and (3) there is little maintenance. Let's add $60 for overhead each week. How much should she charge for a permanent?

Weekly costs are:

```
    $180 (salary)
      60 (overhead)
 +   240 (supplies; $8 ×  30 perms = $240)
    $480 total expenses per week
```

The total cost ($480) divided by the number of perms done per week (30) equals $16 per perm. This is the amount the beautician must charge to break even. Next, add the desired profit margin to the calculation. In determining profit she has to consider that other ladies in the area also give perms, so she is reluctant to go too high. However, she has built a faithful clientele by doing a good job and by keeping a pot of coffee perking and available to customers at no charge. (She has a Coke machine but makes money on this.) She also spends some energy keeping track of their personal lives, making notations on each customer's card about such things as special interests and the names of the customer's spouse, children, and so on (this kind of information flows easily from under a hair dryer). The proprietor reviews the card prior to a customer's visit, and as a result of this extra effort, the people who visit her shop feel special and enjoy the time chatting about things that interest them. Her extra effort is worth a few bucks, and she thinks she can add $4 profit per perm without losing business. If this is too much she can lower prices, but it would be more difficult to raise them. Consequently, the price the customer must pay for a permanent is:

```
    $16 (cost for permanent)
 +    4 (profit)
    $20 (the price she will ask for a permanent)
```

The beautician will make a profit of $120 per week ($4 profit for each of 30 perms). She takes two weeks each year for vacation, so she will earn a profit of $6,000 per year ($120 × 50 weeks), besides the $9,000 salary, for a total of $15,000 per year.

Other ways to figure the price of a permanent, based on formulas discussed previously:

*Formula 1*

| | |
|---|---:|
| Materials | $8.00 |
| Labor cost | |
| (30 perms in a 40-hour week, $4.50/hour) | 6.00 |
| Overhead ($60/week ÷ 30 perms) | 2.00 |
| Profit | 4.00 |
| Price | $20.00 |

*Formula 2*

| | |
|---|---:|
| Materials | $8.00 |
| Wage × overhead factor | |
| ($4.50 × 2.3) = $10.35/hour | |
| 30 perms in 40 hours = 1⅓ hours per perm | |
| $10.35 × 1⅓ | 13.80 |
| Profit | 4.00 |
| Price | $25.80 |

*Formula 3*

(Salary for year ÷ working hours) × overhead factor = hourly cost of labor and overhead

($9,000 ÷ 2000) × 2.3 = 10.35/hour

It takes 1⅓ hours to do a perm, making the labor and overhead cost equal $13.80.

| | |
|---|---:|
| Labor/overhead | $13.80 |
| Materials | 8.00 |
| Profit | 4.00 |
| Price | $25.80 |

Using these formulas as guides, the proprietor could establish a reasonable price. It might be wise to place the price between the two extremes, perhaps around $22.50 per permanent.

## PRICING A MANUFACTURED PRODUCT: POTPOURRI BAGS

Generally, a manufacturer sells a product to a retailer for half the price the customer will pay for it. Thus, a manufacturer receives $1.00 for an item that the retailer sells for $2.00. This subject is discussed further in Chapter 17. The price markup must be taken into consideration when a manufacturer prices products.

The example we will study concerns a manufacturer of potpourri products. This company manufactures small lace bags filled with potpourri and tied with colorful ribbons. The labor to make these items is provided by subcontractors who work in their own homes and are paid according to the number of bags they make, not according to the time it takes to make them. They are paid $.20 for each bag they make. Overhead is kept to a minimum because no manufacturing space is required, although there are many other expenses associated with keeping the operation alive.

| | |
|---|---|
| Cost of supplies | $.20 per bag |
| Cost of labor | .20 per bag |
| Cost of overhead | .20 per bag |
| Cost of management | .30 per bag (explained later) |
| Cost subtotal | $.90 per bag |

Several more items need to be included when calculating the price of the bags. First, these potpourri bags are sold to retail stores through sales representatives (discussed in Chapter 17). The sales reps make a 20 percent commission on everything they sell, and this commission must be added to the *cost* of the product. Secondly, a profit should be included in the *price* of the product. It might be worthwhile to figure backward to arrive at a reasonable price. The question is, how much will a customer pay for one of these little bags? They are classified as "pick-up" items—something shoppers happen to see while shopping, but nothing they would go to the store to purchase. Pick-up items usually need to carry a small price tag so the customer doesn't hesitate or think too much about the price or the purchase. The potpourri bags could probably be sold for as much as $3.50 retail—the cost of a hamburger, fries, and a Coke—which means the manufacturer would need to sell each bag to the retailer for $1.75. In that case the sales rep would earn 20 percent of $1.75, or $.35 per bag. Adding that to the above costs we have:

| | |
|---|---|
| Cost of manufacturing potpourri bag | $ .90 |
| Sales commission | .35 |
| Total cost of making and selling bag | $1.25 |

So, the profit from each bag would be the wholesale price of $1.75 minus the manufacturing cost of $1.25, leaving a profit of $.50. This seems just about right. Still, it doesn't seem quite fair for the person who makes the bag to earn so much less than the sales representative. It would probably be fair and reasonable to increase the amount paid for labor to as much as $.30 per bag and reduce profit to $.40 per bag.

The cost of management was placed at $.30 per bag. This would amount to a $12,000 salary if 40,000 bags were sold, and the profit on this many bags would come to $16,000. But there is a problem. It might be difficult to sell 40,000 individual bags, but if they were sold in units, with maybe an assortment of five fragrances in a small wicker basket, perhaps more would be purchased. Five potpourri bags would normally yield a profit of $2.00 (5 bags times $.40 profit per bag). The cost of the wicker basket must be deducted from this. Small baskets can be purchased in large lots from importers for as little as $.25 each, leaving a profit of $1.75 for a unit consisting of five bags. If *all* bags were sold in units of five, the cost of the baskets would reduce the annual profit by $2,000 (40,000 bags would make 8,000 units of five, and each unit would require a $.25 basket, for a total cost of $2,000)—that's the worst scenario. The actual cost of baskets will depend on the ratio of units of five bags to single bags sold. Thus, profit, after taking a salary, will range from $14,000 to $16,000. If the wholesale price of the bags were just $.25 less ($1.50), the profit would drop several thousand dollars, so you can see how important it is to identify costs accurately and consider the many expenses when setting prices.

I have used this example to illustrate that the formulas, which seemed so straightforward when presented earlier, usually must be adjusted when applied to real business situations. Still, they give a basis for developing a price structure and are of value for this reason.

### PRICING A PRODUCT AND SERVICE: THIS GROCER IS GOING BANANAS!

This example illustrates that pricing to make a profit is very tricky and requires a keen awareness of multiple factors. I used to trade at a grocery store that had a pricing problem in the produce department. The produce was invariably priced higher than at the other groceries in town. On several occasions I heard a shopper grumble about the cost of bananas. Bananas might be priced at $.59 per pound when other grocers were charging around $.29. Many of the $.59 bananas rotted and could not be sold. I don't know if the store carrying the higher priced bananas made more money than the other stores, but I *do* know that the customers were annoyed by the high price and doubly offended when they saw the bananas competitively priced only after they were nearly rotten.

Let's just push around a few numbers and try to determine if the grocer gained much by overpricing the bananas. Let's figure that the wholesale cost of bananas is $.20 per pound (which is too high, but, for simplicity's sake, we'll use this high cost and leave out the cost of labor and overhead). If Store A sells 10 pounds of bananas at $.59 per pound ($5.90 in sales) and the cost of the bananas is $2.00 ($.20 times 10 pounds), then the store made a profit of $3.90 on 10 pounds of bananas. Or did it? Because of the high price, customers did not buy many bananas and many of them rotted. Let's say for every pound that was sold, another two pounds spoiled. In that case, the cost of each pound sold would amount to $.20 times 3 (one sold, two spoiled), or $.60 per pound, so the store actually lost $.01 per pound.

However, let's assume that some of the overripe bananas were repackaged and repriced for quick sale, but they were unattractive and few were bought. There is something very unappealing about overripe produce rewrapped, marked down, and set among the other produce. It gives the impression that business is slow and leaves the customer with a negative feeling. Still, a few of the overripe bananas were probably bought by people intending to make banana bread or cake, for which overripe is acceptable, so maybe the store broke even or even made a little money.

On the other hand, if Store B sells 10 pounds of bananas at $.29 per pound ($2.90 in sales), and they cost $2.00 ($.20 times 10 pounds), then the grocer made $.90 in profit on each 10 pounds of bananas sold. Since the bananas sold for an attractive price, more of them sold and the profit grew. But there is an added benefit to selling bananas at a reduced price. Store B not only made more profit than store A, but it also had the goodwill of its customers who shopped for other items when they came to buy the lower-priced bananas.

The above example illustrates that you won't necessarily earn a larger profit by charging more for your goods. It also is an example of the merchandising wisdom that states, "The lower the price, the more you will sell; and the more you sell, the lower the price" (although this doesn't *always* hold true). On the other hand, guard against setting prices so low that a profit cannot be realized, or so low that you give the impression that the product or service is of poor quality.

## Giving a Quote

Some kinds of businesses are conducted through quotations. A customer inquires what it will cost to have a service performed or a product made and asks for a price "quote" before deciding on who will be contracted for the business.

There are several approaches to use in arriving at a quote for a customer, and you must take the time to make the necessary calculations carefully. Never just "throw out a number," because you may be stuck with that price, and it may be way out of line. If it's too low, your customer will grab it and hold you to it and you will lose money; if it's too high, the customer will look elsewhere for a better price. *Take your time.* Make the appropriate calculations, and base your quote on the calculations. Make sure the quote includes all "reimbursibles" such as reimbursement for faxes, photocopying, and telephone line charges. Leave nothing to question in your quote or you could end up "eating" some charges.

Always remember you are in business to make money, and even though you want the customer's business, do not underestimate the price unless it will open a door for future business. A price too low may well be counterproductive, because you will later have difficulty raising prices because the customer expects a continuation of the unreasonably low prices you initially quoted. So be honest and upfront, and give a quote you can live with.

# 16 Generating Sales Through Advertising and Publicity

Steuart Britt, author of *Spenders*, wrote "Doing business without advertising is like winking at a girl in the dark. You know what you are doing, but nobody else does." Demand for goods or services offered by a business can be brought about in two ways. One way is to *establish* demand by just being available and having people notice that a business is present. The other way is to *create* demand through publicity and advertising. Advertising is the paid part of a promotion program, and publicity is exposure that can be generated without cost. Many businesses depend exclusively on created demand to attract their customers. You will increase sales if you promote your business, whether you are a home-town business or one that appeals to a national or specialized market. As you develop a promotional program you need to determine:

1. The group you are trying to reach
2. The amount of money you can spend
3. The message you want to convey
4. Effective ways to reach potential customers

## Whom Are You Trying to Reach?

The type of promotional campaign you undertake will be based on the potential buyers you are trying to reach. If your business is directed to people who live nearby—in your town, your neighborhood, and the immediate vicinity—the campaign will be conducted using different methods than if your potential customers are distributed over a larger area, maybe throughout the nation. Most home operations are built on business that can be generated in the immediate area. This is especially true of the service-oriented business, such as an income tax preparer, upholsterer, or accountant. Since these kinds of businesses draw customers from nearby, their promotion campaigns are limited to a usually small local area. On the other hand, a mail-order business, newsletter publisher, manufacturer, or seller of specialty goods would seek a more widely dispersed clientele; thus their campaigns would be designed to attract the attention of a larger market. Techniques for reaching these two audiences are described later in this chapter.

Whether you are planning a national campaign or one limited to your town or neighborhood, you must identify your customers and learn to think like them. Don't ever forget that people do business with people, not with billboards, Yellow Pages, coupons, or newspaper ads. Always keep the customer in mind. Ask yourself the following questions:

*Who* are your customers (age, sex, special characteristics)?
*Where* do they live? Nearby? Or are they scattered over a large area?
*What* are your customers seeking?
*When* will they be seeking your service or product?
*How* can you meet their needs and gain their business?
*Why* will they select your business over another?

You will be equipped with the information needed to organize an effective promotion campaign if you can answer these questions about your customers.

## How Much Money Can You Spend?

Advertising costs money—sometimes a lot of money—but it is usually what determines whether or not a business attracts enough customers to make a profit. As you debate whether to sink money into advertising, keep in mind the comment of the playwright Derby Brown, who said, "The business that considers itself immune to the necessity for advertising sooner or later finds itself immune to business."

Plan your advertising budget carefully. You might be thinking, "How much can I afford to spend?"—but the real question is, "How much can I afford *not* to spend?" Your advertising budget will directly affect the amount of business you create. You can expect to pay much more if you enlist the help of a professional advertising agency rather than doing the work yourself. Agencies may have more experience and a better feel for how to conduct a campaign, but many home business owners do a *better* job than the professionals because they are more attuned to the way their businesses can affect others. Later in this chapter you will be led through the various kinds of promotions you might undertake and be given suggestions to help you select the ones that will best fit your business and your budget. The most important concept to carry through your promotional campaign is that *promoting a business is an ongoing process*, and it is necessary to build an advertising budget into your financial plans.

Plan to spend what it takes to attract customers, but only if sales to those customers bring in enough money to pay for the advertising and leave a profit. Otherwise, your advertising would leave you customer-rich but profit-poor. Knowing how much, where, and how to use advertising money is perhaps the most difficult problem a beginning business must deal with. After your fledgling business has attracted some customers, if your goal is to continue growing then you might want to assign a percentage of your net income to an ongoing advertising campaign; initially, however, before potential customers even know your business exists, you will need to use a different method to determine how much money to spend.

While you might like to, don't expect to start off with a bang, because it takes time and money to discover the best promotional techniques. At first your efforts might not yield much response, so don't blow your budget with a splashy all-out campaign. Instead, it is wise to put a little money into several different advertising methods in order to learn which are the most productive for you and your business. But how much money should you put at risk? One approach is to determine the cost of different promotional tactics and to work backward; i.e., if it costs a given amount to advertise in a certain way or ways, and these routes seem to have the best chances of success, then that amount is what should be spent, even if it is borrowed money (within reason, of course).

## What Is Your Message?

Whatever your message, make it consistent and persistent. Plan a promotion that is long-range and that clearly establishes the image you wish to project. Each element in your promotion should reinforce past advertising messages. Many of the large corporations and chains use the same style of advertising over and over again in an effort to build a lasting impression in the minds of consumers. The arches of McDonald's call forth a certain image, as do the bow tie and wire-rimmed glasses of Orville Redenbacher and the nothing-to-do plight of the Maytag repairman. Of course, you will be advertising on a much smaller scale, but like the big corporations you should try to develop an image and use it in every piece of promotional material you put out. Ways to write your message are discussed later in this chapter.

## Promotional Campaigns Directed to the Immediate Area

Promoting a business within a limited area can be just as challenging as promoting one nationwide, and many of the methods used for one are inappropriate for the other.

### SIGNS, SIGNS, AND MORE SIGNS

Signs are one of the easiest ways to get your business message before the public. Some are practically free, costing only the paint and elbow grease needed to apply them, while others can be costly.

The message on a sign should be simple and brief, but with the key words identifying the type of business in large letters. The telephone number should also be in large print. If possible, make a sign unusual so it will be noticed and add something visual so it will be remembered. See the examples in the illustration.

A sign in the front yard or one hanging from the mailbox is one of the simplest ways to let people know about your business. The size of a yard sign will be limited by the rules of the zoning board in your town, but a 2' × 2' sign is commonly acceptable. Some cities prohibit yard signs but will allow signs on a porch or in a window; other cities prohibit all signs on residential property. Elaborate signs with neon and plastic, portable signs, and signs with electronic displays are not appropriate or acceptable in residential neighborhoods.

Any vehicle used for business purposes should certainly bear a sign. Family automobiles could have either a painted sign or a couple of inexpensive magnetic ones that can be removed when the vehicles are converted to personal use (although many home business owners are happy to keep the business signs displayed at all times). Business trucks should display signs with two bits of information in bold print: the kind of service provided and the business's telephone number.

Some home businesses located on busy streets take advantage of their location by using signs on their trucks, cars, and vans as an effective after-hours advertising tool. These businesses park business vehicles where they are readily visible, and at night flood the vehicle signs with light.

A more expensive type of sign is the billboard. Billboards are rented for fixed periods of time, usually a minimum of three months, and the rental fee is based on the size and location of the sign. Larger billboards cost more, and those in high-traffic areas carry a higher rental fee than do those in less desirable locations. Although billboards effectively draw attention to a business, their cost is prohibitive for most home businesses. Placing signs on and in public transportation is still another way to advertise, but again, the cost can be a deterrent for the small business.

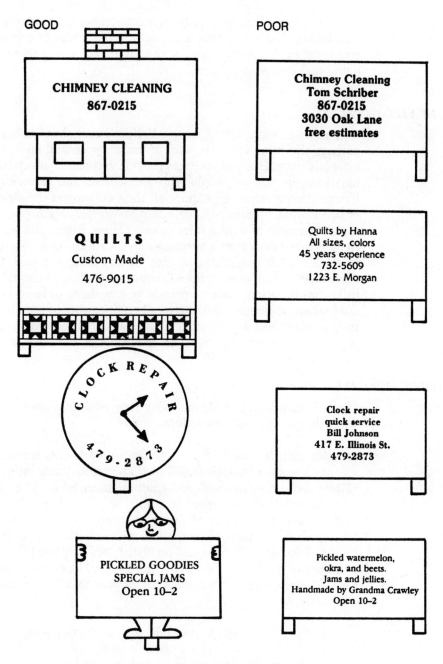

GOOD

POOR

CHIMNEY CLEANING
867-0215

Chimney Cleaning
Tom Schriber
867-0215
3030 Oak Lane
free estimates

QUILTS
Custom Made
476-9015

Quilts by Hanna
All sizes, colors
45 years experience
732-5609
1223 E. Morgan

CLOCK REPAIR
479-2873

Clock repair
quick service
Bill Johnson
417 E. Illinois St.
479-2873

PICKLED GOODIES
SPECIAL JAMS
Open 10–2

Pickled watermelon,
okra, and beets.
Jams and jellies.
Handmade by Grandma Crawley
Open 10–2

*Examples of well-designed signs whose essential message may be seen at a glance, compared with examples of poorly designed signs.*

Small signs can be just as attention-grabbing as big ones. Wearing a name tag on a business suit or uniform has a way of getting people's attention and is another good way to reinforce a business name. Such name tags cost just pennies.

## THE YELLOW PAGES

Yes, it costs to be listed in the Yellow Pages, but such a listing is perhaps the most effective way to inform potential customers about your business. The Yellow Pages provide "targeted" advertising, meaning it is directed to people who are seeking the service or product listed. Many businesses acquire all their customers through this form of advertising. Nordhaus Research of Southfield, Michigan, has shown that 94 percent of adults refer to the Yellow Pages, and 83 percent of them either call or visit a business they locate through this source. The telephone book publisher provides art and design service. Unlike the signs discussed above, Yellow Pages advertisements should be chockfull of information, because people look at them to learn exactly who does what. Someone repairing small engines should list all the brands they service, and a photographer will attract more business by mentioning the events covered, such as weddings, reunions, and dances.

## FLIERS AND CALLING CARDS

Fliers, selectively placed, can bring new business. Some examples of ways they might be used follow:

- A flier calling attention to a résumé preparation service could be tacked on a bulletin board near an employment office.
- Fliers about hospital beds and equipment rental could be tucked under windshields parked at hospitals.
- Fliers advertising air-conditioner preventive maintenance might be stuffed in mailboxes or between doors in early spring; furnace maintenance fliers could be distributed in early fall.
- Notices of hauling services might be posted at auction houses.
- A lawn care or delivery service might post fliers at a senior citizen's center.

Calling cards are an inexpensive yet effective way to attract customers. Cards can be handed directly to the prospective customer or left in a calling-card holder in an appropriate place. Many businesses will allow small businesses offering services that complement their own to display calling cards on a desk or counter. Here are some examples of targeted calling card display:

| Type of business | Display locations for calling cards |
|---|---|
| Furniture refinisher | Antique, paint, and hardware stores |
| Accountant | Office supply stores, banks |
| Music teacher | Musical instrument, record, and tape stores |
| Caterer | Wedding and bridal shops |

## WORD-OF-MOUTH PROMOTION

A word-of-mouth recommendation from a satisfied customer is the best free promotion you can get. Many small businesses have blossomed through the kind words of pleased customers, but just as many have folded because disgruntled people spread the word that the work was inferior or the service lacking. It might be a good idea to send thank-you notes to those who have referred clients to you. This will not go unnoticed, and you will probably get another referral from the source if the opportunity arises.

Businesses sometimes use former customers to convince potential customers their work is reliable. If you plan to use a list of references, ask your customers if they will agree to have their names included, and if they would be willing to have people contact them about your work. This approach is particularly effective if you have done work for people who are well known in the community, because you can benefit from their name recognition.

## WORD-OF-MOUTH POWER

A satisfied customer is a delight, and a talkative satisfied customer can be a great boon to your business.

There is, in the backroads of southern Indiana, a man named Brett Nalley whose home business is timber logging. He depends on his customers to spread the message that he is one of the best. It seems that many people who own wooded land are caught between wanting to cut the mature timber and make a profit and wanting to keep their land intact and unspoiled. Some loggers fell trees with little regard for the damage they leave behind, while others make an effort to fell trees so as to save the young ones and leave the land as unscathed as possible. Brett Nalley and his crew have gained a reputation for selectively cutting trees, protecting the land and standing trees, and getting the best price for the cut timber by having several buyers bid on it. His reputation is worth more than any fancy advertisement could possibly be, and his business grows through the word-of-mouth promotions he gets from satisfied customers.

## TALKING YOURSELF INTO BUSINESS

Any respectable technique that will get your business name before the public is worth pursuing. If you are, for example, a counselor, lawyer, consultant, artist, or tax preparer, make yourself available for speeches and interviews. Just recently I attended a meeting at which a tax consultant spoke to a group of artists. You can be sure the speaker (who works out of her home) will pick up some jobs from that lecture, and, in addition, she was paid $50 for the talk. It seems there are many organizations trying to find speakers for their meetings, and once you give a lecture, you will be surprised at the number of people asking you to speak to their groups.

Public service workshops and participation in community events are good ways to attract free publicity, and community colleges are always seeking speakers with expertise to conduct workshops and seminars. A nurse specializing in home care could become more visible in a community by offering to conduct free CPR classes. A florist could offer an evening seminar on floral design that could either be free or by fee; sales could result if the floral designs are made from flowers the florist sells. This same approach is frequently used by artists in stained glass who teach free classes but sell the glass and supplies the students need. An enthusiastic student attempting to craft the perfect stained glass window can spend a lot of money, and that student may be a customer long after the class ends.

## GETTING INVOLVED, GETTING ACQUAINTED, AND GETTING BUSINESS

People are more inclined to take their business to people they know, rather than to total strangers. Thus, the more contacts you make, the more business will come your way. An insurance salesman might coach Little League, or a real estate agent might pick up business by joining service organizations and social groups. You can make acquaintances and contacts at church; through political and professional gatherings; at alumni, social, and networking meetings—almost any place where people gather. There is nothing wrong with using these contacts to further your business interests. It's an acceptable part of the capitalist system.

## LOCAL RADIO, TELEVISION, AND NEWSPAPERS

The local media can be used in two ways, either for free publicity or for paid advertisements.

***Free Media Coverage.*** Some people are masters at promoting themselves, and they know how to milk the media for a great deal of free publicity. Using a little ingenuity, you can pick up an interview on television or in the newspapers and thus receive the kind of publicity you can't buy. The nurse who offers free CPR lessons would probably have no problem getting a story in the local papers or on radio and television. Of course, a mention of the private nursing business would creep into the story. The same holds true for an artist giving an art show. I've seen artists surrounded by television crews anxious to catch a preview on film, and all that was needed to bring them, with cameras in hand, was a simple news release. Anything that might interest the public—a special collection, an unusual service, a seasonal activity— will be attractive to the media. Don't be shy about initiating the contact, because if you don't "blow your own horn," who will? If nothing about your business seems newsworthy, you can send out a news release prior to National Small Business Week (a nationally proclaimed week in early May) telling about your small business and its place in the community. You may think this isn't news, but it certainly is. Remember that newspaper, television, and radio reporters are looking for stories, and if you provide them with a well-organized news release that can be read or printed as is, or one that is a good lead for a story, they will often jump at the chance to use it. You might also include photographs, because this reduces the reporter's effort in putting together the story and makes it more appealing to use. Once the media people learn you do something a little out of the ordinary, they will keep returning, looking for the next story, and the whole publicity thing will gather momentum on its own.

***Paid Local Media Advertising.***   If you can't find an angle to attract free publicity, then you might promote your business through advertisements. Generally, the printed page is more effective and more economical than radio or television simply because the information is available, on paper, to be studied, circled, or clipped out for later use. Television ads that ask viewers to call a certain number for more information may be unproductive, because few people are ready to jot down a phone number that is so briefly mentioned. When it is available on printed media, the number is available when needed.

A newspaper advertisement can either be a classified listing or a display ad. Classifieds are much less expensive, and thus more accessible to the small home business. They can very effectively target an audience. For example, an automobile painter or mechanic might be listed in the "Cars for Sale" section, or someone who does hauling might be listed under the "Furniture For Sale." The trick is to place the ad in the category most appropriate for the business.

Display ads, if run over long periods, can be useful in establishing a desired image, as discussed earlier. They should always use the same format, even if the information changes. After awhile, viewers learn to associate a certain "look" with the name and function of a specific business. Long-running ads usually cost considerably less per printing than those printed only one or two times. You can design your own display ads or hire freelancers to do this for you. Advertisement content is discussed later in this chapter.

## MISCELLANEOUS PROMOTION TECHNIQUES

There are other ways to promote your business that are either free or very inexpensive. Prior to the Christmas gift-giving holidays, a craftsperson can have an open house and sale, sending invitations to past clients and a news release to the local media. Music and dance teachers or day-care operators might stage recitals or shows that are announced in the media and attended not only by parents of current students, but also by parents of prospective students. Also, chambers of commerce often sponsor business fairs at which members show their wares and attract customers. These events usually pull in lots of buyers.

Would it be appropriate for you and your family to wear caps, T-shirts, or jackets with the family business name emblazoned on them? What about sponsoring a neighborhood baseball team with the team members wearing your commercial name? Calendars work throughout the year—maybe at a subliminal level—reminding the user of the source. Desk pads keep the name of the giver just under the user's nose, and the same applies to pencils and matchbooks. How many times have you absentmindedly glanced at a pencil you were using or

---

## PROMOTION METHODS

### PROMOTION METHODS USED TO ATTRACT CUSTOMERS FROM THE IMMEDIATE AREA

#### Paid Methods of Advertising

Two-step marketing
   Step 1: Classified or display advertisements in local papers
   Step 2: Mailings to respondents to advertisements
Local television and radio
Billboards
Signs on public transportation and in public areas
Fliers stuffed in mailboxes, on doorknobs, under auto windshield wipers
Yellow Pages advertising
Products with business name imprinted on them, such as calendars, pencils,
   matchbooks, telephone pads, shopping bags, and calling cards

*Free Methods of Promotion*

Publicity in local papers—special-interest stories
Local television and radio—news releases
Signs on cars and trucks
Signs in yard
Open house
Word-of-mouth recommendations
Speeches, seminars, and classes given by business owner (related to business)
Exhibitions at malls and shopping centers

*PROMOTION METHODS USED TO ATTRACT WIDELY DISPERSED CUSTOMERS*

*Paid Methods of Advertising*

Two-step marketing
    Step 1: Advertisements (classified or display) in magazines, trade journals,
        special-interest magazines
    Step 2: Mailings to respondents to ads
Direct mail to purchased mailing lists
Television and radio (limited value due to cost)

*FREE METHODS OF PROMOTION*

News release of new product to specialty journals

---

at a matchbook found in your pocket and reflected on when you got it? These articles are doing their job—reminding you of the business that paid for the pencil or matches.

Of course, there are many other ways to promote your business—from searchlights swinging through the night sky to airplanes pulling signs—but many of the more unusual forms of advertising aren't appropriate for the home business. Besides, you don't need theatrics. Instead, your advertising campaign should be a steady reminder to the buying public that you are in business to meet their needs.

## Promotional Campaigns Directed to Widely Dispersed Markets

The methods used to attract customers dispersed over large areas are different from the methods used to attract them to a local business. You will need to either identify and mail advertisements directly to potential customers or reach them through advertisements in the media.

## DIRECT-MAIL ADVERTISING

Direct-mail advertising is the most expensive type of advertising, but it is also the one most preferred by major mail-order companies. It works best for items priced between $50 and $200. It is less effective for more expensive items; likewise, it is not the best sales technique for inexpensive items because the product, if sold, will bring in little more than the cost of the mailing lists, catalogs, and postage.

The problem with direct mail is that a large number of companies are using the same selling technique, which has caused the average household and business to be inundated with piles of brochures and catalogs that arrive through the mail. Many of them are tossed into the "circular file" without being opened. Each discarded catalog cost somebody some money. In fact, it cost somebody quite a lot of money. A simple, rather commonplace mailing costs at least $.50 per piece, and a catalog or brochure printed in color on slick paper costs much more. This includes not only the printing cost but also mailing list rental, mailing preparation, and postage.

The average response to a direct-mail campaign is only 1 percent; if the response reaches 3 to 4 percent, the campaign is exceptional. Accordingly, if 10,000 brochures are mailed, 100 responses can be expected, but there may be as many as 300 to 400 responses. So, the question each advertiser must ask is, "Is direct-mail advertising cost-effective for my product or service?" It takes very little calculating to answer that question. If you receive 100 responses from a 10,000 piece mailing, and it costs $.50 for each piece sent, then *each response* would have cost $50.00 (10,000 × $.50 ÷ 100). Or, if you get the exceptional 4 percent return, then each response would cost $12.50 (10,000 × $.50 ÷ 400)—still pretty high.

The above calculations are based on the response rates you might expect from "cold calling"—that is, trying to sell to people with whom you have had no prior contact. Direct-mail cold calling usually involves using a list purchased from a mail-order listing company. The rate of response increases dramatically if the mailing list is composed of past customers or people who have expressed an interest in your product or service or in related products or services. Developing a profitable mailing list composed of past customers or inquiries takes time and money. It can be done in at least two ways. One way is to purchase mailing lists and make a customized list composed of those who respond to mailings; the other is to get an initial response through an advertisement, which will be discussed shortly.

Finding mailing lists is no problem, as there are companies that specialize in putting lists together. Whether you know it or not, your name is for sale, and you can be sure that whenever you buy something through the mail, join an organization, or subscribe to a magazine, your name will be added to lists and sold to others trying to find customers. The usual minimum rental list is composed of 5,000 names. The cost for a list depends on the targeted group, but it averages around $45 per thousand names (4.5 cents per name and address). These names are supplied on mailing labels. Some direct mail companies will handle the complete procedure, from printing the material to be mailed, to folding and inserting it into envelopes, to metering and mailing; others supply only the list of names and addresses.

Target lists are composed of people with special interests or those with membership in specific groups. Lists are available for such diverse categories as art collectors, book buyers, manufacturing companies, business proprietors, college and university students, short people, fat people, left-handed people, farmers, gardeners, widows, teachers, lawyers, mothers, grandmothers, and on and on. You can request that a list be limited to those within a category but confined to certain geographical areas. Of course, by targeting the correct list the percentage of response will increase and advertising/mailing money will not be wasted on those who have no conceivable interest in a product or service.

An extensive list of firms that sell mailing lists can be found in the free Small Business Association publication *National Mailing List Houses*, but companies selling lists are located throughout the country. You might start by looking in the Yellow Pages to find one in your immediate area.

## TWO-STEP MARKETING

Running an ad for the purpose of locating people interested in a product or service and enticing them to respond and request more information is the first step in "two-step marketing." The second step is to send promotional material to the respondents and ask for an order. Two-step advertising is probably the most cost-effective and thus the most appealing way to bring in business to those operating on a restricted budget.

Because of the tremendous expense involved, it is the very rare home business that can mount an advertising campaign via national radio or television, and for this reason national radio and television advertising is not discussed here. This section is limited to advertisements in newspapers, trade, and specialty magazines.

Your first task in two-step marketing is to locate the publications in which you might advertise. There are several directories that list nearly all publications, of which *Gale Directory of Publications* is probably the best. Other directories list publications according to groups, that is, all those directed to the aging population are listed together, as are those directed to farmers, health fanatics, gardeners, auto enthusiasts, and so forth (see *Ulrich's International Periodicals* or ask your librarian for aid in locating appropriate directories). These directories list the size of the readership and the publisher's address, among other things. If you are considering a publication as a possible place to advertise, write or phone (if there is an 800 number) the publisher and ask for a rate sheet and a media kit. You will receive a profile of the readership, the number of readers, demographics, etc. You will also receive a printed form explaining the various rates for display and classified ads, as well as a schedule of due dates. You will quickly discover that advertisements in large national magazines cost quite a bit, but advertising in specialty or trade magazines is within the reach of many small businesses.

***Classified and Display Advertisements.***   There are two types of advertisements to be considered. The first type, and certainly the most accessible to the home business, is the classified ad; the second type is the display ad. A classified ad is considerably less expensive than a display ad, and for that reason classified ads are the usual ads used by small businesses.

The following example illustrates the difference in cost between classified and display ads. Let's say a travel agency is trying to sell "trips for the retired but young at heart." These trips should be advertised in publications read by older people. A quarter page display ad in *Modern Maturity* costs $3,000. That sounds like a huge sum, but this magazine has a circulation of 17,000,000 and reaches many more people than the circulation suggests, since some of the households to which it is mailed have two or more readers and it is seen in doctors' waiting rooms and other offices. The cost of an advertisement should be divided by the circulation in order to determine the cost per reader. Therefore, you can figure that a display ad in *Modern Maturity* costs no more than $0.000176 per viewing person ($3,000 divided by 17 million). On the other hand, the same size ad in a small newspaper, let's say, in a retirement community in Florida, might cost only $150—but the circulation is only 25,000, so the cost is $0.006 per person, or over 30 times the cost of the ad in the larger publication. So, an apparent bargain is not always a real bargain.

If advertising money is tight—and it usually is for a small business—it makes sense to consider a classified ad. A classified ad in a large national magazine might cost $5 or $10 per word; a classified might cost as low as $0.20 per word in a small newspaper. Thus, the classified ad "Customized trips for the retired but young at heart; write *Wild Life*, P.O. Box 12, Martinsville, IN 46137" could cost less than $5 in a small newspaper and approximately $75 to $150 in a national magazine, as compared to $150 and $3,000 for a display ad. It's obvious why small businesses primarily rely on classified ads to get their message across.

When you evaluate various publications and try to select the ones most appropriate for your advertisements, you should realize that the number of people who see the ad may not be the most important factor. One type of publication could draw more responses per viewer than another. For example, if the above ad for customized trips is placed in a small retirement community newspaper, it could give the impression that the trip is being promoted by a small, exclusive agency, which could make it a more appealing announcement of a travel adventure than if it were advertised nationally. Techniques for assessing advertising success are discussed later in this chapter.

**AN EXAMPLE OF A WELL-DESIGNED DISPLAY ADVERTISEMENT (STEP ONE IN TWO-STEP MARKETING)**

*A well-designed display ad for table pads.*

Note that:

- The name of the item being offered is prominently displayed and is the most visible part of the ad.
- A drawing of the product reinforces the image of the item for sale.
- A toll-free 800 number is provided to entice those interested to call for more information.
- The ad shows which credit cards can be used to pay for purchases through the display of the acceptable cards in the corner of the ad.

Advertising in special-interest magazines is a good way to reach a limited audience for a reasonable price. A pattern maker could advertise in craft magazines for much less than in general-interest magazines, and he or she would probably get a better response because craftspersons read craft magazines. Similarly, a firm wishing to sell hand-tied fishing flys would get a better response by advertising in fishing magazines instead of in general-interest publications.

***Free Publicity in National Trade Journals.***   I am constantly amazed at the wonderful publicity available at the national level for the cost of a single postage stamp. Listing your new products in trade journals and submitting stories about your business are especially effective ways to promote your product or service without spending a dime.

Trade journals are magazines that are directed to a limited audience and geared to a specific subject. There are trade journals written for computer users, financial advisers, aluminum metal crafters, health professionals, pet owners, engineers, real estate agents, gift manufacturers, and so forth. Many of these journals have a special section in which new products are listed at no cost for the listing. A photograph of the product may even be included. Some journals provide a reply card for the reader to request more information. The publisher then sends the manufacturer the list of readers who have indicated they want to learn more about the product—all as a completely free service. It doesn't get any better than this! My family's manufacturing business has had new products listed in this way, and the listings have generated more responses and for a longer period than our regular paid advertisements. Trade magazines are listed in directories such as *Gale Directory of Publications, Literary Market Place,* and *Writer's Market,* which are all available in libraries.

## Writing Your Own Promotional Material

Write your own copy (advertising material) if you can communicate clearly and persuasively. Many successful small business persons produce their own advertisements, catalogs, and brochures, and they have a style that eludes the professional ad writer, who must always be trying to think of something original and catchy. Many business people attribute their success to their own particular writing style. Of course, the criterion on which to judge the quality of a piece of promotional material is, "Does it bring in sales?" If you are not adept at writing copy, seek professional advertising services (look under "Advertising" in the Yellow Pages).

## WRITING A NEWS RELEASE

A news release has a specific format that should be followed. A news release should include the name, address, and telephone number of the sender; the current date; and the words "for immediate release" (or the date to be released) in the top right-hand corner. Start the story with a title that has a "hook" to get the attention of the reader (it may or may not be changed by the editor). The story should be brief and to the point and should contain the basic facts and necessary details. Be sure to indicate who the news service should contact for more information. A news release might be printed in daily newspapers or aired on television or radio as written, or it might be developed into a story by a reporter. As a business owner you'll be glad to take either or both, whatever you can get, because it is free publicity.

## NEWS RELEASE

A news release should include the following information:

The source of the information (name, address, telephone number)
A date or time to release
A headline
The information, limited to one page (basic facts and interesting details)
Where to get more information

The release should be written on plain paper, not on letterhead, with wide margins and a lot of white space above the head for editorial comments.

An example of a news release follows:

FOR IMMEDIATE RELEASE

Gayle Williams, President
Flower Power
2357 Cranbury Neck Road
Martinsville, NY 08512
(609) 628-2997

The Sun Flower Girls, a local gardening club, is holding its annual floral arrangement seminar on May 12, at the Civic Auditorium. Classes are open to the public and will be divided into beginning and advanced students. A $6.00 registration fee will cover morning coffee and a luncheon. The seminar will end with a competition among the participants with the winning prize in each category being 50 pounds of sunflower seeds. Preregistration is required. Entry forms can be picked up at Flower Power, located on Cranbury Neck Road, from 8:30 A.M. to 4:30 P.M. daily.

For more information contact either Gayle Williams at the number listed above or Kathy Parker at (609) 628-4336.

### WRITING ADVERTISEMENTS FOR TWO-STEP MARKETING

In order to write a good advertisement you need to understand clearly its purpose and your goal. The *purpose* of both classified and display ads is to find prospective customers. Ads should provoke a response, whether it's an order or a request for more information. Your *goal* is to make a sale. It would be nice if each reader would slip a check into the mail, ordering your product, but that rarely happens and it is unrealistic to expect it. The usual response to an advertisement is a request for more information.

How can you encourage readers to ask for more information? The answer is simple: Don't tell them everything. An advertisement will provoke a bigger response if it stimulates interest but doesn't ask for an order. Instead, follow-up information should be sent in the form of a catalog or brochure. Some businesses offer to send a catalog in a reader's SASE (self-addressed stamped envelope). This request separates those who are truly interested from the merely curious, which is important because each catalog and brochure costs money to print and mail. On the other hand, quite a bit of money is spent on ads just trying to get a nibble; therefore, it might be worthwhile for you to pay the postage to send the reader your promotional material, because when an inquirer must send a SASE, requests have been shown to be reduced by as much as 35 percent.

Another way to weed out nonserious responders is to charge for the catalog and deduct the cost from the first order. This approach will reduce your expenses but still attract those who are interested enough to put their money on the line. People usually don't like to write checks for $.50 or $1.00; however, they might be more willing to send postage stamps instead of a check or money, so you might charge a few stamps for a catalog. You can always use the stamps for business purposes. Your decision about charging or not charging for a catalog will depend on the type of goods you are selling. If you are promoting something that must be seen to be believed (gorgeous or clever products), or if your line contains a wide diversity of products, you might be better off not charging just to get the merchandise before interested people.

Both classified and display ads should be designed to attract attention and induce readers to ask for more information. Both should follow the guidelines listed below:

1. The product name or description should be stated in the first word or words in a classified ad and should be the most prominent word or words in a display ad.
2. The reader should be urged to write or call for more information.
3. The name of the advertiser should be included.
4. The address or telephone number should be easy to find.

Classified ads are just a few words long, yet contain all of the basic elements. See the examples below:

BABY CLOTHES, customized for your child. Free catalog from TOTS, 1-800-796-8323. (11 words)

JEWELRY, two-for-one sale of the exotic and unusual. Send 4 stamps for catalog now! HANDMADE BAUBLES, P.O. Box 239, Jackson, TN 82633. (21 words)

WORK-AT-HOME REPORT, your business newsletter. Special offer for limited time to new subscribers. For sample copy write, 12221 Beaver Pike, Jackson OH 45640. (24 words)

BODY BUILDING VIDEOS $19.95. Free Brochure 1-800-472-7394. (This last advertisement has only seven words but supplies the essential information.)

These brief ads contain particular words that have been shown in advertising analysis studies to promote inquiries. They include: *free, now, handmade, sale, your, new,* and *special offer.* As you write advertisements, try to incorporate words that appeal to the readers sense of self (*you, your*), sense of greed (*free, save, sale, special offer*), and sense of urgency (*now, limited time*). Other persuasive words are *new, win, easy, love, health, results, proven, guarantee,* and *youthful.*

Display ads contain the same information as classifieds, but they are more difficult to produce because they require a layout. When the

---

### FEDERAL TRADE COMMISSION RULES

1. *The Mail-order 30-day rule* states that it is deceptive to solicit orders through the mail that cannot be filled within the specified time. If no time is stated, then you must fill the order within 30 days. If you are unable to comply within the 30-day limitation, then you must notify the buyer and give the option to cancel the order. Failure to comply with this ruling can result in stiff penalties.

2. *Truth in advertising* maintains that it is unlawful to mislead buyers. Advertisements must not only be true, but they must not give a false impression to the buyer.

3. *Endorsements and testimonials* can be printed if the sources are identified and if the endorsements and testimonials are the result of actual use of the product or service. You must have written permission to use people's names in this manner.

4. A *guarantee* must be clearly explained, including the terms, conditions, and the way the company will meet the guarantee. Warranties inform buyers that products will perform in a given way, and claims made in advertisements may constitute a warranty that places legal obligations on the seller.

ad is submitted to a magazine or newspaper it should be "camera ready," although some magazines and newspapers will provide layout and typesetting services for a fee. If you have no background in graphic design, there are several places to seek help. An advertising agency can do the work for you, or, if you can do the copywriting but not the layout, then you might take your copy to a commercial artist who offers typesetting and design services. Display ads can also be produced through the use of computers that have graphics capabilities. This computerized graphics service is readily available and usually costs less than work drawn by hand.

## Catalogs and Other Sales Material

After placing a few advertisements, don't sit back and wait for the orders to roll in. You'll need to prepare promotional material to send to those who respond. These people warrant special attention because they have indicated an interest in your product, and the promotional material you send to them should be designed to make a sale.

Keep the message in your promotional mailings simple and repetitive. The average American receives thousands of advertising messages every day. Even though the material has been requested, make sure that what you send is easy to understand and that placing an order is easy to do. Good promotion takes customers by the hand and leads them through the message, asks them to buy, and then helps them place an order by phone or mail.

A follow-up mailing might include a brochure or catalog. It should certainly contain a price sheet and an order form with a postage-paid envelope or a telephone number (preferably an 800 number) where an order can be placed. It might also contain samples of fabric, testimonials, or any other materials or information that will convince the inquirer that your offer is worth the inquirer's money. Money-back guarantees have been shown to increase sales by as much as 40 percent, so you might consider such an offer. Don't send too much material in a follow-up packet, because it will only confuse the receiver or take too much time to read, which increases the chances of it being discarded.

Where can you get catalogs and brochures printed? Simple printing on white or colored paper can be done by any printer in town (prices vary, so look around), but slick-papered, colored catalogs need to be put together by professionals equipped to do this specialty work. You can either provide the printer with photographs and copy, or you can pay an advertising agency to provide this service. The latter option can be very expensive. Below is a list of several competitively priced printers that produce brochures, catalogs, booklets, and quality fliers, but there are many others, perhaps even in your area. Consult your telephone directory for listings.

Morgan Printing and Publishing, 900 Old Koenig Lane, Suite 137, Austin, TX 78756. Will do smaller quantities than most other printers (250 to 2,500 copies).

Mohawk Valley Printing, 309 Miller Avenue, Herkimer, NY 13350. Send $2.50 for material that helps in making a camera-ready pamphlet or catalog.

GraphiColor, 3018 Western Avenue, Seattle, WA 98121. Specializes in affordable color printing.

Direct Press/Modern Litho, 386 Oakwood Road, Huntington Station, NY 11746. Offers quality color printing at competitive prices.

## Assessing Advertising Success

Developing an advertising campaign is an ongoing process. Plan your strategy and place ads in different publications to learn which publications bring the best responses. Also, test which type of ad and promotional material provokes the greatest interest in your product or service. Then use your findings to build your campaign.

Accurate records are needed to evaluate the success of each advertisement. If you place several ads in different publications simultaneously, whether they are in local papers or in national magazines, use a "marker" (a slightly different return address) in each so you can evaluate the effectiveness of the various efforts. The return address might include a "Department A" in one magazine, "Department B" in the next, and so on. The source of the advertisement should be noted and tabulated as each response is received.

The cost-effectiveness of each advertisement can be determined by keeping records that include:

1. Place of advertisement (which magazine or newspaper)
2. Cost of advertisement
3. Type of advertisement (classified or display, wording used)
4. Number of respondents
5. Number of sales
6. Dollar volume of sales
7. Cost of advertisement per sale

Similar records should be kept on direct-mail campaigns. Keep these records in the simplest, easiest, least time-consuming way possible, and base future advertising efforts on the success of past ones.

There are several resources that might be of value as you develop your promotional campaign. They include the following:

*Advertising Age.* This weekly magazine addresses current advertising techniques and discusses different advertising campaigns and agencies. Crain Communications, 40 Rush Street, Chicago, IL 60611.

*Associated Press Stylebook.* This book gives detailed instructions for writing promotional material and is considered to be the definitive source for press release writing. Addison-Wesley Publishing Co., Jacob Way, Reading, MA 00867. Revised in 1987. Available in many libraries and in bookstores ($10.95).

National Mail Order Classified. P.O. Box 5, Sarasota, FL 33578. This organization will do the work for you by placing classified ads in different magazines to meet your needs and charging a percent of the cost.

*How to Write a Good Advertisement,* by Victor O. Schwab. This book explains how to write good advertising copy. $16 postpaid, from National Mail Order Association, 5818 Venice Boulevard, Los Angeles, CA 90019.

*The Directory of Directories.* Gale Research. Lists and describes over 9,000 directories and buyer's guides. Found in libraries.

*Product Warranties and Servicing.* If you are thinking of offering consumer guarantees, read this booklet. Free from the U.S. Department of Commerce, Office of Consumer Affairs, Washington, DC 20233.

*How to Write and Use Simple Press Releases That Work,* by Kate Kelly. An excellent how-to guide, with sample press releases and a media resource directory. $7 postpaid from Visibility Enterprises, 450 West End Avenue, New York, NY 10024. Also available from Visibility Enterprises is *The Publicity Manual,* by Kate Kelly. A complete guide on how to get publicity. $29.95.

# 17   Marketing Procedures

Marketing procedures must be tailored to fit business needs, and the procedures used will depend on whether you are selling a product or a service. Procedures and strategies appropriate for each are discussed in this chapter.

## Retail (Direct) Sales of Manufactured or Crafted Merchandise

Manufactured or handcrafted items can be sold directly to consumers at retail prices through fairs or from a home studio or shop, or they can be sold wholesale to buyers who sell them to consumers. The largest wholesale outlets are retail stores, catalog houses, the government, and foreign markets.

### ART AND CRAFT FAIRS

Many people make crafted items during the winter months and spend summer weekends and vacation time making the rounds of art and craft fairs selling their goods. This is the only outlet used by many home crafters, some of whom have mastered the process of locating the best shows, packing and unpacking their wares, setting up attractive display booths, and bringing in the sales. Others become road weary and discover that they prefer to sell through other methods. There is definitely a skill to selling at art and craft fairs and making them profitable and enjoyable adventures.

*Crafty People Go to Fairs!*   Through the years buyers have grown to expect a large selection of handmade items at art and craft fairs, and these kinds of events have become the most lucrative direct outlet for handcrafted items. Several factors should be taken into consideration when you are deciding which fairs you will participate in because there can be a big difference between one fair and another. Selling opportunities depend upon selecting the correct type of occasion to display your wares.

There are two types of art and craft fairs. One type attracts less adventurous artists and craftspeople who make many items from a single pattern. The buyers and browsers who attend these fairs go for the "country look" and are inclined to purchase a lot of knickknacks and doodads to give as gifts. The other type of fair attracts sellers who produce original paintings or original crafted items, and the fair is juried, which means that work must be selected by a certain group of judges before it can appear in the show. These shows attract collectors of high-quality original crafts and artwork who are willing to pay the higher prices such pieces bring. It is important to evaluate your work and decide at what type of show it would receive the best response, that is, where you can make the most sales.

***Which Is the Fairest of Them All?***  Art and craft fairs have become very popular, and practically every community has one at some time during the year. Keep your ears and eyes open to learn about them. Attend fairs in your area and talk to exhibitors to learn which fairs are the most profitable, and contact your state arts commission or the local chamber of commerce for a list of the larger nearby fairs and shows. Also, fairs held throughout the nation are listed in *Craft Horizons*, published by the American Crafts Council, 44 West 53d Street, New York, NY 10019, and the *National Calendar of Indoor-Outdoor Art Fairs*, published by Henry Miles, 5423 New Haven Avenue, Ft. Wayne, IN 46803. These publications provide information concerning dates, fees, type of shows, past attendance, and persons to contact for further information.

As you try to decide if a fair is right for your work, and worth the time, money, and effort to attend, consider the points that follow.

1. *Number of attendees.*  Don't participate in a first-time show, because it will not have an established following. Instead, look for shows that consistently bring in large crowds. Show promoters will indicate the number who attend, but look at these numbers carefully. Is the fair located inside of a mall or outside under the trees in a park? If it is a mall show, do the numbers indicate the number of people who came to the mall during the show period or the actual number of people who browsed through the booths? How is this number determined? If the fair is in a park you can safely assume that most of the people who attend have come for the purpose of looking at the displays, but, again, how is the number of attendees determined?

2. *Facilities.*  Will the show be indoors or out? If it is outdoors,

can the sun, wind, or rain damage your goods, and is there an alternate location if the weather turns bad? If not, is there a rain date? Are tables, chairs, and electricity provided? How big is the booth space? If it is outdoors, will you be under an awning, trees, or in the sun?

3. *Distance.* How far is the fair from your home? Will you be away overnight, and, if so, can you stay in a camper or tent or will you need to pay for a motel room? Maybe it's close enough to go home in the evening and return the next day. Many fairs are two-day, Saturday-and-Sunday events. Is there security during the night, or must you pack up everything and set up your display again the next morning?

4. *Time of year.* Many fairs are held in spring and summer, perhaps because the weather is a delight, but these fairs are not as profitable for the exhibitors as those held in late fall or early winter. In fall, people start thinking about the gift-giving holidays and are inclined to purchase more gifts than in the middle of summer.

5. *Cost.* The cost of attending art and craft shows varies and depends on how far you must travel to reach the show, if you must pay for overnight lodging, and the booth fee. Of course, these expenses are 100 percent tax-deductible (except for the food bill, which is 80 percent deductible), so keep records and receipts for your expenses. Attending some fairs costs more than they bring in, but others can yield a nice profit.

**Preparing for the Fair.** There are several things you should do after deciding to participate in a fair; these things are listed below.

1. Send in the application form with your booth fee.

2. Make overnight arrangements, if necessary.

3. Build an inventory so you will have enough merchandise to make the outing worthwhile. Design products to sell at this type of gathering. Unless you are attending a juried show, don't expect to sell expensive or abstract art; for most shows it makes sense to produce moderately priced items that appeal to less-sophisticated tastes.

4. Design and build a display booth. Make a booth that can be easily assembled and disassembled if you expect to attend fairs as an ongoing activity. Your booth should be able to break down into a tidy package that can be transported from one place to another, yet should be sturdy enough to withstand a gust of wind. You may not always be able to park near your assigned area, so you may have to hand-carry or cart your booth—keep this in mind as you design it. Remember to incorporate into the booth design peg boards or other means of hanging goods.

5. Make a list of the things you'll need, including stapler, tape, display booth, cooler, foods, drinks, books to read, craft supplies (if you intend to craft while selling), change and money box, sales sheets, bags

and packing material for wrapping sold merchandise, boxes for carrying merchandise to the fair, calling cards and a calling card dispenser, electrical extension cords, chairs, a blanket, table coverings, umbrella, plastic sheeting to cover display in the event of rain, and a little more money than you expect to spend.

*Attracting Crowds and Making Sales.* Getting to the fair is just half of the battle—you also have to get the crowd to come into your den. Crowds tend to gather where there is some "action," and one way to draw people to your booth is to demonstrate or work at your craft or art during the show. Talk with people while you work. The longer someone lingers at your booth, the better chance you have to make a sale. Of course, while you are working someone else will need to watch over the merchandise and make sales transactions. Perhaps your spouse or a friend would be willing to take over that part of the operation. Sometimes a sale comes after the show has closed and an attendee has had time to think about where a piece might fit into his or her home. For this reason, have calling cards or printed information available to hand to the interested but not quite committed browsers.

## SALES FROM HOME OR STUDIO

Some artists and craftspeople don't care for the hustle and bustle of the fair atmosphere but prefer to work at home and sell their goods to customers who arrive at the door. You may prefer this type of selling arrangement, but its success depends on getting people to your home or studio. This works well for those who live either in heavily traveled areas or in a place where other craftspeople have gathered to form an art colony, where people expect artwork to be sold. Selling from the home or studio works well in tourist areas where home/studios/shops line the streets. It also works well if the artist has developed a following and people seek out the studio to view and purchase work. Many artists and craftspeople sell all they can produce from their home studios by attracting buyers through word-of-mouth advertising and by selling to family, friends, and neighbors. Also, they might have an occasional show or special event to promote sales, especially around the gift-giving holidays.

Of course, selling from home is not limited to selling your own work. You can sell the artworks and crafted articles of others, and, as far as that goes, you can also sell other kinds of merchandise. Fill a need and you will find your home shop filled with customers.

Although much of the information in this book can be applied to a home retail business, there is much more to retailing than you might suspect. It would be a good idea to look over a few of the many publications dealing specifically with retail shops if you are considering retailing as your home business. The Small Business Administration (SBA) has several pamphlets on the subject, and copies are available at your local SBA office or by writing to SBA, P.O. Box 15434, Ft. Worth, TX 76119. Also, your local library no doubt has books on the subject of retailing.

## Wholesaling Manufactured or Crafted Merchandise

While *retailing* or *direct sales* involves personal contact with consumers through fairs, flea markets, and home sales, *wholesaling* is a form of selling that rarely puts the manufacturer in contact with the consumer. Instead, products are sold in bulk to retailers and other distributors who in turn sell to consumers.

Wholesale orders are usually for multiples of a given item, and most wholesalers have a minimum order to discourage small orders that are more trouble than they are worth. Manufactured consumer products can be wholesaled to different types of buyers, including retail shops, mail-order catalog outlets, institutions, and the government, and they can be exported to foreign markets. Each outlet is discussed below.

The merchandise shipped to buyers must be like the samples used to make the sale, and manufacturers need to be able to respond to orders quickly or within an agreed-upon shipment time. In fact, the time for shipment should be a part of the buy-sell contract.

While sales at a flea market or a craft show can be done with very little paperwork, wholesaling requires a more disciplined sales procedure, and it is necessary to fill in several types of business forms to complete the sales transaction. See the sidebar entitled "Business Forms Used Throughout the Selling Process."

### RETAIL OUTLETS

Retail outlets include gift shops, department stores, apparel shops and boutiques, hospital shops, drugstores, fabric centers, farm stores, museum shops, garden centers, and bookstores, to name only a few. It is to this group of dealers that most home manufacturers seek to sell their goods.

Most retail stores purchase merchandise at wholesale prices and sell at retail prices; the wholesale price is usually 50 percent of the retail price. It may seem unfair to manufacturers, but this heavy markup is needed to cover the costs of acquiring and maintaining the retail store, paying personnel, advertising, the loss that results when

## BUSINESS FORMS USED THROUGHOUT THE SELLING PROCESS

The following forms are used in the sales process, from the time merchandise is being considered until it is paid for. Standard business forms can be purchased from office supply catalogs or stores, or you can print your own.

*Price List:* Two price lists should be available to wholesale buyers, one listing the retail and the other listing the wholesale prices. Conditions of sale should be stated on the wholesale price list, including who pays shipping charges (usually the buyer), the extent of guarantees (if any), the return policy, and minimum order size. Leave space for new customers to list three credit references. If references are lacking, ship COD.

*Sales Order Form:* Some businesses use a sales order book, while others write the order directly on the purchase order form or on business letterhead. Whatever form is used, the order should be signed by the buyer.

*Invoice:* An invoice is a detailed list of goods shipped or services rendered and the price of each. This form should have the vendor's business name and address at the top, with space provided nearby for the buyer's name and address. It should also give the date the order is received, the shipping address, date of shipment, method of shipment, terms of payment, a description and quantity of goods ordered, price per unit, total cost, and shipping charges. From three to five copies of this form are needed for each sale. Use the copies as follows:

1. The original is sent to the customer.
2. One copy is kept in the vendor's files.
3. One copy becomes the packing slip with the prices blocked out.
4. One copy is sent at the end of the month to inform the buyer that payment is due.
5. The last copy is sent if the account is overdue.

*Packing Slip:* A packing slip should be packed with the merchandise so the buyer can check the contents of the shipment received. One of the invoice copies can be used for this purpose. This copy is usually a different color than any other business forms used and may be included in invoice packets. The words *Packing Slip* should appear in large letters at the top.

*Statement:* Statements are needed only for those customers who receive several shipments during a month. A statement states the sum of all invoices issued during a month. In lieu of this, a copy of each invoice can be sent to remind the customer of the total amount due.

*Purchase Order:* If an order is received over the phone, it is written on a purchase order. (When a sales call is made, the order may be written on an invoice or sales order form.) Either the merchandise is shipped immediately or a confirmation is sent to the buyer stating the shipment date. Purchase orders are also used when ordering from suppliers. This form indicates that you are more than a hobbyist, and it may help you get better prices.

merchandise does not move or from bad accounts, the cost of carrying inventory, and a myriad of other expenses incurred while operating a retail store. Retailing is a tough business, and that is why such a low percentage of new retailers become old retailers—most of them fail and go out of business.

Retail outlets can be reached through personal sales calls, sales representatives, trade shows, and merchandise marts (all discussed below), and through direct mailings from rented lists (discussed in Chapter 16).

**Personal Sales Calls.** Many small manufacturers and craftspeople make personal calls to retail shops in an effort to make sales. This is practical for a very brief period, when the business is just getting under way and there is more time than business. However, with any success at all, these people quickly discover that sales calls take too much time away from the other tasks of operating a business, and many of them seek outside help in the form of sales representatives.

**Sales Representatives.** Sales representatives, usually called sales reps, make their living selling for other people. They are the most reliable means for getting repeat orders and finding new customers. A sales rep may work for a single manufacturer or importer, or he or she may sell the products of numerous ones. A sales rep working for a single manufacturer or importer is usually paid a small salary and a commission on the goods sold, while reps who sell for many manufacturers or importers are usually paid only a commission on sales. A good sales rep can make a substantial income, but it takes a lot of "hustle" and requires representing products that sell well. Most sales reps work out of their homes, whether they represent one or many companies.

Do you need sales reps? The answer to that question is yes if you are producing more items than you sell. Sales reps are an effective way to get your products widely distributed. One of the first things you will learn is that if you don't ask for a sale, you won't get it. Your products must be seen to be purchased, and sales reps can get them before the buyers. You can undoubtably increase your sales by using sales reps.

If you are apprehensive about the rate of sales growth, concerned that you will get too many orders too fast, then start with just a few reps and add more as production increases. On the other hand, you may be able to increase production quickly and keep up with orders. My family's business discovered the effectiveness of selling through sales reps and hired many to carry our lines the first year we were in operation. Some of these reps worked very hard and earned a substantial sum, while others rarely sent in orders and were released from our sales agreement, particularly if they held rights to an exclusive territory.

Some important aspects of developing and maintaining a force of sales reps for your product are listed and discussed below.

*1. Locating Sales Reps.* Finding the right sales reps to sell your product is as important as finding the right employee to help you make it. You can hire either individual reps or sales rep organizations. It is easier to work through an organization of reps because the organization oversees distributing commission checks and keeps each of its reps informed about new developments. Also, sales rep organizations keep only aggressive reps in their groups, and thus you are spared the task of always looking for new reps to replace unproductive ones. Sales rep organizations seem to be somewhat more selective about the products they carry than are individual reps, and only handle lines that sell well. Some sales rep organizations maintain showrooms where merchandise is on display and where customers come to view the goods and place orders. These are usually located in large cities. You might get the impression that large-city showrooms are by far the best way to get your merchandise sold; however, you should keep in mind that a lot of merchandise is sold in small cities and in little out-of-the-way places to people who have never seen the inside of a showroom. In other words, there is room for both "uptown" rep organizations and reps who work alone and hit the backroads and small towns.

The easiest way to locate sales reps and sales rep organizations is to place classified advertisements in trade journals directed to the industry most closely related to the products you make. If you manufacture decorative paper plates, a journal directed to retailers of party supplies or giftware might be the place to advertise; if the paper plates are strictly the utilitarian type with no design, then maybe the fast food industry would be the targeted buyer and you would need to advertise for reps in trade journals directed to this segment of the market. In order to locate the appropriate trade journal, refer to the *Directory of Directories* distributed by Gale Research Company or ask for help in your library. After finding what you think might be the correct trade journal, study a few back issues to get a feel for the content and the readers to whom it is directed.

An advertisement to locate sales reps should not cost much— maybe $15 to $20. It should include a general description of the products you make, the territories that need to be covered (state that territories are still open as you start your search), and an address to which interested parties can respond. Also, check the "Lines Wanted" section in the journal; sales reps are always looking for new material to sell, and they place ads in an effort to expand their lines.

Some respondents to your advertisements will write long letters and tell you more than you want to know, others will send a résumé including other lines they carry, and still others will be very cagey and ask to see literature about your products before sending you further information. Follow up the most promising respondents. Ask for three references and, if you have access to credit checks, run a check on each applicant before welcoming him or her with open arms. After making your selection, send each rep an agreement that spells out the modus operandi, specifies the rate of commission and when it will be paid, and clearly defines the territory in which the rep can sell.

You can also find sales reps through agent listings. These are available from the Manufacturer's Agents National Association, located in Irvine, California, and the National Council of Salesman's Organization, located in New York, New York. Directories listing sales reps by industry are also published.

*2. Granting Exclusive Territory.* Most reps insist on exclusive selling rights within a defined geographical territory. They don't want to go into a store to sell your line only to find the products already on the shelves. A territory could be as large as several states, or it could consist of a single city, if the city is a very large one such as Chicago or New York. Some businesses pay a commission on all orders received within a rep's designated territory whether or not the rep actually takes the order (some shops phone in orders, others place orders in showrooms), but other businesses pay only on orders taken by the rep.

*3. Establishing Commission Rates.* When and how much should you pay a sales rep? There is no established across-the-board commission rate. However, there are rate ranges within specific fields. For instance, reps selling giftware usually get a 15 percent commission, but reps selling large industrial equipment or goods in huge lots usually make much less. It is important to offer the going rate in your specific product line, which can be learned by studying the sales rep ads in the trade journals. Reps on the West Coast usually expect a little higher rate than those in the Midwest and on the East Coast. Also, you can expect to pay more if the rep maintains a booth in a showroom, but this is probably money well spent because a permanent sales booth should bring in more orders.

Pay commissions monthly on orders that have been shipped and accepted. *Always pay on time.* These people are your sales force; they make the difference between getting your product sold or not, and you must make sure they are treated fairly and paid on time. Keep a record sheet for each rep and record orders as they are shipped. At the end of each month tally the orders and pay the commission. Never pay commissions on advance orders.

*4. Providing Supplies and Samples.* Each sales rep will need a variety of supplies and a set of samples. When you select samples for reps to show, keep in mind they will be more inclined to cart them around if they are small and easy to handle. Usually your reps will also have samples from other companies they represent that they are expected to carry into each stop on their sales route. You can be sure that big, unwieldy samples will get tossed into the back seat of the car and the smaller samples will get displayed.

*Charge the reps for their samples.* This point is very important because sample costs can become a big expense if you give samples to reps. You shouldn't make a profit on sample items—just cover the cost. The generally accepted charge for samples is 60 percent of the wholesale price. You can deduct that amount from the first commission check. If a rep wants more of your goods to use as personal gifts or for some other reason, charge the regular wholesale price for the extra items.

Besides samples, reps will need descriptive literature to leave with clients as they make sales calls. Most reps carry folders containing information and photographs of the various lines they represent. Design your literature to fit into these folders, and protect it within clear plastic sheets—the type that fit into three-ring notebooks. Reps will also need several business forms, including price lists, order forms, and perhaps business cards. Supply each rep with around 30 to 40 copies of each, replenishing the supply as needed. (Some reps prefer to use their own order forms and business cards since they represent other firms besides yours.) The supplies you must provide to all your reps mounts up to quite a lot of material.

*5. Keeping in Touch.* Generally, you will be hiring reps in areas far removed from where you live and work. In most cases you will never meet these people face to face but will deal with them through the mail and by telephone. You may deal with a rep for many years without ever meeting, although as your business grows you may attend some trade shows and meet with and discuss business with them on these occasions. It's important to keep in close contact with reps to let them know of new-product development and policy changes. Also, continually encourage those who are a little slow gathering orders and compliment those who are bringing in business. Ask reps for suggestions on how you can help them accomplish their goal of selling. If you have a lot of reps, it's easiest to keep in touch through a newsletter, leaving a small blank area where you can write in a note to each individual rep. The newsletter can be included with the monthly commission checks.

*6. Evaluating Sales Performance.* Some reps aggressively push the products they represent and steadily bring in orders, while others fail to perform adequately. When a rep fails to get a sufficient number of orders, it is best to terminate the sales rep agreement (be sure to include a termination clause in the initial agreement!). Ask for the return of all literature and supplies (but if the rep was charged for samples they are the property of the rep). Then look for someone else to take over the territory. It may take awhile to find the right person in a given area, but there are good reps out there and it's worth the effort to continue your search until you find the right ones to sell your products. For further information about sales reps see *Selling Through Independent Reps*, by Harold Novick; 1988, American Management Association, New York, New York.

***Trade Shows and Merchandise Marts.*** Trade shows and merchandise marts are similar in function, but they have a time-frame difference. Trade shows are held periodically for the purpose of gathering people together to show new (and old) merchandise and to take or place orders for the merchandise. Trade shows last from a couple of days to a week. In contrast, merchandise marts are places where goods are permanently displayed and where buyers come to view and order merchandise. They are located in metropolitan areas.

The purpose of trade shows and merchandise marts is to promote sales. They are valuable to both buyers and sellers. Wholesalers, including manufacturers, importers, sales rep organizations, and distributors, display their products in an effort to attract buyers. Retailers, exporters, and catalog house representatives view the goods and place orders. Suppliers attend trade shows looking for manufacturers who can use their products. As you can surmise, a trade show is a gathering of people who need each other to make money.

Besides selling, there are other reasons to attend trade shows. Attendees can size up competitors' wares in person and also, perhaps more importantly, identify trends within the industry. Manufacturers and importers can make contact with sales reps who are looking for new lines to represent.

Selecting the right shows to attend is very important. Attend shows that attract the kind of buyers who are interested in your product line. If you produce gift items, then attend gift shows; jewelry manufacturers should go to jewelry shows; clothing or accessory manufacturers should attend wearing apparel shows; and so forth. Upcoming shows are listed in trade journals.

There are regional and national trade shows. The national shows are in cities like New York, Chicago, Dallas, and Los Angeles, with regional shows taking place in smaller cities such as Louisville or Indianapolis. Booth space might be just 8' × 10' or 10' × 10' and can run from $150 to $1,000, depending on the show. Space at regional shows is less expensive than at national ones, but fewer people attend. The trade show entrance fee will usually include, besides the booth space, the use of tables, chairs, and a source of electricity. Also, the names and booth numbers of all displayers are listed in a guidebook that is distributed to all attendees.

The cost of attending a show is not limited to the cost of booth space. Since these are several-day events, expenses will include lodging and food, and you might also have to pay for delivery and a decorator's fee.

Plan your display to attract attention. You must provide everything needed to assemble your booth, such as a backdrop, table coverings, scissors, tape, staple gun, and so forth. Also, take selling supplies, including samples, order blanks, and sales literature.

The results of attending a show cannot be measured in the number of orders written during the event, although sometimes such orders can be significant. A show has long-term benefits that result from the value of contacts made and information received. Also, you may run into somebody who doesn't seem especially interested in your products, but stuffs your literature into his or her briefcase. Weeks or months later that individual might send you an order and become a long-lasting customer—which is one reason why it is so important to encourage attendees to pick up your literature.

## SELLING TO CATALOG HOUSES

Approximately 20 percent of all merchandise is purchased through mail-order catalogs. Maybe you produce something that can be marketed effectively in this manner. Some manufacturers function as retailers and sell their own products through the mail to consumers, but others sell wholesale to mail-order catalog houses, who, in turn, retail the products to consumers. Catalog houses provide a large outlet that is often overlooked by small manufacturers and importers.

Refer to the directory *Mail Order USA* for a listing of over 2,000 top mail-order catalogs in the United States and Canada. *Mail Order USA* may be in your local library, or it can be purchased from B. Klein Publications, Inc., P.O. Box 8503, Coral Springs, FL 33065. Another good book is *Selling to the Catalog Houses*, by Ron Playle, available for $15.00 from R and D Services, P.O. Box 644, Des Moines, IA 50303.

You need to know several things about selling through this route. First, large quantities might be ordered so you must have the capacity to produce on a large scale; and secondly, the markup is huge, maybe three to four times your wholesale price (rather than double, as in retail stores), so you must decide if you can still make a profit with this price structure.

There is a specific procedure for submitting merchandise for consideration, with submission deadlines for each season's entries. Study the various catalogs or listings in the directory and decide which catalog houses seem most appropriate for your merchandise. Write to learn when and how the goods should be presented. Catalog companies rarely want a sample submitted but prefer a good-quality photograph with a descriptive write-up of the products to be considered. Don't stop with three or four submissions. Apply to a lot of catalogs, because each one that accepts your merchandise can result in many sales; however, note that some catalogs insist on exclusive rights.

## SELLING TO THE BIGGEST U.S. MARKET: THE FEDERAL GOVERNMENT AND THE VETERANS ADMINISTRATION

*Selling to Federal Agencies.* Many small business people look past the largest single customer in this country, while others have discovered this is where their future lies and have built successful businesses by dealing with the federal government.

In fiscal year 1986, the federal government contracted for $200 billion worth of goods and services directly from the private sector. Of this total, $36.3 billion was purchased from small businesses (businesses with fewer than 500 employees). The government buys more goods and services than any other customer in the free enterprise system, and you have just as good a chance of being one of its suppliers as anyone else. The government buys from very large corporations as well as small, singly owned ones. Firms seeking to expand their operations should consider doing business with the federal government because, while it may be in debt up to its ears, the Government pays its bills regularly and makes a good customer. However, you should be aware that the government pays on its own schedule, often as long as 30 to 45 days after it receives an invoice.

The government needs a huge variety of products and services. It needs general types of things, such as office equipment, computers, janitorial supplies, and transportation services. It also needs specialized goods, such as seeds, fertilizers, insecticides, and fire-fighting equipment. If you can think of it, the government probably needs it. In fact, the government needs so many things that every Monday through Saturday, the U.S. Department of Commerce publishes the *Commerce Business Daily*, that lists proposed procurements. Suppliers have at least 30 days to offer a bid.

In order to take advantage of the opportunities to sell to the government, you need to know where in the federal structure to market your products, how to make yourself and your products known, how and where to obtain the necessary forms and papers, and how to bid for the opportunity to sell specific goods or services. These procedures intimidate some owners of small firms so they do not pursue the government as a customer, but others have found that the rules are easily managed, that help is available to them, and that the government can be their best customer. In fact, in many cases, it is a business's *only* customer.

Purchasing agents for the government make an effort to encourage a broad spectrum of the American business community to do business with Uncle Sam. There are special provisions that spread opportunities among all business segments and geographic areas of the country. The chances of small firms are boosted by the efforts of two programs. One is the Business Service Center Program that offers trained counselors to assist entrepreneurs in their search for government contracts and furnishes step-by-step help with contracting procedures.

The other program that offers help to individuals and small enterprises is the Small Business Administration (SBA). The SBA works closely with purchasing agents of the federal government in developing policies and procedures that lead to increased contract awards to small business concerns. It also provides a wide range of services to individual small businesses to help them obtain and carry out government contracts.

SBA Procurement Center representatives are stationed at each of the 12 major buying centers of the federal government. They assist small firms with contracting problems and advise them on how to do business with the government. These representatives provide small business owners with information concerning government buying methods, products and services bought, and ways to get on bidder's lists.

A computerized system has recently been devised and instituted by the federal government to aid and assist the small business owner in the procurement process. This system is known as PASS, or *Procurement Automated Source System.* PASS is a high-tech, computerized network that contains the names of businesses and the goods or services they provide. If you wish to be considered for federal contracts and subcontracts, simply register your company with PASS. Thereafter, computer identification of your firm is made whenever work of an appropriate nature comes along. You can be listed in the system at no cost. A PASS application and the free pamphlet *Your Business and the SBA* can be obtained by writing or calling SBA, 1441 L Street NW, Washington, DC 20416, (202) 653-8200.

Another valuable resource for learning about dealing with the federal government is the 47-page booklet *Doing Business with the Federal Government.* This booklet costs $2.50 and can be ordered from

R. Woods, Consumer Information Center-J, P.O. Box 100, Pueblo, CO 81002.

***Selling to the Veterans Administration.*** The Veterans Administration spends more than $2 billion each year as it serves over 27 million veterans. It actively solicits the small business people of this country to offer their goods and services for its consideration.

If you are interested in getting a piece of the Veterans Administration pie, complete a Bidder's Information Form (Standard Form 129) and send it along with catalogs, price lists, and other material about your products to the proper purchasing center. This will place you on the active bidder's list, and you will be informed when the product or service you provide is needed.

For Form 129 and further information on how and where to be listed to become a supplier to this expanding market write to Director, Office of Procurement and Supply (90), Veterans Administration, Washington, DC 20420.

## TAPPING FOREIGN MARKETS

Almost any U.S. firm with good products and services has export potential. There is money to be made in foreign markets, and sales to overseas customers not only help the firms making the sales but also help the U.S. economy. On the average, $1 million in U.S. export provides 31 jobs to U.S. workers. Sales to foreign markets also help to reduce our trade imbalance.

Too often the suggestion to export sends small business managers running for cover, but what they don't realize is that exporting makes good business sense. If you sell in Indianapolis or Cincinnati, why not sell in Paris or Heidelberg? It is both practical and profitable—not only for giant corporations, but also for small firms that may have more limited resources. Approximately 60,000 U.S. firms exported $250 billion worth of goods in 1989 alone, and these goods range from barbeque sauce, skiwear, and shoes to handcrafted dolls and high-tech equipment. I am convinced that this is the new frontier for the many home businesses that produce handcrafted items. A good example of one company that is tapping into this market is Arbor Hill, a home business in Evansville, Indiana, that produces handcrafted products. Arbor Hill has discovered a world market that has grown weary of plastic and machine-made items and is enthusiastically buying the company's handmade products fabricated from natural materials.

An array of programs have been designed to inform and help the fledgling exporter. If you are interested in entering the export field, the

Department of Commerce's International Trade Administration (ITA) will be a valuable source of information. You can get personal counseling at your nearest Department of Commerce ITA District Offices (see your telephone directory under "U.S. Government" or contact the SBA and ask how to locate the ITA). The ITA provides a variety of foreign trade services, trade assistance, and information; it also puts out brochures on every aspect of the export business, as well as other publications that can keep you informed of international business developments.

A new initiative of the U.S. Department of Commerce called EXPORT NOW informs the business community why *now* is the time to export. EXPORT NOW is designed to increase awareness of the many export assistance programs and services provided by the government and the private sector. Assistance can be obtained by calling the EXPORT NOW office at (202) 637-3077 or by writing to EXPORT NOW, Room 5835, U.S. Department of Commerce, Washington, DC 20230.

The SBA and the Department of Commerce cosponsor export workshops and training programs. The SBA offers financial assistance for small exporters and even has an Export Revolving Line of Credit Loans. The U.S. Export-Import Bank (Eximbank) is an independent U.S. Government agency whose primary purpose is to provide export financing support for Americans seeking to market their products overseas. To encourage small businesses to sell overseas, the Eximbank maintains a special office to provide information on export financing, including discount loans, credit insurance, and foreign bank credits extended to finance the sale of U.S. goods and services abroad. Its toll-free number is (800) 424-5201.

Another aid for businesses considering the export market is the Export Information System (XIS) Data Reports. These reports provide small business owners with a list of the largest import and export markets for their products, as well as the trends within the markets and the major sources of foreign competition. This information can be used to help a business owner decide if it is wise to pursue the export market, and if so, which markets might provide the best chance of success. If you are attracted to the exporting market, see the free brochure *Is Exporting For You?*, available from SBA, Office of Public Information, Room 100, 1441 L Street NW, Washington, DC 20416 (or perhaps from your local SBA office).

The Agency for International Development is another source of export help. It has developed a computerized system to link U.S. suppliers of manufactured goods with foreign buyers. Information on these export opportunities may be obtained by writing to the Office of Small and Disadvantaged Business Utilization, Agency for International Development, Washington, DC 20523 or by calling (202) 235-1840.

## Marketing a Service

Many of the methods used to market manufactured goods are also used to market services, and they will not be repeated in this section. Still, there is a basic difference between the two. A customer can inspect a manufactured or crafted product before buying it, but a customer who contracts for a service to be performed acts on the faith that the promised service will be performed satisfactorily, perhaps according to some written specifications or guidelines. If you are in the business of providing a service, strive to convey a sense of confidence and reliability. Give prospective customers the impression that you are the one for the job. Whether a service business flourishes or falters depends a great deal on the quality of the work delivered. If good service is delivered, satisfied customers will recommend the business to others; however, word will also spread quickly if service is inadequate. A few examples illustrate the long-range effect of past work performance. Each of the examples presented below has actually occurred and has influenced the business involved.

*Example 1:* A child was left unattended for a brief time and was injured while at a day-care facility. The parents talked about the incident among their co-workers, friends at church, other young parents at social gatherings, and family members. Many of these people mentioned the incident when talking with others who were looking for child-care. Imagine: "You don't mean you'd take your kid to that place where so-and-so's kid got hurt!"

*Example 2:* A lawn care business over-fertilized a yard, and large areas of grass turned brown and died. Everyone who passed saw the problem, and the name of the business that caused the problem was quickly passed around as one to avoid.

*Example 3:* A furnace maintenance company sends out notices in late summer reminding customers it is time for a furnace inspection. The maintenance people go through a set routine of maintenance, replacing worn components and cleaning up the area after they are finished. Word has spread that this is a reliable service.

*Example 4:* A furnace maintenance company was called during a severe cold spell to a home where the furnace had stopped working and the lady of the house was struggling to keep warm with space heaters. Her husband was in the hospital recovering from a heart attack. The repairman went to the basement and returned in a couple of minutes with the news that a new furnace was needed, which would cost around $1,500. The women called another furnace company for a second opinion. The inspector from the second company arrived and disappeared into the basement. Before long the furnace rumbled and started heating the house. The repairman had reattached a couple of loose wires and declared the furnace fit and functional. Four years later the furnace is still working. You can be sure the name of the business that tried to take this woman to the cleaners while her husband was indisposed has been spread around town.

*Example 5:* Several hair stylists worked together in a hair salon. One of them colored a young woman's hair and left the coloring chemicals on too long. The young woman's hair turned orange. The stylist finally got the color corrected, but the hair was damaged because several powerful chemicals were required to resolve the problem. The young customer continues to visit the salon, but now she asks for a different stylist to work on her hair.

The number of examples I could cite showing the impact that quality service has on the growth of a service business could fill this book, but enough have been given for you to see how service quality influences future sales.

## Terms of Sale, Credit, and Collections

The days of selling for hard cash seem to be over. While cash sales have their advantages, you need to be open to other types of selling and decide what terms of sale will help you attract sales and collect money owed to you. It is a well-known fact that selling on credit increases sales, but as Ed Howe, an oft-quoted social critic observed, "No man's credit is as good as his money." Still, if you want to pick up those extra noncash sales you will need to think about the kind of credit you will offer and to whom you will extend it.

Credit has become the motivating force in most sales, but it is only effective if it is managed well. The goal of credit and collection is to achieve the most sales with the fewest number of losses. As you develop a credit policy it's worth keeping in mind that the investment in accounts receivable is often the largest single asset on a company's balance sheet. Also, in order to maintain good credit ratings with *your* suppliers, you need to have a credit policy that will ensure that your accounts receivables are indeed received, enabling you to pay your bills.

*Trade credit* is the credit extended from one firm to another. You will probably be on the receiving end of this type of credit as you purchase supplies but will probably extend this type of credit if you sell wholesale to other firms. Trade credit usually carries a sales discount to encourage prompt payment. Common terms of sale are 2/10, n/30, as explained in detail in Chapter 12. Also, after 30 days some firms add one or two percent for each 30 days the bill remains unpaid.

*Consumer credit* is credit extended to the customers who are the final users of a product or service. A discount is rarely offered for early payment. Instead, most retail credit sales charge extra if payment is postponed beyond a due date.

## CREDIT CHECKS AND TRADE REFERENCES

The primary cause of bad debt loss is a credit decision based on an inadequate credit investigation. There are several ways to evaluate credit risks, and it is foolhardy to extend credit without first checking an applicant's credit history. The granting of credit must always be based upon an applicant's ability to repay debts within a specified time period, but, admittedly, it is difficult to know for certain whether or not a customer is a good credit risk. You can only base your judgment on a customer's past credit record, which can be ascertained through credit ratings and credit checks.

If you are planning to deal with a business you haven't dealt with before, find out how long it has been in operation, its credit rating, and at least three references or suppliers it buys from regularly. Check these references to learn the amount of credit that has been extended and how promptly bills were paid. Chances are, if the firm has paid other suppliers on time, you will also be paid promptly.

Credit organizations can evaluate credit risks for you. Credit ratings are assigned to businesses and individuals based on their records of paying bills. A good credit rating indicates the business or individual can be trusted to pay on time. In order to obtain credit information from credit organizations, you need to be a member and pay a yearly fee that covers a limited number of reports. An additional payment is required for each report thereafter. This type of service may or may not be cost-effective for you. Try to estimate how much you might save in avoiding uncollectible debts and compare that with the cost of the service. (It might be helpful to have one or two credit organizations give you a sales pitch before you decide whether to use such a service at all.) If your sales are local and you wish to use a credit organization, join a credit organization that investigates local businesses; a national credit organization would be required if your customers are widely dispersed. Organizations that perform credit checks can be found in the Yellow Pages under the listing "Credit Reporting Agencies" and include Dun and Bradstreet, the National Association of Credit Management, and many others.

## WHAT KIND OF CREDIT SHOULD YOU OFFER?

Several kinds of credit are used regularly in the business world, but it might be wise to ship COD (cash on delivery) if you are selling to a new customer and feel apprehensive about the firm's credit rating. There is an extra charge for COD service, but most small firms realize that this is the price of getting a new business channel opened. After one or two orders, you might offer the new customer the terms extended to other customers, such as 2/10, n/30, but don't allow a company to run up a big debt until you are convinced it is reliable and will pay on time. Of course, the system works the other way too, and you might find that your business is the one being investigated. If your suppliers question your ability to pay, you may need to accept COD terms until your relationship is established.

*Open Account Credit.* Open account credit means customers can make purchases and say, "Charge it," or "Put these on my account." In order to use an open account, customers must apply for and receive permission to have such an account. Open account credit is usually extended to customers whose credit has been checked and who make a lot of purchases. Each purchase is recorded, and at the end of each month the customer is sent a statement listing the purchases and the amount owed. Open account credit has some extra costs associated with it. It takes more bookkeeping, more printed material (statements, extra letterhead and envelopes), extra postage to mail statements, the cost of collecting from delinquent accounts, and the bad debts which are never collected.

*Credit Card Credit.* Paying for purchases with a credit card has become the modern way to shop. The biggest use of credit cards today is for the purchase of consumer products and services. "Plastic" is used to pay for everything from wearing apparel to mortuary services. Churches and political parties even accept contributions via credit cards.

Most credit cards are issued free of charge to qualified applicants, although some credit card companies charge an annual usage fee. Each card specifies a maximum amount of credit the holder may charge.

The advantage of selling to credit card customers is that full collection of the sales, less the credit card company charge, is assured each month—it's just a matter of tallying the credit card sales slips and submitting them to the credit card company. The credit card company charge generally ranges from 3 to 5 percent, depending on the volume of credit card sales and the average dollar sale. Most small businesses don't realize it, but the charges are negotiable since there is so much competition between credit card companies.

Is it better to allow customers open accounts, credit card charges, both, or neither? To answer this question you need to measure the costs of open account credit against the cost of credit card credit. It pays to have open accounts available if the total cost of bookkeeping, printing, postage, interest, collection costs, and bad debts is less than the fee paid to the credit card company. But credit card selling is preferable if your business does not have the sound financing needed to carry accounts receivable, if you don't want to bother with the bookkeeping and the administration of a credit program, and if your clients do not insist on open accounts. Many small businesses use both types of credit, but the trend is toward credit card selling.

***Checks.*** Accepting checks for a purchase is another way of extending credit. When you allow a customer to pay by check you run the risk of receiving a bad check (a check written against an account that contains insufficient funds to cover the amount of the check). The number of bad checks being written has caused many companies to encourage customers to pay with credit cards. Normally, after a check has been returned for insufficient funds you can resubmit it to the bank in an effort to collect the money. The account may have been temporarily overdrawn, in which case the check may clear the second time through. However, if the check is for a sizable amount, it would be a good idea to inform the writer that it bounced and that you are resubmitting it. If the check does not clear on the second submission, notify the check writer that you intend to turn the matter over to your attorney if payment is not forthcoming. Send a *copy* of the check with each communication about it, but keep the check as proof of the amount that is owed to you. Further methods of collection are discussed later.

If you operate a mail-order business and customers submit checks to pay for their orders, deposit the checks immediately upon receipt, then wait two weeks before sending the orders. By this time you will have received notice if the check has bounced, and you can either send the check back to the customer or cancel the order. (As mentioned previously, according to Federal Trade Commission regulations you have 30 days in which to mail an order.)

You are at a disadvantage when you are selling at a fair and a customer asks to pay for purchases with a check. Your only recourse is to use your intuition, but I've learned through the school of hard knocks that the nicest-sounding and nicest-looking people can be the worst thieves, while others who look a little suspicious can be trusted. If you decide to accept checks at these types of selling events, there are several precautions to take. Accept checks written only for the amount of purchase; don't accept third-party checks; and ask to see two forms of identification, including a major credit card and a driver's license.

Compare the photograph on the driver's license with the person standing before you. If the address, telephone number, and social security number of the person writing the check is not imprinted on it, write this information on the front of the check.

### COLLECTING ON BOUNCED CHECKS AND UNPAID INVOICES

***Bounced Checks.*** Bad checks written with intent to defraud are unlawful. You have several options if you hold a bad check that was written for a substantial amount. If it remains uncashable after having been submitted to the bank a second time, you can either contact the individual, asking that the bill be paid in cash and indicating that you will turn the matter over to the police if it is not paid, or you can go directly to the district attorney's office or your local police and let them handle the matter. I did this on one occasion when I got taken for a significant sum (at a time when that amount of money could make my fledgling business go under), and the police put the defrauding shop out of business. This action may seem drastic, but I felt it was justified after I learned that the shop's shelves had been filled with merchandise from many small businesses and paid for with bad checks.

You can also ask the bank to help you collect on a check that has bounced. For a small fee your bank will send the check back to the bank from which it originated and ask that they hold it and cash it when money is deposited into the account. The check will be returned if nothing is deposited within a month.

***The Challenge of Unpaid Invoices.*** Some customers don't bother to send bad checks—they just don't pay their bills, which may leave you with past-due accounts receivables. This is a big problem for the small business and one that can cause a severe cash-flow crisis.

Establish a set pattern for dealing with unpaid bills. The collection effort should be a systematic and regular follow-up. This organized approach establishes credibility with the customer concerning your company's credit terms.

There is a Proverb that says, "Creditors have better memories than debtors." It is very important to start your campaign to collect as soon as it becomes apparent that a bill is overdue, because customers who are behind in payments to you are also probably behind in payments to others, and they will receive another batch of overdue bills the following month. *The older a bill gets, the harder it is to collect.* As soon as it is appropriate, start sending notices of unpaid bills, with each notice being more insistent. These notices can be either letters or copies of the unpaid invoice on which you write a message, urging remittance.

Another way to induce a customer to remit is to hold further orders until the overdue bill is paid. Some small businesses allow customers to run up large bills just because they are glad to get the business, but this puts the small business in a precarious financial position. Instead, inform customers with overdue accounts that shipping of further orders will be delayed until the accounts are paid. When the account is cleared, ship the new orders, but if you are concerned about payment it may be wise to ship COD.

If badgering with increasingly demanding letters and threatening to cease shipment of further orders doesn't bring a response, you can use other collection techniques. One is engaging the services of a collection agency and the other is taking the case to small claims court. Before using either of these options, send one last letter telling the customer of the action you will take and warning that this action will destroy the customer's credit rating. Some will pay up upon receiving such notification, but others won't.

***Collection Agencies and Small Claims Court.*** The goal of the collection agency is to collect unpaid bills for a fee. That fee is a percent of the unpaid bill and is based on the size of the bill and how much effort it takes to collect it. Sometimes the fee can be such a large percent of the money collected that you wonder if it's worth the bother. It usually is because it is better to get a portion of the money owed you rather than none at all; besides, you will have the feeling that the delinquent customer isn't getting away with any shenanigans.

Collection agencies are listed in the Yellow Pages. Dun and Bradstreet, mentioned earlier as a credit reporting agency, is also a well-known collection agency that operates throughout the country and is affiliated with local credit bureaus. For an annual fee, Dun and Bradstreet provides clients with official-looking stickers to affix to overdue bills. These alone are enough to cause some people to pay, but if this effort is unsuccessful, then the agency will take over the collection of the debt. Different agencies charge different rates, but generally the agency retains only a small percentage if a bill is paid after the first collection letter. The percent retained by the agency can increase to as much as 50 percent of the collected money if collecting it requires lengthy and involved procedures, such as locating the delinquent client and using the services of a lawyer.

Small claims court is another way to settle a debt. If someone owes you a bill you can't collect, you can take them to court for a modest filing fee. This is called "small claims," but sums amounting to several thousand dollars can be collected by this method (the amount varies in different areas). Call the county clerk or city courts (in your local government listings) to learn how to proceed in this type of action.

## SELLING ON CONSIGNMENT

Still to be discussed under the topic of terms of sale are consignment sales. Under this arrangement, merchandise is supplied to retail stores, but the supplier is not paid until the merchandise is sold. Consignment selling is a way of getting a foot in the door and is usually limited to those stores the consignor can service personally. This arrangement works very well for many small manufacturers, especially craftspeople, and you might find it an effective way to move your products.

You might consider offering merchandise on consignment if you are seeking new and expanded markets for your products and are having trouble getting stores to stock them. Or, if your products are perishable (for example, potted plants), or seasonal, with a limited selling season, dealers may be concerned about exposing their businesses to financial loss if they purchase the goods outright; in such cases, consignment selling is a way to get goods before the buying public without much risk to the dealer. Small shops are especially receptive to the idea of consigned inventory because many of them operate on a tight budget and have little money to invest in stock.

There are advantages and disadvantages to this type of merchandising. On the one hand, if consigned merchandise is sold, the consignor gets a larger percentage of the sale price than if the articles had been purchased outright by the retailer. On the other hand, dealers may fill the highly visible positions on their shelves with merchandise they have purchased and are anxious to sell, but they may place consigned goods in less desirable locations where the goods do not get maximum exposure. For this reason, it might be wise to avoid consigning merchandise to shops that normally buy their stock.

If you are considering offering products on consignment, keep in mind that you will not get a return on the merchandise until it is sold, whereas you would be paid "up front" for goods sold wholesale to the retailer. Also, since the merchandise remains your property, you may have to bear the cost of items that get shopworn, damaged, or shoplifted before they are sold.

What percent of the sale price do you get? Who is responsible for loss due to theft, fire, damage? How long should the goods remain in a shop on consignment? When will you receive payment for sold merchandise? When should you cease to offer a consignment deal and go for straight purchase by the retailer? You will need a contract that deals with each of the above questions. The contract should be prepared and signed before delivery of the merchandise. Also, each time merchandise is delivered to a shop it is essential that you make an accurate list of all items and have the dealer sign a receipt for them.

Normally, the markup in retail shops is 100 percent and the retail shop sets the price. However, when merchandise is consigned, the consignor usually sets the price, with the consignee (shop owner) receiving 20 to 40 percent of the selling price; or the consignor and consignee can work together to come up with a fair price. Another arrangement is for the consignor to state the minimum price he or she will accept and the consignee to charge whatever the market will bear.

When is the consignor paid? If the merchandise is inexpensive, the consignor is paid monthly or when a given number of sales have accumulated; however, the consignor is usually paid immediately after a very costly item is sold.

The usual agreement concerning returns states that the consignor can remove goods from the shop if after a given period the goods remain unsold. Alternatively, an agreement can be reached in which the merchandise will be left for a specific period after which either the goods can be removed or the time period renegotiated. Also, the consignee can include in the contract the right to request that the merchandise be removed if it does not sell and is taking up valuable shelf space.

The consignor remains the owner of the merchandise and is legally responsible for losses due to theft, fire, or other damage, but this is a negotiable issue and the two parties may agree to share the cost of damages. This important point should be spelled out in the contract. If a consignee won't share responsibility for losses, it is worth reconsidering if it is in your best interest to deal with that particular dealer, because there is little incentive for the dealer to take care of your products.

After a shop carries consigned merchandise for awhile and the merchandise has been shown to sell, it is reasonable to ask the dealer to purchase goods outright rather than continue the consignment arrangement. While this will decrease your profit on items sold, you will receive immediate payment, and it becomes the shop manager's responsibility to sell the merchandise. In the long run you will probably make more money if your products are sold to retailers rather than consigned to them.

An important part of the consignment arrangement is the bookkeeping that keeps you apprised of how much merchandise you have supplied to each shop, the amount that has been sold, the amount and when you are paid, and the amount of goods that remain in each shop. Keep a separate sheet for each business you deal with so you can evaluate the selling pattern of the different shops and determine which ones you should continue to supply with merchandise.

It is important to keep in touch with each store you supply with goods. That's no problem if the merchandise is moving, because you will receive checks and resupply the shelves, but it becomes somewhat of a chore when the store is off the beaten track and your products don't move. In these cases, the whole process seems like an act of futility, and these businesses usually aren't worth the bother. When it becomes apparent that a shop does not sell much of your merchandise, you might as well retrieve it and find another outlet.

## Marketing Written Work

This special section is devoted to the subject of selling written work, because such a large number of home workers are writers and many of them are still trying to figure out how to get published. The goal of this section is to move such workers from being writers with reams of unpublished material to being published authors who earn money for their compositions. As you will learn, being able to write well is just half of the job—finding a publisher tends to be the "big half."

Writing includes writing fiction books, nonfiction books, how-to books (like this one), magazine articles, business brochures, and newspaper articles and columns. Writing and producing newsletters is another option.

### DEFINE YOUR WRITING GOALS

Which is more important to you, to be published or to earn money? You can be published *and* earn money, but being published doesn't necessarily yield a profit. Many writers are anxious to get into print, and they look forward to the time when they get something accepted for publication and finally see their name in a byline. Even if you are paid for your work, it's one thing to have an article or a book published every once in awhile but quite another to earn a living by writing. Not many freelancers can actually bring in enough money to support their habit of eating. It might be instructive to figure out how many articles, books, or other types of writing must be sold to earn a modest income.

Can you make a living writing magazine articles? Probably not. Larger publications pay more than smaller ones, and prices per article range from copies of the publication (can you believe!) to $1,500 (only a few magazines pay more), with an average price running around $200 per article. You would need to sell 50 articles, or one each week, at an average price of $200 per article, just to earn $10,000 per year. You might be able to write one each week, but the calculations above assume they are all sold, and selling an article is often harder than writing it, especially for writers new to the field. However, the amount a writer earns goes up dramatically if he or she is consistently published and becomes known to editors. The truth is, earning a living writing magazine articles is a tough job, although there are ways to ease the work. I've sold well over 500 magazine articles and have learned to use the information in one to build the next. A single topic can yield 20 or 30 articles, each with a new beginning and a different set of photographs (photographs help sell articles and can earn additional fees).

Can you make a decent income writing books? While a writer receives a single payment for a magazine article, a book continues to produce royalties for as long as it remains on the market. What can a writer expect to earn from a book? First, you must find a company willing to publish it, and you can greatly increase the probability of being published by selecting the right subject. There are nine times more nonfiction books published than books of fiction. If earning money is the goal, most of us should forget about writing a great novel and concentrate on writing a book of nonfiction on a subject that has wide interest. Even after a publisher has been found, the amount of money you earn depends on how well the book is produced, how aggressively the publisher markets the book, and the amount of interest that can be generated for the subject. Some publishers keep a title on the market for a long time, while others quickly remove those that don't sell well and replace them with new titles. If you intend to make money writing books, never settle for a publisher that wants to make a first printing of less than 5,000 copies, and always try to get a bigger first printing. Let's try to get a ballpark figure on what you would earn from the sale of 5,000 books. If the book sells for $15.00 to the customer, the bookstore buys it wholesale for around $7.50. The author gets around 10 percent of the wholesale price, or $0.75 per book. Multiplying that by 5,000 books, yields $3,750. As you can see, if you concentrate on writing books, you need to write popular books to make a living. On the other hand, if you write books that continue to sell for several years, and write one each year or so, the accumulation of royalty payments can amount to a reasonable sum. Also, authors of books have the information to write magazine articles and the prestige, as the author of a book on the same subject, to get the articles published. These articles increase book sales, and the author is paid for what is essentially a free advertisement for his or her book. So, writing a combination of books and articles is one way to earn a living via the written word.

Columns and articles in newspapers is another outlet for writers, but these are notoriously poor paying and hardly worth your time, unless you just want to see your work in print. Even the big newspapers pay very little for a piece. For instance, *USA Today*, with a readership of over 5 million, pays only $150 to $200 per piece, and smaller publications pay much less.

A writer's income is very unstable—it's often a case of feast or famine. When a new book hits the market, the author can count on a good return, but then the sales drop and the income decreases. And selling magazine articles seems to run in cycles—one month quite a few might be sold, but the next month sales might be very poor. Writing newsletters and copy for a business or organization on a regular basis (weekly, monthly, or quarterly) can lend a little stability to a writer's income, but again, these kinds of jobs pay poorly. On the other hand, they usually don't take much time to do and are probably worth the effort for someone who must have a steady income.

## HOW CAN YOU SELL YOUR WORK?

Publishers are always looking for manuscripts for magazine articles. You should understand three things about magazine articles: (1) editors need a lot of articles to fill the many publications that come out daily, weekly, or monthly; (2) even though much material is needed, the competition is keen because writing has become a popular cottage industry; and (3) a well-written article with useful information on a topic of widespread interest will sell.

Publishers are also looking for manuscripts for books, but they are in business to make big money and most of them are only looking for writers who can deal effectively with subjects that will attract many book buyers. Therefore, if you intend to attract a publisher, write on a subject that has widespread interest.

Before doing much writing on a subject, send query letters to editors in order to locate a publisher. Contracting with a publisher *before* you write a book or article will enable you to fulfill the editor's expectations regarding length, format, and content; however, if you write a piece and then find a publisher, you may need to do a great deal of rewriting. Also, articles sold *before* they are written (in response to a query letter) usually bring a better price than those sold *after* they are written.

Editors know that a query letter is a quick way to separate writers from nonwriters and subjects of interest from subjects that are inappropriate for their publications. Therefore, it is important to study the market to identify the appropriate publications for the articles or books you plan to write, and then to send query letters to the editors of the targeted publications. Send the same query letter to several editors simultaneously because some don't respond for several months (although others respond promptly). Sending one query letter at a time can result in a long period of apprehension and waiting.

Spend time and energy refining your query letter because your writing ability and competence will be evaluated on the basis of that single page. Photographs and illustrations help to sell books and articles, and if you have them available or can get some you should always mention this fact in your query letters. If the photographs are especially striking, include one with the query. Be sure to accompany each query with an SASE (self-addressed stamped envelope) and keep detailed records of where and when you send material and when you get replies.

Several books are published annually that list thousands of publications looking for new material. The most widely used is *Writer's Market,* which is usually available in the library. A serious writer needs a personal copy, which can be purchased at most bookstores. Publications are listed in *Writer's Market* according to type (all women's magazines are in one section, health in another, and so forth). There is a brief description of each publication indicating the circulation, the amount paid for articles, when payment is made (upon acceptance or on publication), the length of articles used, and other pertinent information. *Literary Market Place* also lists the many markets open to freelancers.

There are some tricks to getting into print. Look for ways to set your work apart from the rest of the material that is cluttering editorial

---

### TIPS TO HELP YOU GET PUBLISHED

The tips below apply to both books and articles.

- Become knowledgeable about a subject before writing about it (do research).
- Write nonfiction because nine times more nonfiction is published than fiction.
- Write on timely subjects.
- Write on subjects of general interest to a wide audience.
- Write on subjects of narrow interest for specialty or trade publications.
- Use marketing books such as *Writer's Market* or *Literary Market Place* to locate publishers.
- Send a well-written, one-page query letter to a targeted publication's editor. The query letter should
  1. Explain the subject you plan to write about and tell why you are qualified to write on this subject
  2. Indicate if photographs are available
  3. State past writing experiences and include tear sheets, if appropriate
- Send queries to several or many editors simultaneously. Be sure to include an SASE. Write with authority and edit mercilessly.

desks. If you submit articles and book ideas to publications listed in *Writer's Market*, purchase the new edition as soon as it is released (usually in late October) and quickly study the new listings (they are marked with an asterisk). Get your material off to the new listings as quickly as possible, while the editors are looking for material to fill their publications. These are the easiest publications to "crack." Several months after the new edition of *Writer's Market* appears in bookstores, it is much more difficult to make a sale because the editors will be flooded with submissions.

Another way to get into print is to become an authority in a field that is not overcrowded with authorities. Many people think they want to be writers, but they don't know what they want to write about. It doesn't usually work that way. You must first become knowledgeable about something and then use your writing skills to communicate that knowledge. This is where experiences can be put to use. For example, a lawyer could write about wills, child support, marriage contracts, or any number of topics that would be of interest to women and the articles would be well received in the editorial offices of women's magazines. A gardener could write about ways to prolong a growing season or methods to ward off insect damage, and these articles would get a good reading by the editors of magazines that contain a section on plants (for example, *The Mother Earth News* and *Organic Gardening*). In other words, write well about something of interest, and you will find publishers and readers.

## COMPUTERS AND WORD PROCESSORS ARE CHANGING THE FREELANCE MARKET

Never before has manuscript preparation been so easy. When computers and word processors first hit the market, and writers learned to master them, there was a sense of euphoria. The labor of writing and editing was replaced with neat and tidy programs that allowed writers to spend their time grappling with ideas and words instead of "white out" and carbon paper.

Unfortunately, the computer has attracted far too many people who have mastered the use of word processors and the technique of putting words on paper but have failed to master the craft of writing. Untrained and poor writers are now producing professional-looking—but poorly written—compositions.

Before computers took over the mechanics of writing, an editor could glance at a submission and know a little about the writer; a neat article would usually get a second look. Now, editors must sift through the bad to find the good. They are finding the task to be overwhelming and, consequently, are using more staff-written material or assigning regulars to provide their basic needs. Thus, the market for freelance writing has dwindled drastically.

Another mixed blessing of the computer age is the printer that cranks out copies on demand. Writers are taking advantage of the ease of making copies that look like an original and are submitting their work to many publishers simultaneously. This, too, contributes to the glut of material in the freelancer's market. While it's understandable why freelancers use the simultaneous submissions procedure—it allows their material to be seen by more editors and increases the chance for a sale—the practice puts editors in the position of having to read and evaluate a piece, only to learn that it has been sold and is no longer available. If you make simultaneous submissions, it is only courteous to withdraw the material from consideration after it has been sold.

As you are trying to enter the writer's market, I advise you to keep another job until you learn what is needed to make a living in this very competitive business. Get some query letters circulating among editors and see what kind of responses you get. You might be surprised at how long it takes to get the ball rolling—to have multiple articles or books in press, others in query, and others in manuscript form—but that is what is required to make writing more than a hobby and turn it into a paying business.

# Part Six

# *Understanding Taxes and Insurance*

# 18    Business Taxes

Each business has different tax obligations, and every business decision, purchase, and transaction has tax implications or built-in tax advantages or disadvantages. Understanding the many types of business taxes and learning how to take advantage of tax breaks is so important that it can literally make the difference between business survival or failure. Your goal is to operate in such a way so as to avoid (legally) as many taxes as possible. The government expects as much and has written the laws with the full realization that this is the prerogative and goal of each tax payer. You can take deductions for home maintenance and improvements, automobile expenses, telephone expenses, office and work space, inventory space, major purchases, as well as such items as safe deposit box rental, credit bureau fees, and stationery and business cards. You can also use your business to take advantage of tax-deferred retirement plans, tax-deductible medical insurance, and a host of other legal tax advantages.

When I started gathering information for this chapter, I visited the local IRS office and asked for the current instruction manual for small businesses. The woman working there handed me a book containing 181 pages of instructions written in tiny print, much of which required slow and attentive reading, and told me that scores of other publications were available on a variety of tax subjects but that she couldn't gather them for me. "But," I protested, "I am a small business owner and need the information." She then informed me that I would need to tell her what I needed before she could provide me with an appropriate publication. And that is a major flaw in the system. Most people trying to understand their tax obligations don't have the background to know what questions to ask or where to start. The following information will give you a start, but if you are truly starting from scratch in understanding tax law and practices, I urge you to "talk taxes" with your accountant before your business gets too far along.

An awareness of how to use the tax system to your advantage will influence your purchasing practices, record keeping, and other business activities, and the sooner you learn the ropes, the more money you will save.

## Kinds of Taxes

Business owners must pay taxes to the federal, state, and local governments. This section will explain the federal taxes you are obligated to pay and briefly explain the most common types of state and local taxes, although you will need to learn if they apply in the area where you live. Keep in mind that tax laws change. They have not been written in stone for several millenia, and what you knew to be true yesterday may not be true tomorrow. Therefore, use this chapter as a guideline, but consult current references or an accountant who can advise you of the changes in tax laws.

### FEDERAL TAXES

The kinds of federal taxes that apply to sole proprietors, partnerships, and S corporations (see Chapter 6) and the tax forms that are used to figure and submit them are listed below. The tax obligations of regular corporations are more complicated, and since few home businesses are organized as regular corporations, such obligations are not presented here. (Consult an accountant if you need this information.) The tax forms listed below can be obtained from your district IRS office, or by writing to the U.S. Government Printing Office, Superintendent of Documents, Washington, DC 20402 or calling the IRS 800 number listed in the Blue Pages of your telephone directory under "United States Government, IRS Forms."

The federal tax forms needed if you have *no employees* include:

1040   Individual Income Tax Return.
1040C   Profit or Loss from Business or Profession. This form is used to itemize business deductions. You will need to determine your end-of-year inventory to complete this form. (See Chapter 12 in this book and IRS *Tax Guide for Small Business* for procedures used to evaluate an inventory.)
1040ES   Estimated Tax for Individuals, paid quarterly.
1040SE   Computation of Social Security Self-Employment Tax. Your estimated tax payments will also include payment into your Social Security fund.
4562   Depreciation and Amortization.

If you *have employees*, you will need to submit the following additional forms:

SS-4 with Circular E. This is the application for the Employer Identification Number (EIN). *Circular E, The Employer's Tax Guide,* explains the federal income and Social Security withholding requirements.

940  Employer's Annual Federal Unemployment Tax Return. This form is used to report and pay the Federal Unemployment Compensation Tax.

941  Employer's Quarterly Federal Tax Return. Use this form to report income tax withheld from employees' pay during the previous calendar quarter, and Social Security tax that was withheld and matched by you, the employer.

W-2  Employer's Wage and Tax Statement. This form is used to report to the IRS and to your employees the taxes withheld and compensation paid to employees.

W-3  Reconciliation/Transmittal of Income and Tax Statements. This form is used to total information from the W-2 and sent to the Social Security Administration.

The following is a brief discussion of some of the taxes reported and the information required on the forms listed above.

***Social Security Taxes (FICA).***  All self-employed people must file a Self-Employment Form when the profit claimed on Schedule C reaches $400. At this point the self-employed start paying into a personal Social Security account at a rate specified by the government (13.02 percent as of 1989).

Social Security benefits are available to the self-employed just as they are to wage earners. Your payment of the self-employment tax contributes to your coverage under the Social Security system, which provides you with retirement benefits and with medical insurance benefits (Medicare). You can learn the amount in your account by contacting the Bureau of Data Processing, Baltimore, MD 21235.

You do not need to pay Social Security taxes on wages paid to your children if they are under the age of 21, but as of 1988 all wages paid to spouses are subject to the FICA tax.

***Employer's Identification Number (EIN).***  Partnerships, corporations, and sole proprietors who have employees are required to have an EIN, and they must use the number as their taxpayer identification number. Sole proprietors without employees can also use the number instead of their Social Security number. The purpose of the number is to facilitate record keeping by the government, and failure to use the number on the appropriate forms results in a fine of $50 each time it is omitted. Apply for an EIN by filing IRS Form SS-4, available from the IRS or where other tax forms are distributed.

*Estimated Tax Payments.* Taxes are withheld throughout the year from the wages earned by people working for someone else. But as a self-employed individual, you are responsible for making periodic payments of your estimated federal income tax. These payments are due by the 15th of January, April, June, and September. You must pay at least 90 percent of the taxes owed or you will be penalized. Request estimated tax payment forms from the IRS.

## STATE TAXES

Taxes vary among the states, but most have an *income tax*. This tax is calculated on net income and is usually due at the same time you file federal tax returns. In some states the tax is calculated on gross income, less certain qualified deductions.

A *sales tax* is also imposed in many states. The sales tax is usually collected by the retailer when the goods are sold to the final user, the consumer. The sales tax is sent to the state with the appropriate form, and this form should be submitted monthly, quarterly, or annually, depending on the quantity of sales. To facilitate record keeping you will need to apply for a sales tax number from the office of the Secretary of State (see Chapter 12).

Some states require employers to carry Worker's Compensation Insurance for all employees. While this is called insurance, for the employer it is merely a tax by a different name. The program can be managed by the state or by the insurance agent who carries your other business insurance. Contact your state administrators to learn about this insurance (tax).

## LOCAL TAXES

Many localities (cities, counties) levy a property tax, which may include a tax on business equipment, inventory of unsold goods, and supplies. This tax inspires many businesses to "clean house" prior to taking inventory. Businesses mark down prices and go through other promotions in an effort to reduce the inventory on hand and, in so doing, reduce the amount of tax owed to the local government.

## Business Deductibles

Federal taxes are paid on net income. Net income is determined by deducting expenses from gross income. Business deductions are allowed for expenses incurred in the course of doing business. Refer to the lists in the accompanying sidebars to see what kinds of expenses you can deduct from your gross income as you figure net income on which taxes will be calculated. Your business may have many other deductible expenses besides those listed, and it is to your advantage to keep track of all expenses and deduct them when you figure taxes.

### ALLOWABLE BUSINESS DEDUCTIONS

Here is a sampling of tax-deductible expenses, but each business has its own peculiar expenses, so be alert for others that may apply to your business.

Accounting and bookkeeping services
Advertising expenses
Bad debts and bounced checks
Books and manuals dealing with business
Briefcase
Business gifts
Christmas cards for business associates
Cleaning services
Commissions to sales reps, agents, and others
Consulting fees
Conventions and trade show expenses
Delivery charges
Donations given in name of business
Dues to professional organizations
Education expenses for business seminars and workshops
Entertainment of clients (this alerts the IRS, so document carefully)
Equipment lease costs
Equipment purchases (these may be depreciated or expensed)
Freight and shipping charges
Insurance premiums, including special riders on homeowner's policy and other
　　business-related insurance
Interest on business loans
Labor costs for independent contractors
Legal fees
Licenses and permits
Mailing list rental
Maintenance contracts for equipment
Office supplies
Post office box rental

Postage
Printing
Promotional costs, including signs, displays, fliers, etc.
Refunds to customers
Research and development expenses
Safe deposit box rental used for holding business documents
Stationery, business cards
Subscriptions to business periodicals and trade journals
Supplies and materials
Tools
Travel expenses, including transportation, meals (80 percent), lodging, tips, and
    tolls
Uniforms used in trade
Wages to employees, including those paid to family

## HOME-USE DEDUCTIONS

A home business owner qualifies for deductions that are not permitted by other businesses. The amount of the allowable deduction is based on the percent of the home used for business purposes, with the two exceptions discussed in Chapter 7.

The percent of the home used for business purposes can be figured in either of two ways. The preferred method is to divide the square feet in the home by the number of square feet used for business purposes; thus, if in a 3,000-square-foot home 1,000 square feet are converted to business use, then 33⅓ percent of home expenses can be claimed as a tax deduction. The other method for figuring space is to count the number of rooms (if they are nearly equal in size) and divide the number of rooms used for business purposes by the total number of rooms. For example, if one room is used in a five-room house, then ⅕ or 20 percent of the home expenses are legitimate home-use business deductions.

Calculate the amount of deductibles attributable to business use by multiplying the total home expenses (utilities, repair, mortgage, etc.) by the percent of space used in your business. For example, if it costs $5,000 for total home expenses and 10 percent of the home is used for business purposes, you can deduct $500 for the business use of your home. You can also deduct the *complete* cost of decorating, painting, or remodeling the business portion of the home. Thus, if a porch is enclosed to create a work area, and the remodeling cost $8,000, you can add that amount to the $500 arrived at earlier for a total deduction of $8,500.

The amount of deduction allowed for home use in a given year cannot exceed the gross income your business generates. However, starting in 1988, an important change was made that affects all beginning and struggling home business owners. Home use expenses greater than the gross income of your business can be carried forward to the next year or years until the gross income is large enough to deduct the entire amount. This change turns out to be a windfall for small business owners!

You should be aware of one other point regarding business use of your home. Usually when an asset is sold you must pay a capital gains tax, but the one exception to this rule is when a home is sold. In this case, the seller is not required to pay capital gains tax if the money is reinvested in another home within a specified period of time. However, the business portion of the home is not included in this exception, and capital gains tax must be paid on the portion of the home that is (was) used for business purposes plus any depreciation that was claimed in previous years on that part of the home. This can amount to a sizable amount of money, but there is a way to avoid this tax. According to a 1982 ruling, the IRS will look only at how the residence is being used *at the time of sale.* If you can anticipate a move and do not claim the business-use deductions for your home *for one year prior to the sale,* you are not liable for the capital gains tax and are not required to reimburse depreciation claims.

## HOME USE TAX-DEDUCTIBLE EXPENSES

A *percentage* of the expenses listed below can be deducted from income. The percentage is based on the percentage of your home used for business purposes.

Rent
Mortgage interest
Insurance premiums on home
Utilities, including gas, electricity, and water
Services such as trash and snow removal, house cleaning, and yard maintenance expenses. If clients visit your home you may claim a percent of these expenses.
Home repairs, including labor and supplies

The *total* amount of the following expenses are tax-deductible:

Decorating, painting, and remodeling costs for the part of the home used for business purposes
Telephone—all long-distance business calls and charges for extra business-related services (see Chapter 20).

It is advisable to enclose a photograph or two of your home office and work area with your tax returns so the examiners can see and more fully understand how you are using the space you are claiming as a deduction. This type of documentation goes a long way toward warding off an audit.

## BUSINESS-RELATED TRAVEL EXPENSES

Expenses associated with travel undertaken for business purposes are tax-deductible, whether the travel is by air, rail, bus, or personal automobile. Traveling by air, rail, or bus provides you with ticket stubs and checks to present as evidence of the travel expenses, but travel by car cannot be documented so easily.

If you use your car for business purposes, the expense of maintaining the car is tax-deductible. Expenses include the costs of gas, oil, tires, repairs, insurance, depreciation, interest on car payments, taxes, licenses, garage rent, parking fees, and tolls. You can figure expenses either by keeping a record of the actual expenses or by using the standard expense mileage rate of 24 cents for the first 15,000 miles driven and 11 cents per mile thereafter. If you use the actual expenses to calculate deductibles but use your car for both business and personal purposes, then you must allocate your expenses based on the percent of the total mileage that is related to use for business purposes. For instance, if you drive 50,000 miles each year and 25,000 of them are business-related, then 50 percent of all expenses can be claimed as a business deduction.

Records are needed to determine how much of a deduction to claim. The records should show the business miles you drive during the year and the total number of miles driven during the year. The easiest way to collect that information is to place a record book in your car or truck and record the date, mileage, and destination each time you turn on the ignition. These records are needed to prepare your tax return, and they are also supposed to be of value for documenting expenses in the event of an IRS audit. You might question the value of these kinds of records for documentation purposes because a year's worth of travel logs can be created in just a few minutes. It seems a little naive for the IRS to put so much emphasis on these records, but it does, so you must go along with the system. Keep records and be ready to present them if your expenses are questioned.

## EXPENSING AND DEPRECIATION

Expensing means deducting the entire cost of an item in the year it is first purchased, up to a limit of $10,000. Depreciation is a way of taking a deduction for business property that has a useful life of more than one year and spreading the deduction over a period of many years. There is the misconception that only certain kinds of property qualify for depreciation, such as machinery, buildings, vehicles, patents, and furniture—big-ticket items—but you can also depreciate smaller articles, such as books.

Expensing is usually preferable to depreciation because a tax write-off is more valuable the earlier it is used, but under certain circumstances depreciation is preferred. Expensing versus depreciation is a somewhat involved issue, and I suggest you ask your accountant which method would serve you most advantageously or refer to the IRS Publication 334 for small businesses.

## Records Needed for Tax Purposes

Records and record keeping were discussed in Chapter 10, and the methods discussed in that chapter were designed to satisfy the IRS and to help you prepare tax returns without undue anxiety. Just to reiterate: (1) Keep all receipts for business expenses, and (2) keep all miscellaneous receipts for out-of-pocket purchases, noting what was purchased on the back of each. Stash the receipts in an envelope, using a different envelope for each month, and note the date and the total amount on the outside. It might be worth categorizing the expenses on the outside of the envelope so you won't need to do it at tax time. Your business checkbook will also contain valuable records that will be needed to figure and document tax-deductible expenditures.

The IRS can investigate a return for up to three years after it has been filed, so you should certainly keep all records for at least three years. In fact, it might not be a bad idea to keep them for six or seven years.

## Tax Sheltering and Tax Benefits

A tax shelter is a way to reduce taxes by investing a portion of taxable income in special nontaxable programs. The taxes are not avoided but are simply deferred, but the deferral can result in a tremendous benefit because of the extra interest earned on the money not being paid out in tax. The money is taxed at a later time, usually at retirement, when presumably the investor is in a lower tax bracket. A tax benefit plan can also result in reduced taxation, and under such a plan some taxes are not deferred but are instead totally avoided.

Tax-sheltering and tax benefit plans are worth studying and implementing. Some of the many legitimate programs are not explained in IRS publications, but you should learn about and take advantage of them in order to ease the tax burden of your business. Again, the advice of an accountant or tax adviser should be considered.

## INDIVIDUAL RETIREMENT PLANS

The retirement plans discussed here enable the participant to *defer* taxes, not avoid them.

*Individual Retirement Account (IRA).*   In 1974, Congress enacted legislation that gave every wage earner an *opportunity* to establish a personal retirement program using tax-sheltered money. To encourage IRA savings, the original plan allowed the money contributed to an IRA plan to be tax-deductible. After looking more closely at the numbers, new rules were established in 1988, and now the savings are only tax-sheltered if you meet *one of two conditions*. The first condition is that you do not participate in any other type of retirement plan (other than Social Security), and the second is that your adjusted gross income is less than $40,000. If you qualify under *either* of these conditions (and many home business owners do), then the amount saved (on deposit with a financial institution) and the earnings that are generated by this type of account are not currently taxable and the tax-free status continues until retirement. Taxes are paid as the money is received during the retirement years when the tax payer is usually in a lower tax bracket. Even if you do not meet either of the conditions specified above, you can still put money into an IRA, but the money you deposit is not tax-deductible. However, money the account *earns* is not taxed until it is recovered after retirement, so it is still an attractive investment.

An IRA tax-sheltered account will accumulate much more than will a taxed account over a given period of time. For instance, if at the age of 25 an individual starts depositing $250 each quarter ($1000 per year) into a tax-sheltered account and continues to add money at that rate until the age of retirement at 65, and if the account grows at 8% compounded quarterly to 8.23% annually, over the 40 years the account would grow to $290,316.31, which is $250,316.31 over the $40,000 that was invested. Yes, those numbers are astounding, but correct.

An IRA is not taxed until payments are received from it at retirement. As early as age 59½ you can choose either to receive a lump sum or to have payments spread out over a number of years. Any portion removed prematurely (before age 59½) is assessed a 10 percent penalty. However, if an individual becomes disabled, IRA funds can be withdrawn without penalty, and in the event of death the funds are paid to one's beneficiary.

There are many IRA plans available: IRAs can be administered by banks and savings and loans (the money is usually placed in certificates of deposit); money market and mutual funds can be used for IRAs; stockbrokers offer self-directed IRA accounts; insurance companies offer annuity plans into which you can place IRA money; and, U.S. minted gold can also be used for an IRA, provided the gold is held for you by a trustee, such as a banker or broker.

*Keogh Plan.* The chief difference between an IRA and Keogh Plan is the eligibility requirements and contribution limitations. While contributions to an IRA can come from earnings from any type of employment, contributions to the Keogh Plan are based only on self-employment income. Also, while the maximum amount you can contribute to an IRA is $2,000 yearly, you can contribute up to 20 percent of your earned self-employment income, up to the maximum contribution of $30,000, to your Keogh Plan each year. For example, if your annual income is $40,000 through self-employment, you can contribute 20 percent of $40,000, or $8,000. You can contribute to a Keogh Plan even if you participate in some other type of retirement plan, IRA, or tax-sheltered annuity.

Operationally, there is little difference between the Keogh Plan and an IRA, but the Keogh has the advantage of the lump-sum averaging rule. If, after age 59½, an individual elects to remove the total amount from the Keogh account, a favorable tax treatment keeps the tax rate low. For example, the averaging rule applied to a $100,000 distribution yields a tax rate of about 15 percent. Also, the tax rate on lump-sum withdrawals is totally independent of other taxable income.

*Defined-Benefit Keogh Plan.* This plan is remarkable in that it can shelter from taxes up to 100 percent of self-employment income. This can be a tremendous tax break for people who earn income through self-employment.

Defined-Benefit Keogh Plans work like other tax-sheltered plans. A full deduction can be taken on your tax return for any contributions made to the plan. The money in your plan is invested, and all earnings (interest, dividends, etc.) are compounded and are exempt from tax until they are withdrawn. Also, the same averaging break that applies to lump-sum distributions from regular Keogh Plans applies to Defined-Benefit Keogh Plans as well.

The chief advantage of a Defined-Benefit Keogh Plan is that far more can be contributed to it (and sheltered from taxes) than to a regular Keogh Plan. The amount, which is based on a person's age, sex, marital status, and self-employment earnings, results in a huge tax savings. Also, you can function as the manager of your plan, in charge of the money you have contributed. You directly control the investments in and disbursements from the plan, or you can delegate this responsibility to a professional investment adviser. Setting up this type of program is a little more complicated than the regular Keogh because an actuary must be involved in making the appropriate contribution calculations and sending in the proper certification forms to the IRS, but the fees for such services are tax-deductible as a business expense.

If you are interested in investigating these plans, talk with an adviser at a bank, savings institution, or mutual fund. Such an adviser can direct you and provide the forms you need to establish your Defined-Benefit Keogh Plan.

## TAX BENEFITS

The tax-free status of fringe benefits such as medical plans makes them especially useful methods to *avoid* taxes. While the salary you take from your business is taxed, certain qualifying fringe benefits are tax-free to both the business and the recipient. In other words, the benefits are not reported as income on your tax return, yet they are taken off as a deduction by your business. To give you an idea of how powerful a money-saving tool these can be, medical benefits are discussed below, but be aware that there are many more benefits that a tax adviser can help you understand and implement.

*Medical Reimbursement Plans.* A corporation can agree to pay all the medical and dental expenses of its employees and their spouses and children, as well as the premiums on a disability policy for its employees, and the corporation receives a tax deduction for these costs as business expenses. To take advantage of this arrangement, you can set up a corporation and be hired as its employee. By doing this, you will receive a tax deduction of 100 percent of the medical expenses you pay for yourself and your family and the premiums on your disability policy.

A sole proprietor can't use this arrangement. Instead, a home business owner who operates as a sole proprietor or works with others in a partnership can set up a plan to cover the medical expenses of all employees and their dependents. Then, if the owner hires his or her spouse to help in the business, the medical expenses of the spouse and the spouse's dependents (including the owner) are covered. A business deduction can be claimed for the medical expenses paid under this plan, so the sole proprietor receives what is equivalent to a tax deduction of 100 percent for the family's medical expenses. Of course, in order to make this arrangement fair, the spouse should work in the business and receive wages.

***Paying Family Members.*** There are several tax advantages to hiring family members, but the tax reform act of 1988 has severely curtailed many of the advantages previously available to employed family members. Different rules apply to children and spouses.

The IRS has ruled that wages paid by a parent to a child are no longer tax-deductible. Prior to the tax reform act of 1988, some earnings were tax-deductible for children under age 21, but now all earnings of children employed by their parents are taxable. This change was brought about because the IRS realized many parents were claiming that their children worked in order to gain a tax advantage. That advantage no longer exists. However, the earnings of a minor child working for a parent will probably be taxed at a lower rate than the parent's earnings, and thus the total tax bill is reduced. Also, the wages of a business owner's children (employed in the business) are exempt from Social Security tax and unemployment insurance.

Payments made to a spouse for work done in a home business become taxable income, and if a joint return is filed there is no change in the amount of tax due. Also, as a result of the 1988 tax changes, all wages paid to a spouse are subject to the Social Security tax. Still, there are some ways that these payments can result in a lower tax bill. For instance, a wage earner can contribute up to $2,000 to an IRA, but a nonworking spouse can contribute only $250. By earning an income, both you and your spouse can contribute $2,000 or a total of $4,000 annually to an IRA.

You could qualify for still another tax break if both you and your spouse work. Tax law allows for a tax *credit* for expenses for household services and child care, but the credit cannot exceed the earned income of the spouse with the lower earnings. A credit is different from a deduction. It is subtracted directly from the amount of taxes owed, whereas a deduction only reduces the amount of taxable income. The maximum amount of expenses to which the credit can be applied is $2,400 for one qualifying dependent or $4,800 for two or more qualifying dependents, but the amount is based upon your adjusted gross income.

## The IRS Wonders, "Is It a Hobby or a Business?"

Many small home businesses look more like hobbies than businesses, and the IRS is watching for people who take business deductions for hobby expenses. This is especially true of craft businesses, but others can also draw the attention of the IRS.

If you make money selling crafts, even though you consider the activity a hobby and not a business, you are expected to pay taxes on your income, but you can deduct the expenses associated with the hobby from the earnings it generates to arrive at your taxable income. You are required to report this hobby income on Form 1040, line 22, under "Other Income." If you *lose* money at your hobby, by spending more than you take in, you are not entitled to a deduction. However, if you pursue the same hobby, organize it into a business to earn a profit, but *lose* money instead, then you can deduct the expenses of your craft business and can offset the loss against your other income. That seems straightforward, but there is some confusion over this point, and the confusion comes in deciding when an activity ceases to be a hobby and becomes a business.

A business is defined by the IRS as an activity engaged in for profit. Some taxpayers do not understand the ruling that states if an activity makes a profit in three out of five years it is presumed *not* to be a hobby. They interpret that to mean that if an activity loses money three out of five years it is considered a hobby, but that is *not* the case. The question to be considered is, "Is the activity engaged in for profit?" The IRS has ways to evaluate if an activity is engaged in with a profit-making motive, and each case is decided on its own merits. If the profit motive is evident, then the business can lose money for an extended time and the expenses can be deducted from other income.

The following are the kinds of evidence that will convince the IRS you are intending to earn a profit:

1. Your business is conducted in a businesslike manner, with separate banking accounts, appropriate records, and receipts.
2. You spend a reasonable amount of time and effort to make it successful.
3. You are skilled at your activity and show success at least part of the time.
4. Your financial status doesn't suggest that you are looking for a tax write-off, but rather it suggests that you are trying to earn some income. You spend money for advertisement, stationery, and the other trappings of a business.
5. While you can enjoy the activity, enjoyment or recreation is not the prime purpose of the activity.

The reason these rules are necessary is that some people try to cheat the government and take deductions for an activity that is nothing more than a hobby. They don't intend to earn money, but would like to have the public help support their hobby. An example would be a horse enthusiast who keeps horses for riding. Horses eat a lot of oats, and it would help the owner if the oats would be tax-deductible. However, if there is no evidence that the horses are used to generate income—and more income than they eat—then they would be considered a hobby. For instance, if on Sunday afternoons the owner makes the horses available for riding to paying customers, but the horses are not used to gain income at any other time, then it would be impossible to bring in enough money to support them and to leave some for profit. Therefore, since there is *no chance to make a profit* at this venture, it would be considered a hobby, and the paying customers are doing nothing more than helping with the horses' oat bill. If, however, the horses are made available to paying customers frequently enough that it *would be possible* to make a profit (even though the profit is *not* made, at least for several years), then the cost of feeding and maintaining the animals would be tax-deductible.

If you have a business that could be questioned, be sure to use Schedule C to report business income and expenses. The very fact that Schedule C is used indicates that you intend your activity to be a trade or business engaged in for profit. Hobby income is reported as "Other Income" on line 22 of the 1040 form, and allowable hobby expenses are reported on Schedule A as miscellaneous deductions.

Remember: Keep good records and act like a business, and you probably won't have any trouble with the IRS.

## How to Survive an IRS Audit

It is frightening to get a letter with the IRS return address on the envelope. Sometimes those letters are asking for more information, but at other times it is apparent that the IRS thinks something needs to be investigated. In some cases returns are drawn for a thorough review through random selection. If your return is to be reviewed, you and your accountant should prepare for the event.

There is no reason to panic if you have done your best to present an honest appraisal of your business when you prepared your tax return. You may have made a mistake, but the IRS has ways of detecting an honest mistake from those that are purposely perpetrated.

Think ahead when you prepare your return, and prepare for the moment when you might be asked to explain it. I have frequently used the IRS information line (in the phonebook Blue Pages under "Federal Government") and have based my calculations on the information I received. Sometimes the answers aren't correct. In fact, a recent survey discovered that nearly a third of the answers are incorrect, and thus the calculations based on those answers are incorrect. Therefore, *always* ask to whom you are speaking when you receive information, and record the person's name and date of the conversation. This simple documentation can be very important when the IRS is determining whether you will be required to pay a fine for an incorrect return that resulted in an underpayment of taxes.

There are several ways to make your return less conspicuous and reduce the probability of an audit. Using a home office as a tax deduction attracts the attention of the IRS, but it's a legitimate claim and one you should surely take. Just make sure you meet the IRS requirements outlined in Chapter 7, and be prepared to substantiate your claims.

The IRS is also alerted when large amounts are spent on entertainment and travel. These deductions can be used by dishonest proprietors to reduce their profits and thus their tax bills. Keep especially detailed records of these kinds of expenses, and make sure they don't look like expenses incurred by taking your spouse to Las Vegas for the weekend or to dinner each week. It might even be wise to record the business topics discussed, if you are claiming dinner expenses, and precisely why you needed to travel, if you are claiming travel expenses. These kinds of records will go a long way in convincing an investigating agent that the travel expenses claimed are for more than personal R and R junkets.

Most examinations are handled by mail, and it's just a matter of supplying the requested information. If your examination is to be conducted through a person-to-person interview, go to the interview prepared. If possible, arrange to have the examination in the IRS office, because in your office all the business records are too readily available for further study. Of course, if the investigation is questioning the expenses you have taken for the use of your home, the investigator will want to see the space and how you are using it. Before he or she arrives for the inspection, be *sure* to remove anything that might smack of family trappings. If you keep a baby playpen in the room, move it to another area during the review and do the same for any other articles that might be questionable.

The IRS investigator will tell you which aspects of your business the IRS wants to review. Do not reveal all of your records, but only those specified. At the same time, don't make it appear that you are withholding information. This type of review will make you appreciate all of those receipts you have painstakingly kept. Also, the value of separate bank accounts for family and business will become abundantly clear when the IRS investigator is looking over your shoulder.

Don't be intimidated by the IRS investigator. If, after the review, you and the investigator don't agree, you can appeal the examiner's report. Such an appeal is actually a rather common practice. An appeal is done through the Appeals Office or the Appeal Courts. Ask your examiner for Publication 5, *Appeal Rights and Preparation of Protests for Unagreed Cases.*

For further information see the newsletter *Tax Savers for Small Businesses.* It is available for $49.50 per year from ProPub Inc., 49 Van Syckel Lane, Wychkoff, NJ 07481.

## TAX INFORMATION PUBLICATIONS

The following free tax-related booklets, prepared by the Internal Revenue Service, can be obtained by contacting the U.S. Government Printing office, Superintendent of Documents, Washington, DC 20402.

*Index to Tax Publications* (No. 048-004-01695-8). This is an index of current tax publications. It includes those listed below and dozens of others.
*Your Federal Income Tax* (Publication 17).
*Tax Guide for Small Business* (Publication 334).
*Business Use of Your Home* (Publication 587).
*Employer's Tax Guide* (Circular E).
*Self-Employment Tax* (Publication 533).
*Tax Information on Depreciation* (Publication 534).
*Information on Excise Taxes* (Publication 510).
*Tax Withholding and Estimated Tax* (Publication 510).

The above publications were prepared by the IRS, whose job it is to *collect* taxes. Two books written by Julian Block show you how to *avoid paying* unnecessary taxes. They are *Guide to Year-Round Tax Savings* and *Small-Time Operator,* both available in bookstores. Other excellent books on this subject are also available in most bookstores.

# 19    Dealing With Risks

Risks are a part of business just as they are a part of one's personal life. You take a risk each time you climb into an automobile or a bathtub, and you will also take a risk each time you extend credit or develop a new line of products. Risk is the chance of damage, injury, or loss. Every business operates with a set of risks, and you need to decide how you will deal with them.

The financial responsibility for some types of risks can be shifted from your business to an insurance company through insurance policies. A sound insurance protection plan is important to the security of your business, because without this protection a lifetime of work can be lost. Insurance premiums are the price you pay for the freedom from worry about economic loss from conditions outside your control.

The insurance you buy may turn out to be one of your most important purchases, and while it is a complex subject, it is worth the time and effort to become a knowledgeable consumer. Good insurance management includes recognizing risks that can be covered by insurance and locating an insurance representative who will help you buy adequate insurance at the best price.

The main risks faced by the small home business that can be covered by insurance include:

1. *Liability to the public.* Personal liability and product liability are risks that must be protected against. These risks include both personal injury and damage to the property of others.
2. *Damage to property.* Inventory and business space are at risk from fire, storms, earthquakes, and other perils.
3. *Liability to employees.* Workmen's compensation insurance provides protection should an employee be injured while working for you.

Organize your insurance program. First, think about the risks and the ruinous misfortune that could strike, then investigate the ways to insure against loss and decide what perils to insure against. You will need the help of a qualified agent, broker, or consultant to explain options and recommend the right coverage. If possible, consult an independent insurance agent, because unlike agents who represent a single company the independent agent can pick and choose from numerous companies to put together an insurance package that best fits your needs.

There is the misconception that insurance costs are about the same among the different insurance companies, but equivalent policies can vary by hundreds of dollars from company to company, so shop around to find the best deal. Also, take advantage of special offers. For instance, some companies offer discounts on homeowner's policies if smoke alarms, fire extinguishers, and deadbolt locks are used in the home, and some companies offer a good rate on automobile insurance to those with good driving records. After your insurance program is in place, you may discover a more cost-effective arrangement with another company and want to switch companies to take advantage of the lower rates. Did you know that you can cancel a policy at any time and receive a part of the premium back? While this might be done occasionally, don't make a habit of jumping from company to company. Also, insurance companies can cancel with a five-day written notice, and this sometimes happens when too many claims are made and the insured party is considered a poor insurance risk.

Before accepting any policy, be sure to read and understand the fine print and know exactly what the policy covers (although you won't *really* know until you have a loss). Keep all insurance records and policies in a safe place, but if you keep them at home for convenience, then give the policy numbers, insurance company names, and other critical information to your accountant or put them in your safe deposit box.

Review all policies periodically to make certain the coverage is adequate and your premiums are as low as possible while giving sound protection. Don't try to save money by underinsuring or by not covering some perils that could cause loss just because you think the probability of their occurring is very small. If the probability of loss is small, the premium will also be small.

A home business should carry at least three kinds of insurance: homeowner's, automobile, and business liability. You might also want to carry several other types of insurance that are discussed below because they will add to the security of your business and personal life.

## Homeowner's or Renter's Insurance

A homeowner's policy normally provides two types of insurance: property protection and liability protection. *Property protection* reimburses you for loss or damage to your house and its contents. *Liability protection* reimburses others (up to $100,000 is common) for injury or damage caused by you or a family member, or for an injury they receive in or around your home. It also pays at least $1,000 of the medical bills of someone who is injured on your property, but through no fault of yours. Liability insurance also applies if you, or a family member, cause injury to someone while away from home.

There are many differences among homeowner's policies. Some offer limited property protection, while others offer comprehensive coverage. Coverage to protect from perils such as vandalism, smoke, and windstorm, and even from such things as damage caused by burst pipes and ruptured hot-water heaters, can be added to a basic fire insurance policy. If you are interested in broader protection, it might be less expensive to get an all-risk policy that offers comprehensive coverage. The term "all risk" is a little misleading because these policies do not cover damage from floods, earthquakes, war, and nuclear contamination, although these types of risks can be covered through an addition to the policy.

Buy the amount of coverage you need—too little would leave you vulnerable to losses, and too much would make your premiums excessively high, leaving you "insurance poor." Your homeowner's coverage should be based on *replacement value*, which means that you would receive the amount it would cost to replace the lost property, regardless of its condition or age. If replacement value is not specified in the policy, the insurance company will award the current value after depreciation, which could amount to much less than what it would cost to replace the structure and its contents. It will cost an extra 10 to 15 percent to have replacement value written into a policy, but that could be money well spent considering the added protection. As an example, the cost of a new filing cabinet would run around $200, but one that is five or six years old would bring a garage sale price of $50 or less.

A rider should be added to your homeowner's policy to cover business equipment and supplies. Without this rider to specifically cover business damage, your homeowner's policy will not cover your property if it is damaged by a fire caused by something associated with your business, such as an electrical fire caused by a business machine. A standard fire insurance policy will not cover the loss by fire of accounts, bills, currency, deeds, evidence of debt, and securities. It is important to discuss this with your insurance agent.

You can speed up the collection of a claim that results from destroyed or damaged property by documenting your possessions. Make an inventory of all home furnishings, business furniture, and appliances, listing model numbers, prices, and purchase dates. Photograph or videotape each room including the insides of cabinets and closets. Keep the inventory list, photographs, and/or videotape in a safe deposit box or some safe place other than in your home.

Review your homeowner's policy at least every three years or any time you redecorate or undertake a remodeling project costing $5,000 or more. Make adjustments in your insurance coverage to reflect the changing value of your home.

## Liability Insurance

The number of liability lawsuits in recent years makes liability insurance an absolute necessity. There are two basic kinds of liability insurance. *Personal liability insurance* protects against lawsuits from people who suffer bodily harm while on your property (discussed above) and against lawsuits from people who suffer damage as a result of auto accidents (discussed below). *Product liability insurance* protects you from claims by consumers who have been injured or allege injury while using articles produced by your business.

Product liability insurance is becoming increasingly important in the business world due to the litigious nature of modern society. It is amazing how some consumers can convert a seemingly safe product into a dangerous item. For this reason you must take great care to childproof and adultproof your goods. Design products with safety in mind, and put warning labels on anything that could possibly cause injury. Still, even the greatest care is to no avail if products are used unwisely. An adult article with small detachable pieces can become dangerous in the hands of an infant who is inclined to poke the small pieces into his or her mouth or nose. If you make something that could possibly cause injury, you must protect yourself with product liability insurance. Many catalog companies and retail shops will not carry products not covered by product liability insurance because they fear a ruinous lawsuit.

## Automobile and "Non-Owned" Auto Liability Insurance

When an employee or a subcontractor uses a car, truck, or other vehicle on your behalf, you can be legally liable even if you don't own the vehicle being used. Automobile and non-owned auto liability insurance protects you against damage to your auto and to automobiles driven by you and employees in the course of performing work, and also against liability caused by you and others working in your behalf.

Automobile and non-owned auto liability insurance can be quite expensive, but the cost can be reduced by having a large deductible ($250 to $500) written into the policy. If your vehicle or a vehicle driven by an employee or subcontractor on your behalf is damaged, you are required to pay the amount of the stated deductible toward the repair of the vehicle and the insurance company will pay the remainder up to the value of the automobile or the limit of the policy. Of course, this leaves you paying for damage caused by fender-benders and minor accidents, but if you and your employees are careful drivers and have few accidents, this approach will be less expensive than having a smaller deductible and, therefore, higher premiums. Your insurance company will pay the complete cost of the repairs if you are responsible for damage to another person's automobile.

## An Umbrella Policy

When it rains it pours, but an umbrella policy offers protection if you get caught in a storm. It is wise to have an umbrella policy that makes available at least $1 million to be used in case homeowner's liability, product liability, or automobile liability have been used and more money is needed to bring about a settlement. This added coverage costs relatively little (often less than $200 per year) and is money well spent, considering the unbelievably high settlements being granted by the courts. Policies for larger amounts are rarely suggested by insurance agents, so you will need to ask about them. Also, few people are aware that insurance agents carry large insurance policies on themselves in the event that they, the agents, are sued by clients who follow their advice and later allege that they were poorly advised and discovered, too late, that they were underinsured.

## Other Types of Insurance Coverage

While preparing your insurance program, you might want to discuss other kinds of insurance with your insurance agent.

*Business Interruption Insurance.* This insurance covers fixed expenses that continue if a fire or other disaster seriously disrupts or closes your business. A policy can also be written to insure against losses incurred should some misfortune close the business of a supplier or customer that results in the disruption of your business or if your operation is interrupted because of power, light, gas, or water failure that is furnished by a public utility.

***Disability Insurance.*** If you are responsible for the support of your family, consider the cost of a policy that will provide income in the event you are disabled and unable to work.

***Crime Insurance.*** A comprehensive crime policy is available to small business owners. It covers loss due to burglary, robbery, disappearance of money and securities, and vandalism. A home business located in what is considered a high-crime area may be unable to purchase crime insurance without paying an exorbitant rate, but the Federal Crime Insurance Program subsidizes insurance of this type. Contact your nearest Small Business Association office to learn about this program.

***Key-Man Insurance.*** Key-man insurance protects against loss of a key employee, but this is not applicable to most home businesses since the key employee is generally the owner. Still, some home businesses hire talented workers who become valuable business assets. If the loss of such a worker would jeopardize your business, it would be wise to insure against this eventuality.

***Worker's Compensation and Worker's Disability Insurance.*** Legislation requires that employers provide employees with a safe place to work. Employers are liable for injury to employees that results from unsafe working conditions and for injury that occurs to employees while they are performing their duties. An important feature of worker's compensation laws is that employees are eligible for benefits regardless of whether or not the employer is guilty of negligence. Worker's compensation pays for employee medical bills resulting from an accident at work. The amount of insurance required is based on the number of employees and the kind of work the employees do, with more dangerous work requiring more coverage and higher premiums than less dangerous work. Premiums can be lowered, over time, by demonstrating a low incidence of accidents.

Worker's disability insures an employee of income in the event he or she cannot work as a result of a disability incurred on the job.

You might also carry other kinds of insurance in your employee's behalf, or you could pay a portion with the employee paying the remainder of the premiums. Often offered as employee benefits, such additional insurances include group life insurance, group health insurance, and retirement insurance.

*Insurance Covering Excessive Loss from Bad Debts.* This type of loss can be reduced by carefully evaluating customers to whom credit is extended. Insurance to cover such a loss is very expensive and can only cover the loss in excess of what is normal for the particular line of business being insured.

*Business Life Insurance.* The benefits of personal life insurance are known to most: it offers protection from life's uncertainties. Business life insurance is also needed to protect owners and their families against financial loss due to death or serious injury. An important benefit of this type of insurance is that the cash accumulation in the policy is available as a reserve fund for contingencies or for retirement. There are four basic types of life insurance including whole life, limited payment life, endowment life, and term life.

*Whole life* is the usual type purchased. Under this plan you are covered for the face amount of the policy throughout your lifetime, and payment of premiums continues over your lifetime. Whole life carries a limited cash surrender value, as well as loan privileges.

*Limited payment life* is a policy that requires payment of premiums for a set number of years, but thereafter no more premiums are paid and the insured remains covered for life. Since the premiums are higher than those of a whole life policy, the limited payment policy has a substantial cash surrender and loan value.

*Endowment life* is similar to the limited payment policy in that premiums are paid for a designated number of years, until the policy is paid up. At this point, the accumulated cash value is paid out in a lump sum, or endowment.

*Term life* is purchased for the sole purpose of insurance protection and has the lowest premiums. Consequently, the policy does not accumulate a cash reserve and therefore has no cash surrender value or loan potential.

## Some Service Businesses Should Bond Their Employees

Some service businesses might need to bond employees as an additional form of insurance to assuage the fears of customers. Being bonded means that insurance is carried against damages or losses that result from services performed. It is essentially another form of liability insurance that protects against theft or damage by employees. Any service that presents a significant risk to a client or a client's property should be bonded. A firm that delivers valuable jewels or a house sitter who has access to homes should definitely be bonded. A tree-cutting company should be bonded in case a limb or tree that has been cut falls on and destroys valuable property. As you can see, this is just another way to assure customers that, should a loss occur, their loss can be recovered. Roofers, painters, lawyers, financial consultants, and house/pet/people sitters are just a few of the services that are normally bonded. A bonded service is usually identified as such in advertisements because many people are reluctant to engage unbonded workers.

## Commonsense Protection

There are many ways to protect your business that don't require paying an insurance premium. A few risks, and ways to guard against them, are listed below:

1. Protect against fire damage by placing fire extinguishers in selected spots. Periodically check that extinguishers are operating correctly.
2. Store inflammable materials in closed containers and place them in a cool area.
3. Practice good housekeeping, and don't allow trash to accumulate.
4. Protect against criminal activity including shoplifting, burglary, and embezzlement. Prosecute any shoplifter or any employee caught stealing.
5. Train employees to be alert and to watch for signs of shoplifting.
6. In hiring employees, make sure your screening procedures are good, and let it be known that you expect honesty.
7. Keep good records and check for irregularities.
8. Sign all checks yourself. Never leave a blank check where an unauthorized person has access to it.
9. Review all canceled checks and their endorsements.
10. Periodically remove excess cash from the cash drawer and place it in a safe.
11. Leave the cash drawer empty and open at night.
12. Keep all keys under your care, and issue as few as possible.
13. Place anti-shoplifting signs in the shop.
14. Place convex wall mirrors and two-way mirrors in shop, if appropriate.
15. Place small, expensive items in locked showcases.
16. Have adequate lighting on the premises for night protection.
17. Install an alarm system. Perhaps the family dog can also alert you to intruders.
18. Install pin-tumbler cylinder locks in all doors.
19. Keep monies and important papers in a high-quality, fire-resistant safe that is secured to the floor.

# Part Seven

## *Success Strategies*

# 20    Organization Is the Key to Being Efficient

The importance of being organized cannot be overstressed. It is the key to being efficient. It is a way of living—a mind-set. The organization you have in your private life will naturally be a part of your business life. If your private life is in chaos, it will be an uphill battle to bring order to your business, but it is certainly worth the battle. Discipline and scheduling are both a part of the organization that produces the drive to succeed.

## Schedules

Written in needlepoint and hanging over my desk is the saying, "The faster I work, the behinder I get." That can be true if your work isn't focused, and the best way to keep focused and on track is to work from a schedule. Henry David Thoreau wrote, "It's not enough to be busy; so are the ants. The question is: What are we busy about?"

You will get more done in less time if you make a schedule and work from it. This schedule must be written down in order to be functional. Only then can you compare the various jobs that need to be done and establish priorities.

You might find it useful to write your schedule in a daily appointment book—the type that has a full page for each day. Start each day by checking your schedule and listing all the jobs you hope to accomplish. Next, prioritize the items on the list. Number the events, jobs, and appointments in their order of importance and, starting with number one, work through the list. If the workday ends before the list is completed, transfer the unfinished tasks to the next day's appointment page. If, on the following day, you feel that the transferred tasks aren't important enough to warrant your attention, circle them and move on to the more important things you have scheduled.

Your appointment book will become an excellent source of information, sort of a diary. It will tell you when you did what, and you might be surprised at how frequently you will refer to it to refresh your memory about past activities. In fact, if you sign a contract or take some other important action, it is helpful to record it in your appointment book so the date of the action is readily available. Make notes at the upper corner of the pages to facilitate finding the more important information contained in the schedule-diary.

There is one other factor to consider as you prepare your daily schedule and that is *prime time,* which is *your* most productive period during the day. Try to identify your prime time and arrange your schedule to take advantage of it. Schedule your most difficult physical tasks or those that require creative thinking into this time period. If you are a morning person, one who bounces out of bed ready to take on the world, then tackle your biggest jobs early in the day; if you are a slow starter, put off your more important tasks until later.

## Tips to Help You Get More for Your Time

Time is a valuable resource that must be carefully spent. You may have heard the saying: "Lose an hour in the morning, and you will spend all day looking for it." Sleeping late or lingering over morning coffee can mean a late start on your day's work and can make it seem impossible to catch up.

To squander time is to squander a part of your life, but time is not squandered when you pause for important things, even though they're unrelated to your business. Only you can decide if an activity is right for you, and that decision will be based on your values. Many parents would consider slipping out to a child's school play as time well spent, but others might feel an urgency to work during this time in order to keep their children in decent clothing. Some people find that taking time for a morning exercise routine increases their vitality, while others believe they get enough exercise as they struggle through the day's work. You must balance the things you *need* to do with the things you *want* to do. The quality of your life and the success of your business will depend upon how successfully you master this delicate balance.

Often you can do two things at once. It rarely takes your undivided attention to participate in a telephone conversation, so use phone time to put stamps on a pile of letters or check your appointment book for upcoming events. While waiting for a client, toss in the laundry, make a quick call, file papers, or take a quick look at your balance sheet. Ponder. While packing goods for shipment, practice the talk you're supposed to present, or let the kids stuff packing material around the goods or seal packages. By having them participate, they feel needed (and are!), and you get a chance to share a few moments together.

Consistency is another secret for getting things done. This powerful tactic has alluded many who find themselves swamped with too much to do. I write a lot—books and articles—and am often asked, "How can you find the time to write all of those books and articles?" The answer is simple: every day, on a regular schedule. That is the secret to getting a job done—to work at it consistently, on a schedule, chipping away at a seemingly impossible task a little at a time. To this day I marvel at the feats of man, from building pyramids and bridges to hopping planets, but each of these feats was accomplished one step at a time, and that is how you will build a business. To the old Latin proverb "Make haste slowly" we might add, "but consistently."

Your business may require a lot of running around—picking up supplies, delivering parts, or meeting with clients—and that can take a large chunk of time out of your workday. Make these outings when traffic is at a minimum and it's easier to move around. Except for emergencies, avoid making trips for a single purpose, but wait until several stops must be made. Think through possible routes, and number the stops so you don't backtrack or lose time.

Procrastination is a huge time waster. When a difficult task must be done, tackle it immediately, before you can think of a reason to put it off. It has been said that "Work is the greatest thing in the world. We should always save some for tomorrow." However, tomorrow will have its own jobs, so do today's work now and start tomorrow with a clean slate.

## The Benefits of the Telephone

Your telephone will save your time, feet, patience, and energy. "Let your fingers do the walking" is a good slogan, and it points out the value of a telephone. The amount of information you can gather without moving from your desk is astounding. A telephone can connect you with the customers, suppliers, services, and information you need to make your business work. If you can't find the information you need in the phone directory, call your local library information desk. Quite often someone there will be able to help you. Also, keep the numbers of the Better Business Bureau and your local chamber of commerce at your fingertips, because they are valuable sources of information.

If you work alone and do not want to draw attention to your home as a business location, you may not want a separate business phone line. A carefully kept phone log can be used to divide business calls from personal calls, and it takes just a few minutes each month to separate charges when the bill arrives. However, you might consider a separate business line if you attract customers through advertising. This will not only separate family and business affairs, but it will also be an excellent form of targeted advertising, since your business will be listed in the Yellow Pages of the telephone directory. Although a business phone and listing costs about two-and-a-half times more than a private line, the listing could and should bring in enough business to more than cover the cost of this tax-deductible expense. Also, a separate business line allows you to leave work behind at the end of the day by simply not answering or by having an answering machine pick up the calls. When choosing a telephone, be sure to purchase a timesaving memory phone that can be programmed to dial frequently called numbers by pressing one or two buttons.

Many business contacts and deals are made by phone, and it is important to develop a good telephone personality. You should come across as straightforward, knowledgeable, and eager to be of service. These qualities will go a long way in convincing clients that you are worthy of their business. It is also important to learn how to control the length of a conversation. If you get caught by a client, friend, or family member who wants to chat when there is work to be done, bring the call to a close by thanking them for calling or by saying, "It's been nice talking with you" and then hanging up.

Before making a call, jot down the points you wish to discuss and the information you are seeking. Don't allow a secretary or anyone else to put you on hold unless you have some work that can be done while you are waiting; instead, hang up and call back or have the other party return the call.

*Children shouldn't answer your incoming business calls.*

## TELEPHONE SERVICES

A variety of telephone-related services can help get work done more efficiently. Some are as effective as having an employee, but they require no training and don't cost nearly as much.

The simplest way to pick up calls while you are busy or away from the office is by using the increasingly common answering machine. This device answers incoming calls with a prerecorded message and records messages left by callers. When these machines were new and unfamiliar, callers were intimidated and would hang up without leaving a message. Now answering machines are so common that most people willingly leave a message. If you wish, you can adjust the machine so you can hear incoming calls and answer them immediately or return them at your convenience. One advantage of receiving calls on an answering machine is that it allows you to decide how you will respond to the caller. It gives you the edge of a little preknowledge before returning the call.

Call forwarding is a valuable but inexpensive telephone service that transfers calls from one number to another. It is activated by dialing a prefix and the forwarding number where the calls will be received. Many small businesses employ an answering service to receive their calls when there is no one in the office or shop to answer the phone. If an answering service intercepts a call that needs your immediate response, you can be contacted through a paging device. By the way, answering services themselves are almost exclusively home businesses, and most of them charge by the number of calls intercepted. They are listed in the Yellow Pages under "Telephone Answering Service." There are other telephone services available that might be of value to you, including conference calls, call waiting, and many others. Ask your local telephone company about them.

Telephone service can be costly, but there are many ways to reduce the expense. Whenever possible, use the 800 number of the party you wish to call. A directory is available from the telephone company that lists all the 800 numbers in use nationwide. The cost of operated-assisted long distance calls can be reduced by nearly 60 percent by dialing direct; therefore, keep your personal directory of business telephone numbers up to date.

Another way to reduce long-distance costs is to take advantage of lower rates during off-hours. If you are phoning the eastern part of the United States, call before 8:00 a.m.—the difference in time zones will work to your advantage because people will already be working. If your call is to the western part of the country, call after 5:00 p.m. when the rates are lower but people are still at work.

And finally, look for the best deal. Formerly AT&T was the only choice for telephone services. Now we can select between several long distance carriers that offer different services and rates. Do some comparative shopping, and select the company that best fills your needs.

## MAINTAINING AN 800 NUMBER

It may be advantageous to get a toll-free 800 number if your business caters to the national market or if your clients are widely dispersed. Toll-free numbers are especially valuable to businesses that advertise nationally because the number can be listed in the ads and result in a significant increase in advertisement response. (For further information see Chapter 16.)

At one time, only the larger companies could afford the rather expensive 800 numbers, but now, with several communications companies vying for long-distance business, the cost has decreased dramatically and 800 numbers are within the financial reach of the small business. In some areas an 800 number costs as little as $10 per month plus a cost-per-minute usage rate of around 25 cents, or even less.

## HOW A TELEPHONE FACSIMILE MACHINE (FAX MACHINE) WORKS

In order to transmit documents, both the sender and the receiver need a fax machine joined by a regular telephone line.

*Sending a Message:* Original handwritten or printed documents are inserted into the sending fax machine. A photoelectronic pickup device scans one page at a time, line by line, and converts the images into digital electronic codes for transmission through the telephone line.

*Message Transmission:* A regular telephone line is used to transmit the digital codes. An average document takes 12 seconds to travel to its destination anywhere in the world.

*Receiving a Message:* The receiving fax machine translates the digital code back to its original pattern, and pinlike heating elements inscribe the image on thermal-sensitive paper as each line is received. The result is an exact copy of the original documents. There is no additional charge for the use of the telephone connection if the material is faxed within a calling area; the costs are the same as for a direct-dial long-distance phone call if the material is faxed outside a calling area.

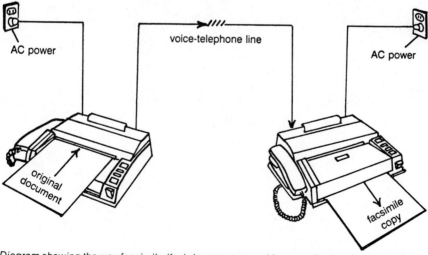

*Diagram showing the way facsimile (fax) documents travel from one fax location to another.*

### FACTS ABOUT FAX (FACSIMILE MACHINES)

Many businesses are now using a piece of equipment in conjunction with the telephone that communicates information without speaking. The fax machine (short for telephone facsimile machine) can transmit written material, photographs, and drawings. This device is becoming increasingly popular in offices across the country because it enables the transmission of documents by telephone in as little as 12 seconds. A document is fed into the machine (which looks somewhat like a small copy machine), and a facsimile of the document is recreated on a similar fax machine at the other end of the telephone line. The cost of owning and operating a fax machine is well within the reach of the small business, with desktop models now selling for under $1000. If a document is transferred within a calling zone, no fee is charged, but if it is faxed between zones, the cost is the same as for a long-distance call.

# 21    Reviewing and Evaluating Your Business

"How's business?" Some entrepreneurs know the condition of their business at all times, while others check the books every once in a while just to make sure their checks won't bounce. It takes perseverance and ingenuity to keep a business functioning, and you might get so engrossed in the daily chores that you fail to take the time to sit back and take stock of things. That approach can be dangerous. Don't wait until the end of the month, quarter, or year to evaluate your business, but make it a continuous process.

If a problem develops, fix it. That simple admonition is behind the success of some of this country's finest corporations, and it can help you be successful. As you go about your business, *look* for trouble! Be alert to problems, and move quickly to resolve them. Your problem may be with the supply pipeline or in the way your family responds to your business. Problems may be caused by sales reps who write up orders incorrectly or by customers who delay paying bills. Whatever the problem might be, confront it as soon as it becomes apparent.

Of course, it follows that if something works, leave it alone. We've all been told at some time or the other, "If it's not broken, don't fix it." You will find that many of the ideas you put into action are good ideas and yield the results you desire. Identifying successful business practices is as important as spotting poor ones, because you can use these successes to build on.

## Take Stock

Here are a few questions that might be appropriate to ask when evaluating your business. The numbers in parentheses are the chapter or chapters in which the question topic is discussed.

- Is your product or service needed, used, or wanted by enough people to support the growth you have projected for your business? (4)
- Are advertising methods bringing in customers? (16)
- What is the cost of advertising per customer? (16)
- What costs can be reduced? (12, 13, 14, and 16)
- Is inventory current and are records kept up to date? (12)
- Is too much money tied up in inventory? (12)
- Can supplies be purchased for less? (12)
- Do you really need employees? Would part-time help be enough? (14)
- Are you taking advantage of tax breaks? (18)
- Are your prices competitive? Do they yield a reasonable profit? (15)
- Is your credit policy attracting customers who pay their bills? (17)
- Is your shipping method fast enough, and do you ship at the best rate available? (13)
- Does your merchandise arrive at its destination intact? (13)
- Do customers return for repeat business? (21)
- Do you waste time throughout the day, or are you disciplined enough to maintain your business schedule? (22)
- Do you study business records in search of clues that can help improve your business procedures? (10)
- Do you see any trends developing in your industry? (2, 4, and 17)
- Should you change products or services to adapt to trends? (4, 17, and 21)
- Are you attracting any of your competitor's customers? (15)
- Are your finances as good as you anticipated at this stage? (8 and 10)
- *Are you making a profit?* (8, 15, and 21)
- How can you increase profits? (8 and 15)
- Have you forecasted next year's sales? (8)
- Do you need to expand business space? (7)
- Is your business life compatible with your family life? (22)
- *Are you happy?*
- *What would make you happier?*

Thinking about these and other questions directed to your particular enterprise can help you find ways to increase and/or improve your operation. A couple of topics that touch at the heart of any business are explored more thoroughly below.

## Keep the Profit Motive

Sales − Costs = Profit. That formula must be understood and used as you direct your energies to make a profit. Remember that there are several ways to measure business success, but profit is surely one of the most important. A business without profit will not endure or prosper.

In order to act effectively you need to keep informed; thus, it is important to analyze business records with a critical eye. Records should tell you about profits, costs, and sales. Study your profit and loss statements because they are the clearest indicators of your business's health. Compare statements from similar time periods to evaluate trends. Is your business in better financial health than it was a year ago? What area is yielding the best profit? Is any sector losing money? Are costs under control? Where can they be reduced without causing a reduction in quality or a loss of customers? Are prices in line with the competition, or would you do better changing some prices? Are you spending enough but not too much, and are you spending it in the right places?

Be flexible and work with the realization that business needs change. A business decision that was right in the past may no longer be relevant to your present goals. Use your financial records but also use your intuition and good sense to help you decide on new directions. We are often told to act, not react, but reacting to profit and loss statements and changes in the market is necessary to improve the profit margin of your business.

## Think Customer!

Customers pay your bills and are your source of profit. Whether you realize it or not, you have a service business even if you are a manufacturer. One of your goals should be to provide good service to customers. Always *think customer!* Glance over the following suggestions concerning customers and try to incorporate their principles into your business life.

- Strive to earn customer loyalty.
- Try to think like your customers and respond to their expectations.
- Understanding customers will enable you to profit by providing the satisfaction they seek from either a product or service.
- Care about your customers and they will reward you with repeat business.
- Listen to and learn from your customers.
- Try to understand customer needs and apprehensions and to anticipate why they might take their business elsewhere—so you can keep them from doing so.
- Respond to customer complaints as quickly as possible.
- Offer service and reliability.

- Be customer-driven and you will be successful.
- Getting the sale is one thing, but the after-sale service is a step toward the next sale.
- Every time you strive to make a sale, act as if you may lose the customer, and try to find the key to saving that customer.
- Develop a service philosophy. Deliver satisfaction. If you make service excellence your prime objective, customers and profit will follow.
- Don't lose sight of the individual customer.
- Keep your promises, but don't promise more than you can or want to deliver.
- Let customers know they can depend on you.
- Find ways of fulfilling customer expectations better than your competitors.
- Let customers help shape your business by using their suggestions.
- Keep in touch with customers by sending thank-you notes, notices of sales, and seasonal greetings.
- Reinforce your business message by sending desk pads, newsletters, and other attention-getting materials to your customers.
- Make customers feel special. Keep personal notes on repeat customers, and take the time to follow up on past jobs with a phone call to determine customer satisfaction.

## Managing Growth

Most business owners want growth, and the faster the better! Growth is highly desirable, but premature or uncontrolled growth can destroy a small business. In fact, most businesses do better with conservative growth rates. The goal is to grow at a pace that will allow the business to continue to function well. When growth is uncontrolled, (1) profits are imperiled, (2) liquidity is threatened, (3) administrative controls collapse, and/or (4) the staff is unable to meet the new demands. If one or two of these conditions exists, it is apparent the business has grown too large, too fast.

It costs money to expand, and the most serious risk of rapid growth is financial instability. The increase in business does not always lead to increased profits. It sometimes destroys them.

You can plan for growth, just as you planned before starting your business. The growth should be based on your winning edge. Whatever it is that has brought success to your business should be expanded on. Sometimes the very key that has brought success is lost when a business expands, so guard against this possibility. We've all seen little shops or restaurants that attract customers and do very well, and then expand into something quite unlike the original business. Very often, an enlarged business will lose the charm, personal attention, or quality service that brought in customers before the expansion.

Some of the questions you need to consider as you contemplate expanding your business are as follows:

- What impact will growth have on costs?
- How much added responsibility will you have?
- Will you need more employees?
- Will the increased paperwork require more sophisticated accounting and administrative procedures?
- Can you maintain product quality and service?
- Can schedules be kept and orders delivered on time?
- Is adequate cash available to support the growth?

# 22    Success Depends on You

Managing the boss is an important part of managing your business. Your health and energy are business assets, and your success will be influenced by the attention you pay to your own well-being. Being the boss can be rewarding, stressfull, fulfilling, lonely, exciting, and demanding. You must learn to balance your professional and personal life. You must learn to control your work schedule, establish good work and health habits, manage your time and energy, and control stress. This chapter presents a few guidelines that can help make living with the boss a little easier.

## Keeping Yourself Fit

Be the best you can be, both for personal reasons and for the success of your business. Eat properly, exercise, sleep an adequate amount, and develop other healthful habits.

Eat for energy and for health. These days it's difficult to avoid hearing about which foods promote health because the media spreads the word about diet and the latest research findings with missionary zeal. It's up to you to make the commitment to select the right foods and the right quantity of food.

How can smoking and drinking affect your business? They can't help it, that's for certain. While reading this paragraph about the dangers of smoking won't induce those of you who indulge to forgo a long-standing habit, it is still worthwhile to reiterate the message that you have heard before and will keep hearing: smoking decreases working days due to increased physical problems that range from chest colds to lung cancer. And, evidence is overwhelmingly convincing that the average life span of smokers is significantly shorter than that of non-smokers. It has been estimated that smoking a single cigarette reduces and individual's life span by an average of five minutes. In simplistic terms it comes down to deciding if you are willing to give up five minutes of life for a cigarette. If you smoke a pack a day, then you must decide if you are willing to relinquish 25 days of life for each year you continue to smoke. It's up to you to make the choice, but try to make the choice consciously rather than acting without thinking.

Next, the subject of drinking. A cocktail before dinner is one thing, a six-pack to carry you through the evening is quite another. Moderation is the key to controlling the influence drinking has on your life and business. While some doctors recommend a cocktail before dinner for their heart patients, a single cocktail might be too much for another person. Know what is appropriate for you, and don't overdo.

"Early to bed, early to rise, makes a man healthy, wealthy and wise." Don't you wish it would be that easy? Still, there is a message in that saying, namely, get your rest but don't waste working hours in bed. In other words, "time's a'wastin!"

The routine of sleeping is a habit just as eating is a habit, and, like food, sleep is needed to restore energy. Some people fall asleep easily and feel rested in the morning, while others toss and turn and rarely get a full night's sleep. Develop the sleeping habit by going to bed and getting up on a regular schedule. While it's nice to sleep late on weekends, that deviation from the schedule can upset the habit of sleeping.

You can program yourself to require a certain amount of sleep. For decades we have been told we needed eight hours of sleep each night, but now research has shown that six hours is enough for most people, and as little as four hours is all that others require. If you are in the habit of sleeping eight hours each night, try sleeping seven hours and see how you respond, and gradually reduce sleeping time until you find the amount your body actually requires. Reducing sleeping time a single hour each night can result in 365 extra waking hours each year. If you work 40-hour weeks, one hour less of sleep each night will amount to over 9 extra work weeks a year. It takes very little pencil pushing to realize that reducing your sleep by a single hour each night can result in a significant number of extra waking/working/playing hours over your lifetime.

Exercising can increase your energy level, ward off chronic fatigue, and slow the aging process. In the previous paragraph it was suggested that you rise early and get on with your day. One good way to start your day is with a brisk run or some other type of exercise. Research has shown that exercise increases stamina and produces a feeling of vitality by strengthening the energy-producing organs. Regular and sustained exercise builds a stronger heart, which in turn pumps more blood with less effort, resulting in a larger supply of oxygen to the lungs and muscles.

Exercising not only makes the body function more efficiently, but it also has a direct effect on mood. It reduces anxiety, stress, and depression by stimulating the brain to produce norepinephrine, a naturally occurring chemical. Depletion or lack of norepinephrine can result in depression.

As you can see, it is a good idea to build a fitness program into your day and exercise your way to a healthy body, clear thought, and creative thinking. With regular exercise your health will improve, your stress level will drop, and your trim look will inspire you and others to have confidence in your abilities.

## Networking to Keep in Touch and Informed

Some people are reluctant to work at home because they fear isolation and the loss of social skills. One way to fight the debilitating force of isolation is to seek and find others with whom you can network. Networking is a growing phenomenon among home workers, who are finding it to be a source of information, interaction, and socialization. Breakfast and luncheon groups have formed to talk shop, exchange ideas, share successes, solve problems, boost morale, pat each other on the back, and share a few laughs. These gatherings can go a long way in improving your business image and reaffirming your sense of purpose.

A networking group can be an official club, but it can also be just a group of business people who reinforce each other. They might gather at the country club or on stools at the corner donut shop. If you are looking for a networking organization, contact the local chamber of commerce, which will probably know of the larger ones in your area. Or just call a few other home workers and get together to talk. The group will grow from there. Many communities already have an assortment of networking organizations, such as clubs for woodworkers, photographers, artists, and writers. There are several national networking organizations, such as Women in Networking (a group that will probably suit someone who is more into "clubbing" than sharing hard information). A couple of networking newsletters are *Alliance,* a quarterly published by National Alliance of Homebased Businesswomen, P.O. Box 306, Midland Park, NJ 07432; and *National Home Business Report,* which is also a quarterly (NHBR, P.O. Box 2137, Naperville, IL 60565).

Trade organizations can also be a valuable contact for home workers. These associations offer technical advice and guidance through regional and national meetings. Attending these kinds of meetings takes time and money, but the cost is tax-deductible.

Other possible networking groups that can help you make valuable business and professional contacts include your local chamber of commerce, Kiwanis Club, Exchange Club, and other business organizations.

## Building a Business Image

Projecting a business image is an important part of building credibility with your customers and suppliers, and it contributes to your own professional self-image. Your image is built by your speech, dress, and demeanor—the total of how you present yourself to others.

Some clients will never see you, and contact will be confined to telephone conversations or letters. Make sure these contacts convey the right message. Practice your conversational style so you come across as confident, capable, and reliable.

Dress for work. It might be very tempting to shuffle into your office and get started on the day's work while still clad in robe and slippers, but that will automatically reduce your efficiency. And, you certainly don't want a customer to catch you in such garb. Make dressing for work another habit. Dress comfortably but appropriately.

## Controlling Interruptions

Interruptions are a normal, yet time-consuming, part of life, but as you strive to make your business successful, you will need to control them. As you start your business, people with whom you have shared your time will still want to chat or drop in. A wit once said that "Busy souls have no time to be busybodies"—it pays to remember that bit of wisdom as you go through your workday.

Some interruptions arrive at the door. What do you do when an old chum arrives with a gastronomic delight and an hour to spare? Your friends and family probably won't intentionally intrude upon your time, but it is up to you to establish business hours and make sure they are known to them.

If clients visit your work place, it is important to develop a style that informs them when to leave. For instance, if you teach music lessons from your home studio, you should give clear signals to the students when the lessons are over; if you do tax returns and clients bring you information, make sure they know when the session is over. Stand up, shake hands, and move the client toward the door. Developing this skill will help prevent lost time at the end of each session.

Interruptions will arrive with the ring of your telephone, and these can be the most difficult to deal with. You will be shocked at the number of requests that will come your way as your business grows and you become more successful and visible to the public. You will be asked to give talks, chair campaigns, be on public service committees, and so forth. Of course, you may want to do these things, and you surely should "pay your dues," but don't allow an excess of outside activities to interfere with the proper conduct of your business. Such requests are easier to handle if they arrive through the mail because you will have time to think about an appropriate response. In any case, keep in mind that time is your most valuable resource, and learn to deal with interruptions quickly and efficiently so you do not waste it.

## Juggling Business, Family, and Friends

Sometimes the expectations your friends and family have of you will be different from those that you have for yourself, and the question you must resolve is, "Whose goals and expectations will I fulfill?" The bottom line is that for the most part business owners have less free time than they had before beginning a business. Still, the quality of your life will quickly deteriorate if you allow your days to be filled with all work and no play, and it is important to schedule time with your family and friends.

Time and energy are your most valuable resources, and one of the first things you discover when you get a business under way is that you don't have enough of either to do everything you would like. Recognize your time and energy limitations and discard some of your past roles as you acquire new ones. You will need to make choices—to set priorities. Which are your most important nonbusiness roles? You may function as a parent, spouse, friend, cook, and driver—just for starters. Many of you also entertain friends, watch over ailing parents, and support children's and grandchildren's activities by taking them to meetings and watching them compete in sports events. Besides that, you may dine out, dance, attend concerts and stage productions, sing in a choir, play on a sports team, keep the cars tuned up, shop, keep the house tidy and in repair, maintain the yard, and volunteer.

If you have made the decision to work at a home business, you will also need to make decisions about eliminating some of your other activities. Look for help. Since you will be bringing in income and helping to support the family, maybe it's time to delegate some of your work to other family members who will enjoy the benefits of your labor.

You can help your spouse and children adapt to having a business on the premises and to your business work schedule. At first it may be difficult to get new household rules and patterns of play established, but if you consistently respond in ways that reinforce the desired behavior, the household will settle into a pattern that will allow family life and business activities to coexist.

One of the reasons people work at home is to be with their children, but if this is your situation you will need to establish ground rules in order to fill both your parenting and business roles. Actually, you will need to find a way to put a little separation between the two roles. Some home workers achieve this by putting their office or workroom in a remote part of the house or by closing the office door when they are at work. But children don't understand closed doors, especially when they need your attention. It's easier to separate your role as parent and business person with time, spending time with your children when they are at home, but resuming the business role the moment they are on their way to school or busy with other activities. Of course, if you have preschool children who are always underfoot, it may be necessary to arrange care for them so you can concentrate on your business. The care might be given by a spouse who returns home after a workday, by older children, by grandparents, or by neighbors. If these options are not possible, you may need to seek professional child care so you can get work done. This care is partially tax-deductible (see Chapter 18).

## Stop Planning, Start Doing

It's time to go to work. It's time to get your business started—to put your plans into action. Don't expect everything to work as you have planned, but use the best part of your plans and successes to build on. The first step—whatever it is—may be the most difficult to perform because of some internal reluctance, but taking the first step will give you the momentum to continue. The first step may be a call to the telephone company requesting information about rates, prowling through shops that carry supplies, or measuring a room for an office.

You may feel insecure as you get started, but most of us feel a little uneasy when we start doing something different. You will quickly discover that each activity will get easier and your confidence will grow with each try. And you will also discover that running a business is fun! You can do it—and it's time to prove that to yourself and to the world. Get on with it, and good luck to you!

# Index